Personhood in the Byzantine Christian Tradition

Bringing together international scholars from across a range of linked disciplines to examine the concept of the person in the Greek Christian East, *Personhood in the Byzantine Christian Tradition* stretches in its scope from the New Testament to contemporary debates surrounding personhood in Eastern Orthodoxy. Attention is paid to a number of pertinent areas that have not hitherto received the scholarly attention they deserve, such as Byzantine hymnography and iconology, the work of early miaphysite thinkers, and the relevance of late Byzantine figures to the discussion. Similarly, certain long-standing debates surrounding the question are revisited or reframed, whether regarding the concept of the person in Maximus the Confessor, or with contributions that bring patristic and modern Orthodox theology into dialogue with a variety of contemporary currents in philosophy, moral psychology, and political science.

In opening up new avenues of inquiry, or revisiting old avenues in new ways, this volume brings forward an important and ongoing discussion regarding concepts of personhood in the Byzantine Christian tradition and beyond, and provides a key stimulus for further work in this field.

Alexis Torrance is Archbishop Demetrios College Chair of Byzantine Theology and Assistant Professor in the Faculty of Theology and the Medieval Institute at the University of Notre Dame.

Symeon Paschalidis is Professor of Patristics and Hagiography in the Faculty of Theology at the Aristotle University of Thessaloniki and the Director of the Patriarchal Institute for Patristic Studies in Thessaloniki.

Personhood in the Byzantine Christian Tradition
Early, Medieval, and Modern Perspectives

**Edited by Alexis Torrance
and Symeon Paschalidis**

LONDON AND NEW YORK

First published 2018
by Routledge
2 Park Square, Milton Park, Abingdon, Oxon OX14 4RN

and by Routledge
711 Third Avenue, New York, NY 10017

Routledge is an imprint of the Taylor & Francis Group, an informa business

© 2018 selection and editorial matter, Alexis Torrance and Symeon Paschalidis; individual chapters, the contributors

The right of Alexis Torrance and Symeon Paschalidis to be identified as the authors of the editorial material, and of the authors for their individual chapters, has been asserted in accordance with sections 77 and 78 of the Copyright, Designs and Patents Act 1988.

All rights reserved. No part of this book may be reprinted or reproduced or utilised in any form or by any electronic, mechanical, or other means, now known or hereafter invented, including photocopying and recording, or in any information storage or retrieval system, without permission in writing from the publishers.

Trademark notice: Product or corporate names may be trademarks or registered trademarks, and are used only for identification and explanation without intent to infringe.

British Library Cataloguing-in-Publication Data
A catalogue record for this book is available from the British Library

Library of Congress Cataloging-in-Publication Data
Names: Torrance, Alexis, 1985– editor. | Paschalidis, Symeon, editor.
Title: Personhood in the Byzantine Christian tradition : early, medieval, and modern perspectives / edited by Alexis Torrance and Symeon Paschalidis.
Description: New York : Routledge, 2018. | Includes bibliographical references and index.
Identifiers: LCCN 2017060120 | ISBN 9781472472786 (hardback : alk. paper) | ISBN 9781315600185 (ebook)
Subjects: LCSH: Theological anthropology—Christianity. | Human beings. | Orthodox Eastern Church—Doctrine.
Classification: LCC BX342.9.M35 P477 2018 | DDC 233/.50882819—dc23
LC record available at https://lccn.loc.gov/2017060120

ISBN: 978-1-4724-7278-6 (hbk)
ISBN: 978-1-315-60018-5 (ebk)

Typeset in Times New Roman
by Apex CoVantage, LLC

Printed and bound in Great Britain by
TJ International Ltd, Padstow, Cornwall

Contents

Acknowledgements viii
Contributors ix

Introduction 1
ALEXIS TORRANCE AND SYMEON PASCHALIDIS

SECTION I
Ancient Christian, early Byzantine 7

1 Personal relationship as a prerequisite for moral imitation according to the Apostle Paul 9
   CHRISTOS KARAKOLIS

2 Emotional "scripts" and personal moral identity: insights from the Greek fathers 19
   PAUL M. BLOWERS

3 Personhood in miaphysitism: Severus of Antioch and John Philoponus 29
   JOHANNES ZACHHUBER

SECTION II
Early to middle Byzantine 45

4 Hypostasis, person, and individual according to St. Maximus the Confessor, with reference to the Cappadocians and St. John of Damascus 47
   JEAN-CLAUDE LARCHET

5 Mary, the mother of God, in dialogue: the drama of
   personal encounter in the Byzantine liturgical tradition   68
   MARY B. CUNNINGHAM

6 Personification in Byzantine hymnography: *Kontakia* and canons 80
   DAMASKINOS (OLKINUORA) OF XENOPHONTOS

SECTION III
Late Byzantine   101

7 The exemplar of consubstantiality: St. Gregory Palamas's
   hesychast as an expression of a microcosmic approach to
   personhood   103
   DEMETRIOS HARPER

8 Nicholas Cabasilas of Thessaloniki: the historical dimension
   of the person   114
   MARIE-HÉLÈNE CONGOURDEAU

9 Freedom, necessity, and the laws of nature in the thought of
   Gennadios Scholarios   128
   MATTHEW C. BRIEL

SECTION IV
Modern   135

10 Flesh and Spirit: divergent Orthodox readings of the iconic
   body in Byzantium and the twentieth century   137
   EVAN FREEMAN

11 Nikos Nissiotis, the "theology of the '60s," and personhood:
   continuity or discontinuity?   161
   NIKOLAOS ASPROULIS

12 Eastern Christian conceptions of personhood and their
   political significance   173
   NICOLAS PREVELAKIS

13 **Consubstantial selves: a discussion between Orthodox personalism, existential psychology, Heinz Kohut, and Jean-Luc Marion** 182
NICHOLAS LOUDOVIKOS

Index 197

Acknowledgements

We would like to thank all those who helped bring this volume to fruition. In the first instance, we are grateful to the 13 contributors to this volume, whose patience was often tried by us, but never shaken. The work of volume editing is often likened to the thankless task of herding cats, but in this case, it proved a joy. We are likewise grateful to the staff at Routledge, in particular Jack Boothroyd, who was invaluable at shepherding us through the publication process. Several of the contributions to this volume were initially given at a conference held in Thessaloniki in May 2014. We are grateful for the various financial and institutional support that helped make that conference possible, including a European Union grant via Greece's National Strategic Reference Framework, the support of the Aristotle University of Thessaloniki, the University Ecclesiastical Academy of Thessaloniki, and a grant from the Fellowship of St Alban and St Sergius.

Alexis Torrance and Symeon Paschalidis
December 7, 2017

Contributors

Nikolaos Asproulis is Deputy Director of the Volos Academy for Theological Studies (Volos, Greece) and Lecturer at the Post-Graduate Program of Orthodox Theology, School of Humanities, Hellenic Open University (Greece).

Paul M. Blowers is the Dean E. Walker Professor of Church History in the Emmanuel Christian Seminary at Milligan College, Tennessee. He is a scholar of Greek and Byzantine patristics and has published extensively on Maximus the Confessor.

Matthew C. Briel is Assistant Professor of Theology at Assumption College in Worcester, Massachusetts.

Marie-Hélène Congourdeau, chercheur honoraire au CNRS and membre associé de l'UMR 8167 *Orient Méditerranée* (Monde byzantin), Collège de France, Paris. She is presently working on a biography of Nicolas Cabasilas.

Mary B. Cunningham is Honorary Associate Professor of Historical Theology at the University of Nottingham. She has published books and articles on the role of the Virgin Mary in Byzantine and modern Orthodox Christian tradition, as well as on subjects relating to Byzantine preaching, hagiography, and liturgy.

Evan Freeman is a PhD candidate in the Department of the History of Art at Yale University and a lecturer in Liturgical Art at St. Vladimir's Orthodox Theological Seminary.

Demetrios Harper is Visiting Research Fellow in the Department of Theology, Religion, and Philosophy at the University of Winchester and Assistant Editor of *Analogia: The Pemptousia Journal for Theological Studies*.

Christos Karakolis is Associate Professor of New Testament at the Department of Theology of the National and Kapodistrian University of Athens, Greece and Research Fellow of the Department for Old and New Testament Studies at the University of the Free State, South Africa.

Jean-Claude Larchet is a retired *professeur des universités* based in Strasbourg. He is a scholar of patristic and Orthodox theology of international renown.

Nicholas Loudovikos is Professor of Dogmatics and Chair of the Department of Theological and Pastoral Studies at the University Ecclesiastical Academy of Thessaloniki. He is the author of numerous books and articles on Orthodox Dogmatic Theology, and is Senior Editor of *Analogia: The Pemptousia Journal for Theological Studies*.

Damaskinos (Olkinuora) is a member of the monastic brotherhood of the Holy Monastery of Xenophontos, Mount Athos, and serves as University Teacher of Systematic Theology and Patristics at the University of Eastern Finland. His research concentrates mainly on middle Byzantine hymnography and homiletics, as well as the veneration of the Theotokos.

Symeon Paschalidis is Professor of Patristics and Hagiography in the Faculty of Theology at the Aristotle University of Thessaloniki and Director of the Patriarchal Institute for Patristic Studies in Thessaloniki.

Nicolas Prevelakis is Lecturer on social studies at Harvard University. He is also Assistant Director of Curricular Development of Harvard's Center for Hellenic Studies. His teaching and research interests include Eastern Christianity, the history of moral and political philosophy, and the interconnection between modern nationalism and religion.

Alexis Torrance is Archbishop Demetrios College Chair of Byzantine Theology and Assistant Professor in the Faculty of Theology and the Medieval Institute at the University of Notre Dame.

Johannes Zachhuber is Professor of Historical and Systematic Theology at the University of Oxford and Fellow and Tutor in Theology at Trinity College, Oxford.

Introduction

Alexis Torrance and Symeon Paschalidis

Theological reflection on the notion of personhood has from the first Christian centuries played a central role in the articulation of Christian doctrine, particularly in expressions of Trinitarian and Christological dogma. How doctrinal formulations regarding the persons of the Trinity or the person of Christ relate to the understanding of human personhood in the history of Christian thought, however, is a topic that has provoked much scholarly debate. The contention, in particular, that Byzantine Christianity developed a fully formed concept of the person (human and divine) that largely matches, and at times corrects, notions of personhood worked out by modern thought – a view most influentially elaborated by the Greek Orthodox Metropolitan John Zizioulas – is by turns celebrated and condemned.

Among the chief hampers to progress in this debate is the often narrow range of texts and contexts under discussion. If Byzantine Christianity does indeed offer important insights into an understanding of personhood, the debate should not simply hang on a few select passages from the Cappadocian Fathers or Maximus the Confessor (as is often done). The debate needs widening, and in order to make fresh advances on this crucial topic, new tactics are needed. Rather than dwell exclusively on terminological markers (such as the Greek words *hypostasis* and *prosopon*) and their meaning in the sources, such an approach needs to be combined with a broader and more widely focused enterprise, one that is not limited to dogmatic formulas and their conceptual content, but includes reflections on the human person arising from other sources, whether liturgical, hagiographic, iconographic, homiletic, ascetic, and so on. This is the gap that the current volume seeks to fill. By offering focused treatments of different aspects of the question of personhood in specific yet diverse figures, texts, and contexts across early, medieval, and modern Byzantine Christianity, this collection opens up distinct new avenues of research into the theological and anthropological concepts of personhood, thereby contributing not simply to the historical study of personhood in the Byzantine Christian past, but likewise to broader live discussions of personhood and its meaning.

The contributions that make up this volume grew out of a conference held in Thessaloniki in May 2014. They have been divided roughly into chronological order in four sections, ranging from the early Christian period to contemporary

Orthodox Christian debates. This reflects the desire of the editors to highlight the importance of taking a "long view" of Byzantine Christian tradition – a tradition that theologically speaking is neither coextensive with, nor circumscribed by, the historical existence of the Byzantine Empire.

As with any such endeavor, no claim to providing a comprehensive or exhaustive treatment of the subject at hand is being made. This volume does not set out to offer a sweeping narrative arc regarding personhood in Byzantine theology, nor do the editors consider themselves to be "taking sides" in the various debates surrounding the theology of personhood that continue to cause controversy in modern Orthodox theology. It is not, that is, a partisan book, even if some of its contributors may identify themselves with one or another side in the debates. That said, certain accents of the volume are by design, such as the wide spread of subjects broached and methodologies employed, as well as the relatively minor attention paid to some figures so amply discussed elsewhere, such as the Cappadocian Fathers. This collection is an attempt, in short, to give fresh and deeper texture to discussions of personhood, not only as these relate to the Byzantine theological tradition but also in the wider context of efforts to come to grips with the psychological, sociological, historical, political, philosophical, and theological meaning of the person.

Summary of contents

The first section of the volume places the reader at the scriptural source of Christian theology in the person and letters of St. Paul. While admittedly pre-Byzantine, Paul serves as a non-negotiable basis for subsequent Byzantine Christian thought. The presence of this chapter serves a double purpose: first to emphasize the roots of the Byzantine Christian tradition within the New Testament itself and second as a kind of articulation of the need for biblical scholarship and Orthodox theology, so often alienated from one another, to interact. **Christos Karakolis**, a scholar of the New Testament, rises to the occasion by turning our attention to the interdependent categories of personal relationship and imitation in the letters of Paul. The key, claims Karakolis, and one that has direct bearing on our understanding of personhood, is that because of the strong *imitative* dimension inherent in the concept of positive personal relationships, there cannot be for Paul a strong notion of "personhood" that is not also conditioned on the level of behavior and virtue. The central texts for Karakolis in this regard are the series of admonitions from Paul to *imitate* him, even as he imitates Christ (e.g., 1 Cor 11:1), which he exegetes with skill and insight.

We move from Paul to Greek patristic and ascetic theology in the chapter by **Paul M. Blowers**, specifically on the concept of emotional "scripts" and personal moral identity. Drawing on work done in the social science and classics fields on moral psychology and identity theory, Blowers shows, in a clear and constructive way, how the questions and concerns raised in these fields find specific and potentially fruitful answers in early Christian reflection on the content, role, and destiny of the emotions and the "moral self." The chapter proves a particularly helpful transition from the chapter on Paul, dealing as he does with questions of ethics and virtue in Irenaeus and Origen through to the Cappadocians and Evagrius, with a concluding nod to Maximus the Confessor. The scope of the texts discussed allows Blowers to give us a convincing sense of the establishment of "the integrated moral self" as a kind of model for anthropological discourse in early Byzantine theology. Blowers laments that the richness of this tradition would no doubt be unwelcome in secular social and humane sciences, yet holds it up as offering a serious and potentially fertile solution to many of the problems that currently plague these fields.

Turning from questions of moral identity to dogmatic concerns, **Johannes Zachhuber** discusses the theology of two figures not usually associated with the Byzantine theological tradition: the miaphysites Severus of Antioch (465–538) and John Philoponus (490–570). While the miaphysite position was not ultimately adopted in the Byzantine Empire, it is often forgotten that the initial debates over miaphysite doctrine were internal to Byzantium and conducted, for the most part, in Greek (i.e., not along strictly "ethnic" or "linguistic" lines as is often imagined). Thus, at least from the historical point of view, the thought of Severus and Philoponus constitute a legitimate "Byzantine" perspective worth exploring.

Zachhuber brings both of these figures into dialogue with the ontology of the Cappadocian Fathers. In the first case, he suggests that Severus "inverts" this ontology, which in turn "led him to an unprecedented emphasis on the unity and individuality of the hypostasis as the unique existential expression of being (*physis*)." In the second case, he demonstrates that Philoponus goes much further than Severus, denying the possibility of any concept of "universal nature" or essence in his concern to safeguard the primacy of the particular nature or hypostasis. Zachhuber emphasizes the importance of considering miaphysite discussions in broader engagements with the concept of personhood.

Jean-Claude Larchet opens the second section dealing with early to middle Byzantine theology. This chapter, dedicated to the meaning of the terms *hypostasis*, person (πρόσωπον), and individual (ἄτομον) in the work of St. Maximus the Confessor (died 662), is invaluable, gathering together as it does a huge sample of texts in which Maximus uses these terms and discusses their meaning. Larchet further links his discussion to the Cappadocian Fathers that preceded and St. John of Damascus who followed. He makes it clear that he approaches his topic as a careful reader of the texts rather than as a proponent of either personalist or antipersonalist theories. The results are thus more of a philological rather than a theological nature, although this does not prevent him from weighing in (perhaps too harshly some might say) on the positions of prominent Orthodox personalists, Zizioulas in particular. His overall contention is that while personalism has tended to oppose "person" and/or "hypostasis" to "individual," these terms are used virtually interchangeably in Maximus.

The next two chapters, somewhat fittingly for the early to middle Byzantine period, are concerned with the Byzantine hymnographic and homiletic traditions. **Mary B. Cunningham** removes us from the realm of terminological debate and puts us at the feet of the Theotokos, Mary the Mother of God. From a consideration of the person of Mary herself as a place of meeting between God and man, heaven and earth, she expertly introduces the reader to the poetic and typological imagery of the Byzantine liturgical tradition that conveys Mary to the audience as the picture of saintly human life. The dramatic hymnographic and homiletic retelling of Mary's joys and griefs so deftly summarized by Cunningham serve, she argues, both to introduce the person of Mary herself to the listeners, bringing them into intimate personal contact with her, but likewise to speak symbolically of the ongoing task of relating to God and so becoming also, in some sense, a personal bearer of God.

Damaskinos (Olkinuora) of Xenophontos likewise looks closely at hymnography, in particular at the *kontakia* of St. Romanos the Melodist (490–556) and several canons of the ninth century. His interest is in the rhetorical device of personification and how its use differs in the hymns from a straightforward concept of *prosopopoeia*. This comes about from its wider application, looked at in turn under the headings 1) nature and places, 2) Hades and Death, 3) female virtues, and 4) typological images. Olkinuora shows not only the pervasiveness of personification as a literary device in Byzantine hymnography, but also its frequent deployment in underscoring the hymnography's central theological message. This is a new contribution to the field and one that holds promise as a fresh avenue in studying the concept of personhood in Byzantine thought.

Moving from the middle to the late Byzantine period, **Demetrios Harper** treats us to a chapter on St. Gregory Palamas (1296–1359). Any volume promising a multiplicity of perspectives from the Byzantine Christian tradition would be incomplete without a contribution on Palamas, and Harper provides us with a particularly pertinent discussion of the great hesychast's anthropology. In doing so, he argues that Palamas's approach to the human being is deeply indebted to, and dependent on, that of his monastic forbear St. Maximus the Confessor. He makes creative, and perhaps at first counterintuitive, use of the category of "consubstantiality" to describe Palamas's approach to human personhood, understanding it in the sense that Palamas, like Maximus before him, envisages the inner consubstantiality of the human soul and body (a veritable "microcosm") as constitutive of what it means to be a human person. Based on hesychast principles, Palamas sets out a vision of the eschatological destiny of the human person that fully affirms the *nature* of the person, composed of soul and body.

Harper's insistence on the theological importance of life "in the body" is echoed, in a certain way, by **Marie-Hélène Congourdeau** in her close historiographic telling of the life of St. Nicholas Cabasilas (1322–ca. 1392). As a historian, Congourdeau makes use of the prosopographical approach in historiography as a means of shedding light not so much on the "concept of personhood" *in abstracto*, but on the dense and interconnected web of personal relationships that makes up the historical dimension of the person. Her masterful command of the sources related to Nicholas Cabasilas (on whom she is possibly the world's foremost authority) yields a "hagiography" of a special kind. She narrows in on the central importance of the city of Thessaloniki in the formation and development of Cabasilas, thereby raising larger questions regarding the ties between place and person. She likewise shows that the many complex historical dimensions of his life help us better understand his theological priorities and concerns, thereby indirectly cautioning all who would extrapolate elaborate theories of personhood from the Byzantine tradition without paying due attention to historical context.

Our last chapter in the section on late Byzantium concerns the pivotal figure of Gennadios Scholarios (1400–1473), the first patriarch of Constantinople following the fall of the city in 1453. **Matthew C. Briel** offers us a tantalizing look at Scholarios's approach to the vexed philosophical and theological question of the relationship between freedom, necessity, and laws of nature (found in his lengthy *On Providence in Five Tracts*) – an issue at the heart of much discussion of personhood. The impetus for Scholarios's discussion is spawned, Briel argues, from Gemistos Pletho's tract *On Fate*, which put forward a strongly deterministic view of the world and of providence. Scholarios rejected such determinism, working instead with foundations laid in the earlier Byzantine theological tradition (particular by St. John Damascene), which insisted on the coexistence of divine and human freedom and a level of *synergy* in the working of good (the working of evil had only human rather than divine will to blame). Particularly interesting is his deployment of the Christological language of συντρέχειν (running together or concurrence) to describe the coexistence of divine and human action. We eagerly await the publication of Briel's larger project of translation and commentary on these important texts.

The final section of the volume brings us to the modern period. If Orthodox systematic theology is most widely known for its approach to the concept of the person (combined with the doctrine of essence-energies and "Eucharistic ecclesiology"), Orthodoxy as a whole is known to the larger world (if at all) not so much because of this, but by virtue of the Byzantine icon. The relationship between icon and person is crucial yet understudied. The study by **Evan Freeman** does the field an immense service by highlighting divergent interpretations of icons in Byzantium and the twentieth century, demonstrating the strikingly dissonant implications these differing views have not only for understanding icons but also for understanding Christian anthropology more broadly. In particular, Freeman shows that the harnessing of theories of abstraction and non-naturalism in modern art by influential theorists of the icon, such as Florensky, Trubetskoy, and Ouspensky, led to a hyperspiritualized if not entirely disembodied notion of what the "true" icon was depicting. This is put in sharp contrast to the overriding "incarnational" concern in Byzantine defenses of the icon that emphasized the "embodied" and historical basis for having icons in the first place rather than any overly spiritualized sense of depicting non-natural, even "disembodied," holy figures.

From predominantly Russian discussions of the icon, we turn to the complex and little studied figure of Nikos Nissiotis (1925–1986), a Greek Orthodox theologian and philosopher, and an important forerunner to the personalism of the likes of Christos Yannaras and Metropolitan John Zizioulas. **Nikolaos Asproulis** provides us with a helpful overview of Nissiotis, showing us the personalist concerns of his work already embedded in his doctoral thesis of 1956 on "Existentialism and Christian Faith." Nissiotis proves to be an important piece in the "puzzle" of modern Orthodox personalism, and Asproulis serves us well in calling our attention to his thought, together with several of its nuances vis-à-vis the thought of Yannaras and Zizioulas.

Our penultimate chapter introduces the important yet neglected voice of political science to the discourse on personhood in Orthodox theology. **Nicolas Prevelakis** sketches out some of the ways political scientists have linked theological differences between East and West with the political behavior of Orthodox-majority countries. A significant example by Julia Kristeva is discussed, in which she associates Orthodox conceptions of the Holy Trinity with a penchant for permissiveness, violence, and even totalitarianism in the midst of the Yugoslav War. However wrongheaded if not outright bizarre these claims may be, Prevelakis gives due warning of their influence in political science. Having alerted readers to this trend, he discusses the work of Christos Yannaras and Aristotle Papanikolaou on the issue of human rights. While both authors share similar conceptions of personhood, they interestingly draw from it rather different political conclusions.

The final chapter of the volume brings us to the realm of contemporary Orthodox systematic theology, in this case a theology in wide-ranging dialogue with important thought currents in the social sciences, psychology, and philosophy. **Nicholas Loudovikos** here serves by turns as a defender and critic of Orthodox personalism, appreciating the way it connects Christology and Trinitarian theology to discussions of the human person but attacking its deprecation of the concepts of nature, essence, and consubstantiality. In an attempt to capture, in a positive manner, the meaning of the person in Byzantine theology, Loudovikos proposes the notion of "free natural dialogical reciprocity," which points to the "reciprocal intergivenness" between persons. With this basis, he further offers important connections and correctives such an approach to personhood yields when placed in dialogue with the fields of depth psychology and phenomenology.

Conclusion

As the above summary indicates, research and reflection on the concept of personhood in the Byzantine theological tradition continues to flourish in a variety of disciplines and with a range of methodologies, not all of which sit neatly or squarely within the field of "Orthodox personalism" narrowly construed. If that field is to develop further, we suggest that it include the kind of work represented in these pages. That the Byzantine Christian tradition – from its earliest to its latest instantiations – has much to say about the themes and topics that occupy the modern search for the meaning of personhood should not be in doubt. But the precise source or form of those insights may not always be obvious or straightforward. We hope that readers discover, as the editors have done, some of the many scholarly and theological insights and surprises contained herein.

Section I
Ancient Christian, early Byzantine

1 Personal relationship as a prerequisite for moral imitation according to the Apostle Paul

Christos Karakolis

When I received the tempting proposal to read a paper on the New Testament conception of person within the framework of a conference on personhood in Orthodox theology, my first thought was to decline since the New Testament does not seem, at first view at least, to contain anything relevant to the so-called theology of the person according to modern-day Orthodox theology.[1] However, on second thought, I wondered whether the New Testament, while never using the term "person" in its later philosophical and theological sense, does contribute to this issue, although by means of a different terminology. Since in the contemporary Orthodox context a real dialogue between biblical and systematic theology is almost nonexistent,[2] I finally considered this invitation as an important opportunity and a positive challenge.

In the New Testament, the term πρόσωπον[3] should be rather understood in light of its Old Testament usage,[4] meaning physical presence, external appearance, or even just "face," but certainly not in the sense of the contemporary theological concept. For this reason, I chose to focus on the field of personal relationships since, evidently, personal relationships can only be held by persons, while by the quality of such relationships, significant conclusions can be drawn about the traits and qualities of the respective persons and at a second step also of the concept of person as a whole.

From the point of view of New Testament theology, personal relationship should not be examined on an exclusively horizontal axis – namely, with regard to the relations of the faithful to each other and to the world – but also on a vertical axis – i.e., with regard to the relations between the faithful and the Lord Jesus Christ. In the latter case, the dimension of somehow participating in Christ's Passion, as well as in his resurrection, is necessarily included. In other words, personal relationship should not only be understood as communication between different parties but also as apprenticeship, simulation, and even identification, not only on the level of behavior but also on a deeper level of organic unity.[5]

Within the narrow limits of the present chapter, it is impossible to examine all of the parameters of the issue at hand in every single relevant text of the New Testament. Such an undertaking would need the space of a monograph. Therefore, I have limited myself to the epistles of Paul, which provide us with a variety of texts that deal with the theme of this chapter. My attention was especially caught by one of the notable Pauline concepts with regard to personal relationships – namely, that of imitation.[6] In the present chapter, I will argue that in Paul, the theological concept of imitation is a corollary of personal relationship or, conversely worded, personal relationship is a prerequisite for imitation in its theological meaning. Therefore, apprehending this concept is crucial for the clarification of the meaning and the significance of personal relations in Paul.[7]

* * *

As is evident, especially in the *praescriptiones* of his epistles, Paul understands himself as being both a slave (δοῦλος)[8] and an apostle (ἀπόστολος)[9] of Jesus Christ. In the ancient biblical context, an ἀπόστολος was an envoy of someone superior to him running an errand or transferring a message on his master's behalf.[10] Therefore, these envoys could well be slaves.[11] A good slave was not only supposed to be fully devoted to his master but also ideally to know the mind – i.e., the way of thinking and the ultimate will – of his master.[12] On the other hand, the receivers of the master's message would (also ideally) have to welcome the envoy as though he were the sender himself.[13] The famous phrase of Paul ζῶ δὲ οὐκέτι ἐγώ, ζῇ δὲ ἐν ἐμοὶ χριστός ("it is no longer I who lives, but Christ who lives in me" – Gal 2:20) does not only imply Paul's mystical union with Christ[14] but also very practically that Paul is fully identified with Christ as his authorized representative and "apostle" in the sense of his envoy in order for the recipients of his preaching to believe in it and follow it as though Christ himself would be preaching to them.[15] Paul then carries out the will of Christ, represents him, and transfers his message – namely, the gospel – to the world because he already met and got to know him personally outside of the gates of Damascus,[16] where he was assigned with the role of apostleship.

In order to express his own particular relations with the members of his communities, Paul presents himself as their spiritual father,[17] thus drawing from ancient family imagery.[18] The unique relationship of a father with his children does not begin and end with their birth, but is lifelong and includes the appropriate training of the children and their adequate preparation so that when they become adults, the children will be capable of succeeding their father, possibly as heads and protectors of their initial family, and eventually as founders of their own patriarchal families. For their part, the children have to learn their father's profession by watching him practicing it in order to be able to absorb and put into practice everything he knows. An apprenticeship of this kind is realized by means of imitating the father – an imitation that necessarily presupposes personal contact and communication between the children and their father. Only in such a way can the children witness the actions of their father, try to imitate him, and, finally, acquire his skills, thus becoming enabled to succeed him in his profession when becoming of age.[19]

Of course, the relationship between father and son is not exhausted in a simple transfer of the former's knowledge and skills to the latter. In an ideal case, such a relationship is characterized by mutual trust, love, empathy, self-sacrifice, unselfishness, sharing, and self-overcoming, in other words all qualities that are inherent to communion (κοινωνία).[20] It is in this light that we should understand Paul's admonitions toward the believers to imitate him as their spiritual father. There is a number of such direct prompts or references in the Pauline texts:

- I urge you, then, be **imitators** of me (1 Cor 4:16).
- Be **imitators** of me, as I am of Christ (1 Cor 11:1).
- Brethren, join in **imitating** me, and mark those who so live as you have an example in us (Phil. 3:17).
- And you became **imitators** of us and of the Lord (1 Thess 1:6a).[21]
- For you, brethren, became **imitators** of the churches of God in Christ Jesus which are in Judea; for you suffered the same things from your own countrymen as they did from the Jews, who killed both the Lord Jesus and the prophets, and drove us out, and displease God and oppose all men by hindering us from speaking to the Gentiles that they may be saved (1 Thess 2:14–16).

This last passage does not seem to be fully in line with the previous ones, because it presents imitation as a process that takes place without the requirement of personal communication, since, obviously, the members of the newly established community of Thessaloniki as a whole are not personally acquainted with the Christian communities of Judea. However, Paul makes use here of a logical chain, according to which the choice of unjustly suffering as a standard attitude to be imitated, is not limited to the churches of God in Judea, but is also found in the lives of the Lord Jesus, the prophets, and, finally, Paul himself along with his collaborators. Thus although not explicitly mentioned, it is clear that the imitation of the churches of Judea on the part of the Thessalonians is inextricably linked to imitating Paul, the prophets, and the apostles. It would just seem that here the concept of imitation is not yet as theologically as developed, as in Paul's later epistles.[22]

A similar use of the concept of imitation can be found in the Deutero-pauline 2 Thess:[23]

> For you yourselves know how you ought to **imitate** us; we were not idle when we were with you, we did not eat any one's bread without paying, but with toil and labor we worked night and day, that we might not burden any of you. It was not because we have not that right, but to give you in our conduct an example to **imitate**.
> (2 Thess 3:7–9; emphasis added)

Because of the limits of the present chapter, I will not be able to take into account the relevant passages of Ephesians and Hebrews,[24] which differ in significant ways from the more-or-less uniform Pauline line of thought that I previously sketched. This differentiation can be explained by the fact that both Ephesians and Hebrews were not written by Paul himself, but by unknown authors, probably after the apostle's death.[25] With regard to our theme, Ephesians in particular is the only New Testament text that speaks of the possibility of a direct imitation of God himself (Eph 5:1).[26]

Apart from these direct references, Paul formulates even more indirect exhortations that are one way or another connected with the notion of imitation.[27] In this regard, Paul tends to portray himself as the model for the faithful to follow in the moral field. Philippians is an excellent case study in this regard. In this epistle, Paul urges the Christians of Philippi to remain united and warns them of the harmful influence of heretics, projecting himself as a role model. Concretely, at the beginning of Philippians, Paul presents himself not as focusing on any self-centered interests, but as prioritizing the spreading of the gospel and the spiritual interest of all other Christians:

> I want you to know, brethren, that what has happened to me has really served to advance the gospel, so that it has become known throughout the whole praetorian guard and to all the rest that my imprisonment is for Christ; and most of the brethren have been made confident in the Lord because of my imprisonment, and are much more bold to speak the word of God without fear. Some indeed preach Christ from envy and rivalry, but others from good will. The latter do it out of love, knowing that I am put here for the defense of the gospel; the former proclaim Christ out of partisanship, not sincerely but thinking to afflict me in my imprisonment. What then? Only that in every way, whether in pretense or in truth, Christ is proclaimed; and in that I rejoice.
> (Phil 1:12–18)

In the same line, in Philippians 3, Paul presents himself as having willingly abandoned all of his advantages as a Jew in order to find Christ:

> But whatever gain I had, I counted as loss for the sake of Christ. Indeed, I count everything as loss because of the surpassing worth of knowing Christ Jesus my Lord. For his sake I have suffered the loss of all things, and count them as refuse, in order that I may gain Christ and be found in him, not having a righteousness of my own, based on law, but that which is through faith in Christ, the righteousness from God that depends on faith.
> (Phil 3:7–9)

If we scrutinize the interrelation between the narrative (1:12–26) and the exhortative (1:27–2:18) part of Philippians,[28] we can deduce a strong semantic and theological correlation between them. By this means, Paul urges the believers to follow in their lives (imperative) what he has already realized in his own spiritual life (indicative).[29]

Of course, Paul does not consider himself as being the ultimate target of the imitation of the faithful, as he himself imitates Christ. However, he does not imitate Christ as his father – i.e., in the way that the faithful are expected to imitate him as their spiritual father – but, according to the above analysis, as his slave. Because the believers are the (spiritual) children of Paul and because Paul is Christ's slave, the believers are also themselves slaves of Christ, since in the ancient world, slavery was hereditary.[30] On this basis, the faithful are practically urged to imitate Christ himself as their ultimate master by following the example of Paul, their spiritual father.

In the example of Philippians, the fact that the believers are expected to ultimately imitate Christ himself is clearly stated by Paul in his exhortation to them συμμιμηταί μου γίνεσθε καθὼς κἀγὼ χριστοῦ ("be imitators of me as I am of Christ" – 3:17), as well as in the epistle's famous Christological hymn (2:6–11), which is embedded in the exhortatory part of the letter (1:27–2:18). Paul introduces this hymn by the following admonition: "Have this mind among yourselves, which is yours in Christ Jesus" (2:5). The hymn that follows refers accordingly to the Lord Jesus Christ's unity with God the Father, his self-humiliation, and his final exaltation by God in order to demonstrate what the daily moral practice of the faithful should look like.[31]

According to the aforementioned, in order for the faithful to be able to imitate Christ, they must first imitate Paul, who imitates Christ by way of his life because he has personally met and gotten to know Christ as the resurrected Lord, which is not the case for the faithful of his communities. In this regard, 2 Corinthians 5:16 makes a quite important distinction in the way one has to know Christ so as to be able and willing to imitate him, and thus reach salvation. Many have already witnessed Jesus κατὰ σάρκα (according to the flesh), but this is obviously an inadequate knowledge. Paul does not judge anyone according to the flesh because everything has been renewed through the Christ event (2 Cor 5:17; cf. Gal 6:15).[32] Consequently, Christ can only be imitated if he is viewed as the Son of God and the true Lord. Real imitation of Christ presupposes a genuine and deep perception of his true identity.

This certainly applies to Paul himself who was personally called by the resurrected to his apostolic office. However, this does not apply to the faithful of Paul's communities who only have an indirect relationship with Christ through the mediation of Paul being their spiritual father. It is noteworthy that the situation of the faithful within the present world is characterized by Paul as *in Christ* (ἐν χριστῷ). This expression denotes the new life that the believer acquires in baptism, thus organically participating in the body of Christ – namely, the Church.[33] This kind of participation implies the existence of an organic link with all other believers and, on a higher level, with Christ himself as well. However, ἐν χριστῷ does not imply or presuppose the existence of a personal relationship with Christ. Such a relationship is signified in Paul by the expression *with Christ* (σὺν χριστῷ) that refers to the Parousia of the Lord, when believers are expected to meet Christ in heaven and from then on to always be with him (1 Thess 4:16f).[34]

Therefore, we should here speak of an imitation-chain. The believers are able to imitate the Apostle Paul, whom they personally know, while Paul is able to imitate and indeed does imitate the Lord Jesus Christ, whom he also personally knows. On the other hand, the believers cannot directly imitate Christ, but only through Paul, which should, however, be more than enough for them, since Paul has already reached the ultimate level of imitation, which is complete identification with Christ: ζῶ δὲ οὐκέτι ἐγώ, ζῇ δὲ ἐν ἐμοὶ χριστός ("it is no longer I who lives, but Christ who lives in me" – Gal 2:20).[35]

Lastly, it is of significance that in Philippians Paul does prepare the faithful even for the worst case scenario – namely, not only a long or even permanent absence of him from the community because of imprisonment or other unforeseen events (1:27; 2:23) but also his possible death that may even precede Christ's imminent Parousia (1:20, 23). In view of such a perspective, Paul had to give a convincing answer to the question about the possibility of Christ's imitation by the newly converted faithful who had never met him personally and thus were not able to be parts of the aforementioned threefold imitation-chain (faithful-Paul-Christ). In Philippians, Paul's indirect answer to this problem is the recommendation of Timothy not only as his faithful disciple and spiritual child but also as his absolutely trustworthy envoy (2:19–23). Paul implies that Timothy has already imitated him in an excellent way, as a son who imitates his father in learning his father's profession and serving his father at it (ὡς πατρὶ τέκνον σὺν ἐμοὶ ἐδούλευσεν εἰς τὸ εὐαγγέλιον: "as a son with his father he has served me in the gospel" – 2:22), and is thus an exemplary case that should be followed by the members of the Philippian community.[36] This brief recommendation of Timothy clearly extends the aforementioned imitation-chain. In the absence of the apostles, the community members should search for imitation examples in the persons of the apostles' faithful disciples. At this point, Paul practically introduces the concept of imitating Christ through the imitation of the saints, and thus indirectly the long historical and spiritual imitation-chain that connects the present-day Church with her founder, the Lord Jesus Christ himself.

It is probably not coincidental that in Philippians, right after the recommendation of Timothy, Paul even includes a recommendation of Epaphroditus (2:25–30), an envoy of the Philippian community to Paul and probably the bearer of the Apostle's letter back to the Philippians.[37] Paul characterizes Epaphroditus as his *brother, fellow worker, and fellow soldier*, characterizations that position Epaphroditus among some of Paul's closest disciples and associates.[38] Furthermore, Paul urges the Philippians to receive Epaphroditus *with all joy* and honor him, as well as other people like him *because he nearly died for the work of Christ*. Without stating it clearly, Paul presents Epaphroditus as actually imitating him in his self-sacrificial spirit for the sake of the gospel (cf. Phil 1:12–18). Epaphroditus, as an exemplary community member, could be viewed as the missing link in the imitation-chain between the apostles (Paul) and their immediate disciples (Timothy) on the one hand, and the Christian community on the other hand (the Philippian Christians).

* * *

On the basis of the aforementioned analysis, it would seem that the spiritual life, or else the new life in Christ according to Paul's theological terminology, presupposes the practice of imitation, which is based on personal relationships. This kind of imitation ultimately goes back to Christ himself, however always through the individual spiritual master and father or mother who leads his or her children in Christ through his or her example toward their final salvation.

As previously mentioned, eventually, everything goes back to Christ. Every personal relationship reaches its full potential, when it is connected with the person of Christ as the perfect example. In Paul, Christology is the fundament and the source of ethics.

Personal relationships in Christ are based on humility (Phil 2:3f), following the example of Jesus Christ himself (Phil 2:5–8). Humility is inextricably connected with love, which according to Paul is the most significant virtue and the decisive criterion for the value and genuineness of all other virtues (1 Cor 13). Christian spiritual life cannot be realized unless it is truly based on such personal relationships that are characterized by humility and unconditional love.

In my previous analysis, I mentioned that a personal relationship with Christ is the presupposition of Christ's imitation, at least for Paul himself as an apostle who witnessed Christ and was called by him to his apostolic office and mission. Paul, however, awaited the coming of the Lord during his own life span.[39] To him, it was unthinkable that later Christian generations would follow in a time when all apostles would have passed away.[40] Therefore, while he did consider the possibility of Christ's imitation through personal relationship not only with an apostle but also with an apostle's disciple, he did not go as far as to speak of what has later become known as *imitatio sanctorum*, an imitation that is not only necessarily based on personal acquaintance but also on just reading the vitae of the saints or more generally by listening to narratives about them within the ecclesial social space.

I believe that the imitation of the saints, as well as the deeply rooted belief of the possibility of a mystical relationship with Christ, the apostles, and the saints, both on an individual and on a social-liturgical level is to a great extent historically and theologically based on Paul's teaching about personal relationships in Christ as the presupposition of imitation and consequently of Christian ethos and soteriology. In light of this position, it would perhaps be a gain for the contemporary Orthodox theology of personhood if it would turn its attention also to its biblical roots and in particular to the relevant Pauline teaching. Such a shift of focus would in my opinion not only be an enrichment but also could offer an additional possibility for a reorientation in a field of studies that nowadays seems to have reached a theological plateau.

Notes

1 Cf. esp. Yannaras (2007); Zizioulas (1985), as well as the critique on their positions on personhood by Williams (1972); Agourides (1990).
2 Cf. the relevant critical review by Stylianopoulos (1997), pp. 162–85. The only text known to me that criticizes the Orthodox "theology of the person" from the point of view of contemporary biblical scholarship is the aforementioned text of Agourides (1990).
3 There are 76 references of the word πρόσωπον in the New Testament, while in the LXX, it occurs over 1,200 times.

4 Cf. Eduard Lohse, "πρόσωπον," *TWNT* 6, pp. 771–4.
5 Cf. the characteristic example of 1 Cor 12:12–27 in which Paul presents the church as being identical with the crucified and resurrected body of Christ, and her members as organic parts of this body. See on this dimension of Pauline ecclesiology Matera (2012), pp. 136–7.
6 On the Pauline concept of imitation, see the comprehensive presentation of Burridge (2007), esp. pp. 144–8.
7 I will limit my main focus on the Pauline *Homologoumena* according to the current research consensus – namely, Rom, 1 and 2 Cor, Gal, Phil, 1 Thess, and Philem; cf. on the issue of the so-called Deutero-pauline literature Boring (2012), pp. 319–28. This focus should offer a clearer view of the understanding of the historical Paul himself.
8 Rom 1:1; Gal 1:10; Phil 1:1; cf. also the Deutero-Pauline Tit 1:1, in which the author makes a distinction between being a slave of God and an apostle of Jesus Christ.
9 1 Cor 1:1; 2 Cor 1:1; Gal 1:1; 1 Thess 2:7; cf. also the Deutero-Pauline references Eph 1:1; Col 1:1; 1 Tim 1:1; 2 Tim 1:1; Tit 1:1. The two terms are expressly combined in Rom 1:1. There are of course even more indirect references to both terms in the Pauline literature.
10 On the tradition-historical background, and the meaning of ἀπόστολος in Paul, see de Boer (2011), pp. 21–6.
11 Cf. Bash (1997), p. 6.
12 Cf. Harrill (2012), pp. 86–8.
13 See the relevant discussion in Orr (2014), pp. 161–74.
14 Cf. Arnold (2014), pp. 155–6.
15 Cf. Orr (2014), pp. 169–71.
16 Cf. Acts 9:3–8; 22:6–11; 26:12–19; Rom 1:1; 1 Cor 15:10; Gal 1:15–17.
17 On the other hand, it is noteworthy that Paul usually calls the faithful brethren (ἀδελφοί), especially when wanting to stress the fact of their common spiritual adoption by God; see the relevant discussion in Lewis (2016), pp. 97–9, with regard to the relevant references in Rom 1–5.
18 Cf. 1 Cor 4:15: "For though you have countless guides in Christ, you do not have many fathers. For I became your father in Christ Jesus through the gospel" (all English translations of the Greek New Testament text have been taken from the RSV); cf. Stettler (2014), pp. 365–6.
19 Professions in antiquity were usually hereditary; cf., for instance, York (2012), p. 22; Clarke (1971), pp. 110–13.
20 A very important term not only for contemporary Orthodox theology (cf. MacDougall [2015], pp. 19–22) but also for Paul himself; cf. Rom 15:26; 1 Cor 1:9; 10:16; 2 Cor 6:14; 8:4; 9:13; 13:13; Gal 2:9; Phil 1:5; 2:1; 3:10; Philem 6. See on κοινωνία in Paul, Ogereau (2014), pp. 348–50; Matera (1996), pp. 175–7; Thiselton (2000), pp. 103–6, among others.
21 On the basis of the earlier analysis, the expression "through us" should be implied after the word "and." Here Paul states clearly enough that the Thessalonians should first imitate himself and then only at a second step also the Lord; contra Weima (2014), p. 90.
22 1 Thess is Paul's first epistle and the most ancient Christian document; cf. Boring (2012), pp. 209–10.
23 On the Deutero-Pauline character of 2 Thess see *ibid.*, 362–5.
24 Eph 5:1; Heb 6:12; 13:7.
25 On the problems of dating and authorship of these two epistles, see Boring (2012), pp. 345–6 and 413–21, respectively.
26 On the notion of God's imitation, see Lincoln (1990), pp. 310–11.
27 See Gerber (2005), pp. 415–20.
28 Cf. Alexander (1989), esp. pp. 94–6.
29 In my still unpublished paper 'Ο δέσμιος Παῦλος και το ἦθος των πιστῶν των Φιλίππων: Νοηματικές αντιστοιχίες και ηθική διδασκαλία στο Φιλ. 1,12–2,18' (forthcoming in the volume of the conference *Παῦλος – Φίλιπποι δύο χιλιετίες: Τό εὐρωπαϊκό ὅραμα*

τοῦ Ἀποστόλου τῶν Ἐθνῶν, which took place in Philippi from May 20 to 22, 2011), I have attempted a detailed comparative study between Phil 1:12–26 and 1:27–2:18 on the level of both semantics and ethics.
30 See Volti (2012), p. 2.
31 Being actually in a poetic form, the Christological hymn leaves a much more intense effect on its listeners than a simple narrative would do; cf. Travers (2005), p. 595.
32 Cf. Harris (2005), pp. 427–30.
33 Cf. the relevant discussion on the various nuances of ἐν χριστῷ, including the ecclesiological one, in Moule (1977), pp. 54–96.
34 On the use and the significance of the expression σὺν χριστῷ in Paul, see Dunn (1998), pp. 401–4.
35 Cf. Colijn (2010), pp. 281–2.
36 It is in this spirit that Timothy should be received by the faithful of the church community in Philippi, cf. Heil (2010), pp. 134–5.
37 Cf. O'Brien (1992), p. 278.
38 Cf. Rom 16:3.9.21.23; 1 Cor 1:1; 2 Cor 1:1; 2:13; 8:18.22f; 12:18; Phil 4:3; 1 Thess 3:2; Philem 1.7.16.20.24 as well as Eph 6:21; Col 1:1; 4:7.9.11 from the Deuteropauline epistles.
39 Cf. characteristically Rom 13:11; 1 Cor 7:29–31; 16:22; Phil 4:5; 1 Thess 4:14–5:11.
40 On the so-called Pauline *Naherwartung*, cf. Plevnik (1997), pp. 276–81.

Select bibliography

Agourides, S. (1990), "Μποροῦν τὰ πρόσωπα τῆς Τριάδας νὰ δώσουν τὴ βάση γιὰ περσοναλιστικὲς ἀπόψεις περὶ τοῦ ἀνθρώπου; Σχόλια σὲ κάποιες σύγχρονες Ὀρθόδοξες θεολογικὲς προσπάθειες," *Synaxi* 33, pp. 67–78.

Alexander, L. (1989), "Hellenistic Letter-Forms and the Structure of Philippians," *JSNT* 37, pp. 87–101.

Arnold, B. (2014), *Christ as the Telos of Life: Moral Philosophy, Athletic Imagery, and the Aim of Philippians*, WUNT 2/371, Tübingen.

Bash, A. (1997), *Ambassadors for Christ: An Exploration of Ambassadorial Language in the New Testament*, WUNT 2/92, Tübingen.

Boer, M. C. de (2011), *Galatians: A Commentary*, Louisville KY.

Boring, M. E. (2012), *An Introduction to the New Testament: History, Literature, Theology*, Louisville KY.

Burridge, R. A. (2007), *Imitating Jesus: An Inclusive Approach to New Testament Ethics*, Grand Rapids MI.

Clarke, M. L. (1971), *Higher Education in the Ancient World*, London.

Colijn, B. B. (2010), *Images of Salvation in the New Testament*, Downers Grove IL.

Dunn, J. D. G. (1998), *The Theology of Paul the Apostle*, Grand Rapids MI.

Gerber, C. (2005), *Paulus und seine 'Kinder:' Studien zur Beziehungsmetaphorik der paulinischen Briefe*, BZNW 136, Berlin.

Harrill, J. A. (2012), *Paul the Apostle: His Life and Legacy in Their Roman Context*, Cambridge.

Harris, M. J. (2005), *The Second Epistle to the Corinthians: A Commentary on the Greek Text*, NIGTC, Grand Rapids MI.

Heil, J. P. (2010), *Philippians: Let Us Rejoice in Being Conformed to Christ*, ECL 3, Atlanta, GA.

Lewis, R. B. (2016), *Paul's 'Spirit of Adoption' in Its Roman Imperial Context*, LNTS 545, London.

Lincoln, A. T. (1990), *Ephesians*, WBC 42, Grand Rapids MI.

MacDougall, S. (2015), *More Than Communion: Imagining an Eschatological Ecclesiology*, London.
Matera, F. J. (1996), *New Testament Ethics: The Legacies of Jesus and Paul*, Louisville KY.
Matera, F. J. (2012), *God's Saving Grace: A Pauline Theology*, Grand Rapids MI.
Moule, C. F. D. (1977), *The Origin of Christology*, Cambridge.
O'Brien, P. T. (1992), "The Gospel and Godly Models in Philippians," in Michael J. Wilkins and Terence Paige, eds., *Worship, Theology and Ministry in the Early Church: Essays in Honor of Ralph P. Martin*, JSNTSup 87, Sheffield.
Ogereau, J. M. (2014), *Paul's Koinonia with the Philippians: A Socio-Historical Investigation of a Pauline Economic Partnership*, WUNT 2/377, Tübingen.
Orr, P. (2014), *Christ Absent and Present: A Study in Pauline Christology*, WUNT 2/354, Tübingen.
Plevnik, J. (1997), *Paul and Parousia: An Exegetical and Theological Investigation*, Eugene OR.
Stettler, H. (2014), *Heiligung bei Paulus: Ein Beitrag aus biblisch-theologischer Sicht*, WUNT 2/368, Tübingen.
Stylianopoulos, T. G. (1997), *Scripture, Tradition, Hermeneutics*, vol. 1 of *The New Testament: An Orthodox Perspective*, Brookline MA.
Thiselton, A. C. (2000), *The First Epistle to the Corinthians: A Commentary on the Greek Text*, NIGTC, Grand Rapids MI.
Travers, M. E. (2005), "Poetry," in K. J. Vanhoozer (ed.), *Dictionary for Theological Interpretation of the Bible*, Grand Rapids MI.
Volti, R. (2012), *An Introduction to the Sociology of Work and Occupations*, Los Angeles, CA.
Weima, J. A. D. (2014), *1–2 Thessalonians*, Grand Rapids MI.
Williams, R. D. (1972), "The Theology of Personhood: A Study of the Thought of Christos Yannaras," *Sobornost* 6, pp. 415–30.
Yannaras, C. (2007), *Person and Eros*, Brookline MA.
York, W. H. (2012), *Health and Wellness in Antiquity Through the Middle Ages*, Santa Barbara CA.
Zizioulas, J. D. (1985), "From Mask to Person: The Birth of an Ontology of Personhood," in J. D. Zizioulas (ed.), *Being as Communion: Studies in Personhood and the Church*, Crestwood NY, pp. 27–49.

2 Emotional "scripts" and personal moral identity
Insights from the Greek fathers

Paul M. Blowers

In the contemporary social-scientific academy, "moral psychology" is a relatively novel concept and discipline. As two eminent scholars in this emerging field, Darcia Narvaez and David Lapsley, have recently observed,

> The alignment of moral integrity with our sense of self-identity might be one of those facts about ourselves that is so obvious that it hardly bears examination... [which] might go part of the way to explain the odd fact that the moral self does not have a long research tradition in psychology.[1]

"Heretofore," they write, "the fragmented research on moral personality has been mostly a study of cognition without desires, rationality without brains, agents without contexts, selves without culture, traits without persons, persons without attachments, dispositions without development."[2] This state of affairs contrasts sharply with moral psychology in Greco-Roman and early Christian traditions where, absent a clinical science of human development and behavior, the analysis of the psyche as an embodied moral agent was already thoroughly bound up with sustained philosophical and theological reflection on the constitution of the moral self and on its conditioning through ethical experience.

My premise in this chapter, however, is that there are important threads connecting ancient and modern debates on moral personhood, including the question of whether personal moral identity is the teleological actualization of a potentiality immanent within human nature or rather the product of an acquired or cumulative "characterization" known only as the upshot of life lived. In contemporary moral psychology and identity theory, for example, there remain significant differences between neo-Aristotelian or neo-Stoic *naturalists* who, anxious to obviate moral relativism, strive to give an account of the essential human capacity to be a morally virtuous self, *constructivists* who argue that personal moral identity is altogether socially or culturally constructed, and *narrativists* who enhance the self-interpretive and communally intelligible dimensions of personal moral identity over a lifetime.[3]

Even if the philosophical turf was quite different, Greek and Byzantine patristic thinkers in their own ways adumbrated some of the significant problems posed in postmodern moral psychology and philosophy. In particular, they anticipated the basic tension between an account of moral personality as ontologically grounded in human nature or potentiality, and an *a posteriori* account of moral personality primarily as formed or reformed through the contingencies of concrete moral and spiritual experience.

Early on, Irenaeus of Lyons sought to have it both ways. Exploring in depth the "image" (εἰκών) and "likeness" (ὁμοίωσις) of God in Genesis 1:26–7, he occasionally distinguished between the divine "image," located in the body, and the "likeness" granted by the incarnate Christ (the New Adam) and by the Holy Spirit to the whole psychosomatic self as it matures in knowledge and virtue.[4] Even though Irenaeus was not always consistent in distinguishing image and likeness, he clearly enough believed that the *embodied* image provided the stable material groundwork for the ongoing, progressive "assimilation" to God implied by ὁμοίωσις (as opposed to ὁμοίωμα) in Genesis 1:26. Irenaeus was not really innovating here, since Paul already described adoption by God as a redemption of the *body* (Rom. 8:11, 23) and as the *assimilation* of redeemed bodies (and, by extension, whole moral selves) to the glorified body of Christ (Phil 3:21).[5]

Origen too juxtaposed the basic human affinity to God ("image") with a teleological horizon of assimilation to God ("likeness"), but on different terms. It is the intellectual soul, not the body, that is originally imprinted with the image of God,[6] since it is the seat of the active imitation of God by which human beings eschatologically attain the divine likeness.[7] Because, in setting out his vision of divine providence and judgment, Origen famously speculated about the preexistence of spirits (νόες) and souls (ψυχαί) and their downgrading (καταβολή) into material bodies after falling away from contemplative union with God, many of his critics have concluded that the final assimilation to God would have to be purely a return to bodiless spiritual perfection in primordial paradise. But even though Origen favorably compares the blissful end of souls to their original state, he also asserts unmistakably that the final "likeness" of rational beings to their Creator has never yet appeared (citing 1 John 3:2)[8] and will not exclude the body but entail its reshaping as appropriate to perfected souls.[9]

Despite their differences, Irenaeus and Origen could have agreed that humanity's ultimate likeness to God has been revealed foremost in the New Adam and perfect divine image, Jesus Christ, and that the joint vocation of mind, soul, and body is to acquire through historical existence and experience an essentially christoform perfection enhanced by the Holy Spirit. Further variations appear in Greek patristic thinking about the image and likeness of God. Athanasius, for example, is less interested in distinguishing image and likeness than to emphasize the divine grace immanent in the image, preserving corruptible human nature in the face of its attrition through sin and preparing the way for the restorative grace of the incarnate Lord, God's supreme image.[10] Gregory of Nyssa, in his turn, fuses image and likeness from the outset as together designating humanity's dignity and vocation, and yet the upshot is much the same, since attaining likeness to God is but the continuing, indeed infinite, actualization (by grace) of the perfection already latent in the original image.[11] Gregory does not concentrate on exactly "locating" the image, though the created intellect (νοῦς) is a sign (σημεῖον) of its ubiquity in human nature.[12] For Nyssen, as Vladimir Lossky accurately observes,

> The image of God in man, in so far as it is perfect, is necessarily unknowable. . .; for as it reflects the fullness of its archetype, it must also possess the unknowable character of the divine Being. This is the reason why it is impossible to define what constitutes the divine image in man. We can only conceive it through the idea of participation in the infinite goodness of God.[13]

Meanwhile, Origen's memorable distinction between the "image" as endowment and the "likeness" as teleological goal also found its own new expressions and variations in Byzantine patristic authors for centuries.[14] Moral identity was a matter of embodying over time and circumstance what humans were summoned, by nature, to become in the Creator's premeditated plan for rational creatures.

Embodying is a keyword here. Despite the privileging of intellect (νοῦς) and reason (λόγος) in Greek patristic expositions of moral psychology,[15] the seat of moral identity was destined in Christian thinking to be the *whole* of one's human nature. Athanasius, the Cappadocian Fathers, Maximus the Confessor, and other Eastern authors vigorously insisted on the cocreation and coexistence of mind (νοῦς), soul (ψυχή), and body (σῶμα) not only in order to refute Origenist speculations about spiritual preexistence and the provisionality of the body but also because they projected their coexistence as a prerequisite for the eschatological integration of the moral self (= assimilation to God) in the mystery of deification. Gregory Nazianzen and his commentator Maximus the Confessor relished the sublime irony that the body was at once a yoke and a wondrous, indispensable "coworker" (συνεργός) of the rational soul.[16] Corporeality was a theater for human nature to realize its fullness and transformation. For Gregory of Nyssa, the universal *plêroma* of human nature in its primordial potency is like a single human being and so also like a single moral agent,[17] but it has historically actualized itself only in the vast diversity of embodied persons,[18] each one challenged to become a unified, *virtuous*, and resilient moral self, a truly *free* self, through progressively integrated operation of the component endowments and faculties of human nature.

In Nyssen, and especially in Greek monastic writers from the fourth century on who resonated his influence, the frontier between the rational soul and the body was the center of gravity for such an integration, at the core of which was the work of the intellect, through reason's mediation, to rally the lower, passible soul and its somatically implicated drives of desire (ἐπιθυμία) and temper (θυμός) into the service of virtue. Gregory, however, boldly moved beyond the unsatisfactory polarization of soul and body in earlier Christian Platonism by appealing to Stoic ethics in which the mind (νοῦς), as "ruling principle" (ἡγεμονικόν), coordinates the panoply of judgments and impulses in the hierarchy of the moral self. In his trenchant dialogue *On the Soul and Resurrection*, Gregory sets a crucial precedent for later theologians and ascetics by arguing dialectically that affectivity or passion (πάθος), while not of the core essence of a human being insofar as emotional impulses are not intrinsic to the mind (νοῦς) or higher soul, is nonetheless indispensable to propelling the soul to fulfill its highest vocation, the desire for God.[19] In and of themselves, the epithymetic and thymetic drives are morally neutral and are morally valorized only by being redeemed from their "instinctive" capacity (their orientation to procreation and self-preservation) so as to propel and advance the quest for transformative union with God. As Gregory puts it candidly in the voice of Macrina,

> Such qualities in us are called emotions and they have not been allotted to human life for an evil purpose. For if that were the case and such compulsions to sin had been included in our nature, the Creator would be the cause of evil. *Such faculties of the soul exist because of the need to choose between good or evil.* Think of how iron, forged through the judgment of the craftsman, is formed in keeping with his intention and becomes either a sword or a farming implement. Therefore, if reason, which is the special ingredient of our nature, is in control of the faculties imposed upon us externally, then as scripture has made clear through the symbol of man being ordered to rule over all irrational things, none of these faculties within us is activated towards the service of evil – fear engenders obedience, anger courage, cowardice caution; the desiring faculty fosters in us the divine and pure pleasures.[20]

Concretely, this means that emotional impulses must not simply be controlled or suppressed, but filtered, refined, and, if possible, redirected or recontextualized to enrich the moral and spiritual life of the Christian. Choosing the good without the emotional "texturing" of the will would suggest a Kantian-style *tour de force* of moral reason quite foreign to the ascetical realism that Gregory shared with later monastic theologians such as John Cassian or Maximus or certain of the Fathers of the *Philokalia*, many of whom, like Gregory, employed the Christianized Stoic notion of χρῆσις, or "using" the emotions in morally virtuous ways. The formulation seems odd. Emotions were by definition passions, surges arising from the irrational soul, but some early Stoics, viewing them not simply as psychic disturbances but as errant "judgments" still within the domain of the mind, had accordingly insisted on the mind's moral responsibility for them.[21] One key, as Origen and Didymus the Blind proposed, was to anticipate them at their most preliminary stage as προπάθειαι, or "pre-passions," initial disturbances of the soul that could be closely connected with deviant or demon-induced "thoughts" (*cogitationes* = λογισμοί) or "considerations" (ἐνθυμήματα).[22] Meanwhile, Nemesius of Emesa and others in his debt recognized the physiological dimension of the passions or emotions, and their connections to bodily metabolic functions, as a factor in the self-knowledge necessary to orienting the moral self.[23]

Even though the actual physiological duration of any emotion is extremely short, emotions have "histories" or experiential trajectories. Classicist Robert Kaster, in analyzing the taxonomy of emotions in Greco-Roman thought, has introduced the notion of emotional "scripts," "the narratives we all enact when we experience any emotion," many of which have an obviously *moral* coloring. Emotions are "culturally constructed" to the extent that they represent the conditioning of emotional experience within a culture that has its own preconceptions of what constitute morally appropriate or inappropriate emotions.[24] As the Greek Fathers already recognized, emotions are dynamic registers of one's moral formation and orientation at any given point in time. And yet individual emotions can be complex "events" of the soul, since they entail impulses or judgments that take different moral tracks as they cross-fertilize, transmute, and play out in experience. Indeed, perhaps no emotion ever appears in a purely simple form, since emotions are constantly coloring each other and can intensify, suppress, modify, divert, and co-opt each other within the dynamism of the affective life of the soul.

So far as emotional "scripts" are concerned, let us take an example from Basil of Caesarea, who describes the slippage between the emotions of envy and pity, both of them species of distress ($λύπη$), in the concrete scenario of a man who, having for years bitterly envied a more privileged neighbor, shows up at the funeral of the neighbor's young son, effusively eulogizing him and mourning his death.[25] Hypocrisy aside, Basil understands that the man's envy is a deep-seated emotional pain pleading to be eased. By one "script," that pain could be assuaged through the relative pleasure of expressing authentic compassion. But the more likely script of the man's envy, according to Basil, is to vent the pain in the form of a false, condescending pity designed to publicize the envious man's now superior lot in relation to his bereaved neighbor. Basil does not explore it further, but by either scenario, an accurate moral reading of the man's pity presumably could come only through observing his subsequent dispositions and actions toward the neighbor, and how the script plays itself out over time in the trajectory of emotions involved in his response to the neighbor. Basil himself does not pursue it further, since his principal concern in this scenario is to expose envy in its pathological complexity. But in another best-case scenario, the envious man's pity could potentially transmute into authentic compassion, as the emotional energy of his condescending pity might yet become the stuff of agapeic mercy.

Missing in Basil's story, of course, is a full description of the man's formation and habituation as an "envious" human being. The point of his *Homily on Envy*, where this anecdote appears, is rather to profile how envy is a classic case of an emotion that can take on a script of its own in the soul – indeed, many scripts – that disintegrate the powers inherent in human nature and utterly undermine the moral freedom of the person. Ontologically, envy is an abuse of the epithymetic and thymetic faculties, while existentially its scenarios are self-destruction at best and homicide at worst.[26] Basil and numerous other Greek patristic and monastic writers thus addressed the healing of envy at considerable length. He and Maximus, and several of the monastic Fathers whose writings appear in the *Philokalia*, heavily emphasized the role of deep self-knowledge and of conscience as an introspective moral inventory.[27] To understand and anticipate the scripts of various emotions, after all, went far in stabilizing or redirecting them. Evagrius Ponticus, Maximus, and other monastic pedagogues who closely associated envy and the vicious passions with demonically induced "thoughts" ($λογισμοί$),[28] sought apotropaic strategies for pre-empting the barrages of emotional impulses. As in Gregory of Nyssa, such strategies included the good "use" ($χρῆσις$) of the passions – that is, converting surges of desirous or irascible affect into the raw materials of virtue (e.g., lust into *eros* for God, wrath into righteous indignation).[29] But even prospectively virtuous emotions such as pity or mercy were vulnerable to new and deviant scripts. Augustine had noted in the Latin tradition how easily pity can degenerate into an illicit pleasure since, as Aristotle first recognized, it involves comparing one's own lot with that of another of similar standing to oneself who is undergoing suffering. Pity can then transmute merely into a solipsistic catharsis of the fear of suffering that has little to do with Christian compassion or empathy.[30]

At last, let me connect this discussion more directly to the issue of personal moral identity. I do not have the space here to plumb the complex issue of the Greek patristic ontology of "person" and "individual identity,"[31] and shall restrict myself to the Fathers' thinking on the self as an integrated moral subject and agent. Alasdair MacIntyre, the contemporary moral philosopher deeply influenced by Aristotelian virtue ethics, has drawn close connections between moral *identity* and moral *integrity* for contemporary ethics, since integrity is about acting wisely and consistently across multiple social-relational contexts.[32] The same holds true, I think, in many of the Greek Fathers, who broadly drew on classical virtue ethics while drawing their exempla from the Bible. In their perspective, virtue (singular) was about excellent moral reasoning, to be sure, but also about morally healthy dispositions of the soul and salutary alignments of the soul's multiplex faculties, all for the purpose of overcoming a "divided self" and thus supporting the unity of the will and the integrity of moral agency. The Cappadocians and the monastic Fathers actually give less attention to moral reasoning per se (i.e., the mental process of discerning worthy ends) than to "reading" the soul, including the soul's emotional "scripts," and enacting – with prudence and virtuosity – healthy scripts that would build up and sustain virtuous emotional states and strengthen volition. Evagrius Ponticus, for his part, closely aligns the contemplative reading of the mind, itself a microcosm of the cosmos infused with divine ideas and intentions (λόγοι),[33] and the "shepherding" of the morally laden "concepts" (νοήματα) of the external world amassing in the soul:

> The concepts of this present world – these the Lord gave to man, like sheep to a good shepherd: for it is written, *He has placed the ages in his heart* (Eccl 3:11); yoking to him indignation (θυμός) and desire (ἐπιθυμία) as helpmates, so that with the first he may drive away the wolf-like concepts, while with desire he may lovingly tend the sheep, assailed as he often is by the rain and winds . . . And if, weary from our toil, a certain *acêdia* [listlessness] overtakes us we should climb up a little onto the rock of knowledge and converse with the Psalter (see Ps 48:5), plucking with the virtues the strings of knowledge: let us again tend our sheep as they pasture below Mount Sinai, so that the God of our fathers may also call to us out of the bush (see Ex 3:1–6) and grant us the *logoi* of the signs and the wonders. (See Ex 7:9, 11:9–10)[34]

Evagrius perfectly reflects here the idea that all the soul must be integrated and drawn up into the process of contemplating and enacting the good. Moral or ascetical performance depends on a virtuosity that has been cultivated from across all the levels of the self.

Does this mean that one's moral *identity* as such is simply the status of the interactions between reason, will, and affect at any given moment? Yes and no. In a separate study on Maximus the Confessor's virtue ethics, I have argued that for Maximus (and we could extend this to other Greek ascetical theologians), the self as moral agent is always both *diachronic* and *synchronic*.[35] As diachronic, it is the accretion of its own past (including acquired habitudes, dispositions, moral memory, etc.). Comparable somewhat to Augustine's notion of the soul being "distended" or stretched over time, the diachronic self for Maximus always carries and experiences its past in the present. But it is also stabilized by the inherent *logos* of human nature and retains the divine image that points toward the perfected orientation of all the faculties of the human constitution. As synchronic, the moral self finds itself in an immediate existential condition (κατάστασις), a constant moral threshold, the subject of an acquired configuration of dispositions and habits, with a mixed record of virtues and vices, a conscience variously tainted and convicted, and a will torn between its "gnomic" mode, a vacillation due to "mixed" moral knowledge, and its "natural" mode in the form of godly resolve.[36] As I see it, especially for Maximus, a person's moral identity – as moral integrity – remains ever poised between its chronological and eschatological horizons. It can attain consistency but must strive toward an elusive wholeness.

Reinforcing that identity or integrity, for Maximus and for much of the Byzantine monastic tradition, was thus a matter not only of maintaining ascetical and contemplative protocols from within the soul but also of remaining accountable to a community, a moral culture that cultivates transparency and the imitation of virtuous exemplars. As Alexis Torrance has demonstrated, the Eastern monastic culture of late antiquity was at bottom a culture of *repentance* (μετάνοια), repentance comprehending the whole *paideia* of contrition, self-denial, humility, and radical obedience to Christ (and by extension, obedience to one's spiritual superiors). This repentance, Torrance shows, was universally understood in monastic culture as the sole means to establish individual moral identity. What is more, he argues, "monasticism provided a basis for the formation of Christian identity not only among its own adherents, but among an increasingly aware and attentive lay audience."[37]

In conclusion, I scarcely think I will ever be asked to republish this chapter for any of the contemporary academic journals of psychology, psychotherapy, or moral philosophy and ethics. Were I to do so, however, I would wish to interject into their dialogues that what the Greek and Byzantine Fathers aggregately have offered is a model of the integrated moral self, which, though hardly likely to be welcomed in secular social and humane sciences as the solution to their own fragmentation and compartmentalization, begs still to be taken seriously as a reading of how human moral identity is constructed and sustained. Indeed, the modern conversation on moral personality has, to a significant degree, languished under the weight of the hubris of the social sciences. On the Church as its own moral culture, meanwhile, the Greek Fathers have bequeathed a rich theological anthropology that broadly and imaginatively drew on classical moral psychology and philosophy, extensive traditions of interpretation of the moral narratives and exempla of the Bible, the guiding perspectives of Trinitarian and Christological dogma, and new forms of ascetical and monastic *philosophia* that paid meticulous attention to the internal structures of the self and the interactions of mind, emotion, and will. Especially with the Cappadocians and Maximus, moreover, this patristic legacy includes profound insight into the created gift that is "nature" (φύσις) itself, nature, which Nicholas Loudovikos has appropriately called "the totally concrete incarnation of divine will,"[38] the gift that ever stabilizes, energizes, and enriches personal identity in its individual and social dimensions.

Notes

1 Narvaez and Lapsley (2009), p. 238.
2 Introduction to Narvaez and Lapsley (eds.) (2009b), p. 2.
3 These and other interpretive positions are profiled in Musschenga et al. (eds.) (2002a).
4 Cf. Irenaeus, *Adversus haereses* 5.1.3 (SC 153:26–8); 5.6.1 (pp. 72–80); 5.8.1 (pp. 92–6); 5.16.1–2 (pp. 212–16). On the interpretive complexities of Irenaeus's distinction of "image" and "likeness," see most recently Presley (2015), esp. pp. 96–7, 106–7, 158–9, 185–6; Fantino (1984).
5 As noted by Edwards (2013), p. 95.
6 Cf. *De principiis* 2.10.7 (GCS 22:181); *Contra Celsum* 8.49 (GCS 3:265)
7 *De princ*. 3.6.1 (GCS 22:280). Crouzel (1956).
8 *De princ*. 3.6.1 (GCS 22:280).
9 Ibid. 2.10.1–3 (GCS 22:172–6).
10 Cf. *Contra gentes* 2, 8, 34, ed. and trans. Robert Thomson (Oxford: Oxford University Press, 1971), pp. 6, 8, 94; *De incarnatione* 3, 4, 6, 11, 14 (Thomson, pp. 140, 144, 146–8, 160, 166).
11 See *De hominis opificio* 16, 18 (PG 44:177D-188A; 192A-D).
12 Ibid. 16 (PG 44:185C).
13 Lossky (1957), p. 118
14 Cf. Basil of Caesarea, *Hom. in Hex*. 10.17 (SC 160); Diadochus of Photiki, *De perfectione spiritualis* 4, 78 (SC 586); Maximus the Confessor, *Ambigua ad Johannem* 7 (PG 91:1084A, 1092B); *Capita de caritate* 3.25 (PG 90:1024B-C); *Quaestiones ed dubia* III,1 (CCSG 10:170). For a larger summary, see esp. Camelot (1956); Thunberg (1995), pp. 120–9.
15 See Williams (2007), esp. pp. 44–142, 190–231.
16 *Or*. 14.7 (PG 35:865B); Maximus, *Amb Jo*. 6 (PG 91:1065B-1068C).
17 *Hom. opif*. 17 (PG 44:188A-192A). For analysis of this rich notion, see Gregorios (1988), pp. 185–218.
18 See Corrigan (2009), pp. 201–2; Hart (2003), pp. 409–10.
19 Rowan Williams has offered an incisive analysis in Williams (1993).
20 *De anima et resurrectione* (GNO 3/3:42, l. 4–43, l. 1), trans. Callahan (1967), p. 222 (emphasis added).
21 On the various understanding of the roots and domain of the emotions vis-à-vis the mind in the philosophical background of Nyssen and the Cappadocian Fathers, see Barnes (2002), pp. 476–8. On the philosophical background itself, see Inwood (1985), pp. 130–1; Nussbaum (1994).
22 Cf. Origen, *De princ*. 3.2.2 (SC 268:158–62); ibid. 3.2.4 (SC 268:168–74); Didymus, *Comm. in Ps*., ed. Michael Gronewald et al. (Bonn: Habelt, 1968–1970), pp. 41,26–42,6; 43,16–20; 263,4–12. See also Layton (2000), pp. 262–71; on Didymus's treatment, ibid., pp. 271–81; also Layton (2004), pp. 114–34.
23 See Nemesius, *De natura hominis* 16–27, Greek text ed. Moreno Morani (Leipzig: Teubner, 1987).

24 Kaster develops this notion of emotional "scripts" in Kaster (2005), pp. 8–9, 85, 132–33. On the scripts of invidious emotions, see pp. 84–103; and Kaster (2003), pp. 253–76.
25 *Homilia in invidia* 2 (PG 31:373C-D).
26 Ibid. (PG 31:372B-385C).
27 See Basil's *Hom. 3 in illud: "Attende tibi ipsi"* (PG 31:197–217). Cf. Maximus's notion of an intro-circumspection in *Quaestiones ad Thalassium* 16 (CCSG 7:109). On conscience in the *Philokalia*, vol. 1 (ET), see, e.g., Isaiah the Solitary, *On Guarding the Intellect* 3, 18; Mark the Monk, *On the Spiritual Law* 69–70, 185–6; id., *No Righteousness by Works* 179, 185.
28 See esp. Evagrius, *De malignis cogitationibus* (SC 438), trans. Sinkewicz (2003), pp. 153–82. In Maximus, who speaks as much of νοήματα as λογισμοί, see, e.g., *Car*. 2.31 (PG 90:993C); ibid. 2.71–3 (1008A-B); ibid. 2.78 (1009A); ibid. 2.84 (1009D-1012A); ibid. 3.20 (1021B-D).
29 Cf. Gregory of Nyssa, *Hom. opif*. 18 (PG 44:193B-C); Evagrius, *Mal. cogit*. 5; 16–17 (SC 438:166–70, 206–8); Maximus, *Qu. Thal*. 1 (CCSG 7:47); ibid. 10 (CCSG 7:85–7). See also Blowers (1996), pp. 57–85.
30 I have discussed this at length in Blowers (2010), pp. 1–27.
31 For some fundamental analysis, see Stead (1981), pp. 170–91.
32 See MacIntyre (2007) for his fuller work on virtue and moral identity, also MacIntyre (1999). Cf. Musschenga (2002).
33 *Schol. in Eccl*. 15 (SC 397:82).
34 *Mal. cogn*. 17 (SC 438:208–12), trans. with analysis by Dysinger (2013), p. 33.
35 See Blowers (2013), pp. 338ff.
36 In Maximus, the distinction between "gnomic" and "natural" volition is an enormously significant component in his overall virtue ethics. Gnomic will (γνώμη), denoting deliberation over perceived (but possibly fallacious) goods, is not wholly negative, since it is intrinsic to the rational process of learning how to use one's moral freedom and hopefully to become virtuous (e.g., *Ep*. 2, PG 91:396C-D; *Amb. Jo*. 8, PG 91:1104A; ibid. 10, 1116B, 1117C, 1136B, 1140B; *Capita de caritate* 1.24–6, PG 90:965A-C). Yet gnomic will must ultimately be conformed to the more basic freedom of human *nature* itself, the "natural will" (θέλημα φυσική) and natural desire that are predisposed toward the will of God (e.g., *Amb. Jo*. 6, PG 91:1068A; ibid. 7, 1073C, 1076B, 1084A; *Quaestiones ad Thalassium* 2, CCSG 7:51).
37 Torrance (2014), p. 125; also Torrance (2013).
38 N. Loudovikos, "Hell and Heaven, Nature and Person: C. Yannaras, J. Zizioulas, D. Staniloae and Maximus the Confessor" (Unpublished paper), p. 28.

Select bibliography

Barnes, M. (2002), "Divine Unity and the Divided Self: Gregory of Nyssa's Trinitarian Theology in Its Psychological Context," *Modern Theology* 18, pp. 475–96.

Blowers, P. (1996), "Gentiles of the Soul: Maximus the Confessor on the Substructure and Transformation of the Human Passions," *Journal of Early Christian Studies* 4, pp. 57–85.

Blowers, P. (2010), "Pity, Empathy, and the Tragic Spectacle of Human Suffering: Exploring the Emotional Culture of Compassion in Late Ancient Christianity," *Journal of Early Christian Studies* 18, pp. 1–27.

Blowers, P. (2013), "Aligning and Reorienting the Passible Self: Maximus the Confessor's Virtue Ethics," *Studies in Christian Ethics* 26, pp. 333–50.

Callahan, V. (1967), *Saint Gregory of Nyssa: Ascetical Works*, Fathers of the Church 58, Washington DC.

Camelot, P.-T. (1956), "La théologie de l'image de Dieu," *Revue des sciences philosophiques et théologiques* 40, pp. 443–71.
Corrigan, K. (2009), *Evagrius and Gregory: Mind, Soul and Body in the 4th Century*, Farnham and Burlington, VT.
Crouzel, H. (1956), *La théologie de l'image chez Origène*, Paris.
Dysinger, L. (2013), "An Exegetical Way of Seeing: Contemplation and Spiritual Guidance in Evagrius Ponticus," in Markus Vinzent (ed.), *Studia Patristica* 57, Leuven, pp. 31–40.
Edwards, M. (2013), *Image, Word and God in the Early Christian Centuries*, Farnham.
Fantino, J. (1984), *L'homme, image de Dieu chez Irénée de Lyon*, Paris.
Gregorios, P. Mar (1988), *Cosmic Man: The Divine Presence*, New York.
Hart, D. B. (2003), *The Beauty of the Infinite: The Aesthetics of Christian Truth*, Grand Rapids MI.
Inwood, B. (1985), *Ethics and Human Action in Early Stoicism*, Oxford.
Kaster, R. A. (2003), "*Invidia*, νέμεσις, φθόνος, the Roman Emotional Economy," in David Konstan and N. Keith Rutter, eds., *Envy, Spite and Jealousy: The Rivalrous Emotions in Ancient Greece*, Edinburgh, pp. 253–76.
Kaster, R. A. (2005), *Emotion, Restraint, and Community in Ancient Rome*, New York.
Layton, R. (2000), "*Propatheia*: Origen and Didymus on the Origin of the Passions," *Vigiliae Christianae* 54, pp. 262–71.
Layton, R. (2004), *Didymus the Blind and His Circle in Late-Antique Alexandria*, Urbana IL.
Lossky, V. (1957), *The Mystical Theology of the Eastern Church*, Edinburgh.
MacIntyre, A. (1999), "Social Structures and Their Threat to Moral Agency," *Journal of Philosophy* 74, pp. 311–29.
MacIntyre, A. (2007), *After Virtue: A Study in Moral Theory*, 3rd ed., Notre Dame IN.
Musschenga, A. (2002), "Integrity – Personal, Moral, and Professional," in Musschenga et al. (eds.) (2002a), pp. 169–201.
Musschenga, A. et al. (eds.) (2002), *Personal and Moral Identity*, Dordrecht.
Narvaez, D. and Lapsley, D. (2009), "Moral Identity, Moral Functioning, and the Development of Moral Character," in Daniel Bartels (ed.), *The Psychology of Learning and Motivation*, vol. 50, Burlington VT, pp. 237–74.
Narvaez, D. and Lapsley, D. (eds.) (2009), *Personality, Identity, and Character*, Cambridge.
Nussbaum, M. (1994), "The Stoics on the Extirpation of the Passions," in M. Nussbaum (ed.), *The Therapy of Desire: Theory and Practice in Hellenistic Ethics*, Princeton, pp. 372–86.
Presley, S. (2015), *The Intertextual Reception of Genesis 1–3 in Irenaeus of Lyons*, Leiden.
Thunberg, L. (1995), *Microcosm and Mediator: The Theological Anthropology of Maximus the Confessor*, 2nd ed., Chicago IL.
Torrance, A. (2013), *Repentance in Late Antiquity: Eastern Asceticism and the Framing of the Christian Life, c. 400–650 CE*, Oxford.
Torrance, A. (2014), "Individuality and Identity-Formation in Late Antique Monasticism," in A. Torrance and J. Zachhuber, eds., *Individuality in Late Antiquity*, Farnham, pp. 111–27.
Sinkewicz, R. (2003), *Evagrius of Pontus: The Greek Ascetic Corpus*, Oxford.
Stead, G. C. (1981), "Individual Personality in Origen and the Cappadocian Fathers," in U. Bianchi (ed.), *Arché e telos: L'antropologia di Origene e di Gregorio di Nissa: analisi storico-religiosa. Atti del colloquio Milano, 17–19 maggio 1979*, Milan, pp. 170–91.
Williams, A. N. (2007), *The Divine Sense: The Intellect in Patristic Theology*, Cambridge.
Williams, R. (1993), "Macrina's Deathbed Revisited: Gregory of Nyssa on Mind and Passion," in L. Wickham and C. Bammel, eds., *Christian Faith and Greek Philosophy in Late Antiquity: Essays in Tribute to George Christopher Stead*, Leiden, pp. 227–46.

3 Personhood in miaphysitism
Severus of Antioch and John Philoponus

Johannes Zachhuber

Greek patristic thought and the notion of person: the state of the question

Scholarly interest in patristic ideas about personhood has had a somewhat curious history. It is arguable that its point of origin was denial: theological heavyweights Karl Barth and Karl Rahner both argued, albeit in different ways, that Trinitarian faith today would do well to dispose of the formula "one God in three Persons" given its inescapably tritheistic overtones.[1] This demand was not meant as a late correction to the language of late fourth-century Nicenism according to which the Trinity was one *ousia* in three *hupostases*. Instead, the twentieth-century theologians claimed that "three Persons" was unhelpful as a translation of *treis hupostaseis*. The Church Fathers, in other words, had never meant to confess a Godhead in "three Persons" in our own meaning of the term. Hypostases for them were "modes of existence" and not "independent centres of self-consciousness."[2]

The accuracy of the latter claim, however, proved controversial. Greek theologian John Zizioulas in his influential *Being as Communion* reversed Barth and Rahner's claims, insinuating that in actual fact they betrayed more about the limitations of the Western Trinitarian tradition than about the true significance of Greek patristic Trinitarian theology. Zizioulas attributed to the Cappadocian Fathers of the late fourth century nothing less than an ontological revolution. Where previous Greek thought had emphasized the universal over the particular, according to Zizioulas, the needs of Trinitarian theology prompted a fundamental reevaluation resulting in a privileging of the particular over the universal:

> What does it mean to say that God is Father, Son and Spirit without ceasing to be *one* God? The history of the disputes which broke out on this great theme [. . .] includes a philosophical landmark, a revolution in Greek philosophy. This revolution is expressed historically through an identification: *the identification of the "hypostasis" with the "person."*[3]

Zizioulas subtly ties together a number of strands in modern Trinitarian debate. He clearly weighs in on the side of so-called social Trinitarians who bemoan the alleged modalism of the Augustinian model that has loomed large over all later Western discussions. In doing so, he is eager to present, in the footsteps of Vladimir Lossky,[4] the virtues of the Eastern Orthodox tradition as a potential cure for the ills of the modern, secularized West. For my present purpose, however, these important questions have to be bracketed in favor of a third, historical claim that is central to Zizioulas's major argument: that in the working out of a solution to the Trinitarian controversy of the fourth century, the so-called Cappadocian theologians, Basil the Great, Gregory of Nazianzus, and Gregory of Nyssa, pioneered a notion of the person that is in significant ways a forerunner of the modern idea of personhood. According to Zizioulas, then, and in stark contrast to the contentions of Barth and Rahner, the Cappadocian concept of hypostasis is not at all radically different from modern notions of personhood, but instead its direct ancestor.

Is this claim plausible? One does not do an injustice to Zizioulas by observing that his reliance on the Cappadocians is not of such a kind as to settle this question. Throughout his work, he operates with assumptions whose textual basis is never really made explicit. Yet while later scholarship has attempted to support his contentions by means of more careful textual study, results have remained ambiguous.[5] I shall here follow Zizioulas's "philosophical" reading of the Cappadocians and accept as essentially correct his emphasis on their theological use of the term hypostasis.[6] I shall, however, qualify his claim that the Cappadocians brought about an "ontological revolution" that gave primacy to the individual over and against the universal. There is indeed revolutionary potential in the Cappadocian notion of hypostasis, but within the Trinitarian context, this potential remains undeveloped simply because there ultimately is little "individuality" to be observed in each of the three divine Persons.

I would, therefore, submit at this point that Zizioulas's intuition of a reversal of ontological priority in patristic text is more likely to be confirmed in the context of Christology. Theo Kobusch, in his important, though as yet untranslated, book on the "discovery of the person" (*Die Entdeckung der Person*), did trace modern ideas about the person to Christological discussions.[7] Kobusch did not, on this occasion, go all the way back to antiquity, but chose as his starting point debates about the hypostatic union in the thirteenth century. There may, nevertheless, be a case for extending the implicit logic of his thesis by asking for antecedents of this idea in patristic thought.

It would perhaps appear intuitively evident why Christology might have been the conceptual starting point for the development of notions of personality. It was, after all, one of the most important and at the same time most difficult challenges of this doctrinal topic to explain how divine and human in Christ formed a unity. This question, however, could not be answered without explaining what kind of unity this was. No easy or straightforward answer to the latter question was forthcoming, but it seems plausible to assume that the notion of personality would figure in any account that could hope to solve the problem.

Yet if this premise is granted, the so-called miaphysite opponents of the conciliar decision at Chalcedon would appear to deserve careful scrutiny in any investigation of early notions of personhood. For their most fundamental theological concern was undoubtedly the preservation of the unity of the savior against what they called "Nestorian" tendencies to separate him into two ultimately alien components.

This *prima facie* consideration motivates my present investigation and at the same time shapes its central question. How, I shall ask, did intellectually leading miaphysite thinkers consider the hypostatic union in Christ? Do their attempts to make intelligible the uniquely close union of divine and human lead them to develop notions similar to what we might call the "person" and, if so, what was the precise character of such a concept of personality?

Miaphyisitism in modern scholarship: the long shadow of Joseph Lebon

It can perhaps be taken for granted today that the century-long prejudice, according to which Eastern opponents to the two-nature formula of Chalcedon were "monophysites" who ultimately denied the fullness of Christ's humanity after the Incarnation, has been a malicious caricature. Crucial in correcting this misperception was Joseph Lebon's landmark study from 1909, *Le monophysisme Sévérien*.[8] In this book, Lebon established that Severus, arguably the major theologian of the miaphysite tradition, was by no means a "Eutychian" in the sense in which this heresy was condemned by the Council of Chalcedon. Rather, he was for all intents and purposes a radical follower of Cyril of Alexandria whose inheritance he, together with many others, saw betrayed at Chalcedon. Severus's Christology, consequently, cannot be understood as a failure to give due weight to Christ's humanity, but needs to be perceived from his principal intent to emphasize and maintain the unity of the savior against those who, he felt, were threatening it by dividing human and divine as two separate "natures."

An implication often drawn from Lebon's view of Severus was a revisionist account of the Council of Chalcedon that many twentieth-century scholars perceived as pandering to Nestorianism, for better or worse. Recent authors have, quite rightly, protested against such a reading of the council emphasizing the crucial significance of Cyril's teaching for the decisions of the synod.[9] If they are right, however, the question that becomes all the more burning is why miaphysites such as Severus were so adamant in their rejection of the council's teaching? The answer to that lies, of course, in the adoption of the phrase "in two natures" by the Council of Chalcedon. Yet why was this language so utterly unacceptable to Severus and his friends?

It is sometimes suggested that the basis of the controversy was little more than a terminological quirk. Severus, it is often claimed, understood *physis* as synonymous with *hypostasis*.[10] Therefore, to him any suggestion of Christ as being "in two natures" inevitably meant that he was in two hypostases as well, hence the charge of a "Nestorian" decision at Chalcedon. By contrast, the Chalcedonian Fathers faithfully followed the Cappadocians who had taken *physis* as a universal term and applied this to Christology.[11] Disagreement between the two sides would, in this perspective, be almost entirely reduced to the definition of *physis* accepted by the two factions.

I shall argue that this reconstruction of the controversy is at the very least an extreme simplification that does little to help us understand why Severus and others found the Chalcedonian formula so utterly unacceptable. Instead, the problem lay with an ambiguity inherent in the Cappadocian ontology. This ambiguity came to the fore when their theory was eventually applied to Christology, and in this process, the revolutionary potential of Cappadocian thought was finally actualized. For this reason, we must now briefly consider the principles of Cappadocian ontology.

The Cappadocian background

In order to appreciate the Cappadocian ontology properly, it is important to recall what theological or dogmatic problem it set out to solve.[12] Their famous formula according to which the Trinity was one *ousia* in three *hupostases*, has often been understood as a Solomonic adjudication of the original Nicene theology with its emphasis on divine unity expressed through the central phrase *homoousios* and the Origenist tradition of affirming the separate and eternal (hypostatic) existence of Father, Son, and Spirit. Closer examination reveals, however, that the controversy during the final third of the fourth century was focused on the relative virtues of ontological subordination within the Trinity.[13] The rejection of the *homoousios* among many of its opponents was due to its alleged connotation of ontological coordination between the Persons that was supposed to lead to one of two unacceptable solutions, either tritheism or the postulation of an antecedent substance from which Father and Son were equally derived.[14]

In this constellation, the genius of the Cappadocian solution consisted in their ability to offer a philosophical theory that was tailored to this particular doctrinal concern. It is most concisely summarized in the writing usually called Basil's *Epistle 38*, but which was in all likelihood written by Gregory of Nyssa.[15] This writing starts from the semantic difference between universal and particular nouns to deduce from that distinction a fundamental logical and ontological one: universal names, such as "man" (ἄνθρωπος), refer to natures (φύσεις), while proper nouns, such as Paul or Barnabas, refer to individuals.[16] How is this distinction achieved? The textbook answer to this question is the celebrated Cappadocian doctrine of properties (ἰδιώματα). Universal names connote properties that are shared by all individuals of the same class, whereas proper names conjure up more specific characteristics through which it is possible to identify the particular person. On the basis of that distinction, it is usually held that the Cappadocians achieved a rapprochement between the Nicene theologians and their opponents while neutralizing the problems inherent in the older, "derivative" accounts of the Trinity. *Qua* substance or nature, the three Persons were the same, but *qua* Person or *hypostasis*, they were distinct. This distinction, moreover was achieved without any notion of subordination of the second and the third Person, because the unity guaranteed by a common "account of being" (λόγος τῆς οὐσίας) did not allow for any "more or less" in the *ousia*, as the Cappadocians regularly cite from Aristotle's *Categories* (5, 3b33 ff.):

> If now of two or more who are in the same way, like Paul and Silas and Timothy, an account of the *ousia* of men is sought, one will not give one account of the *ousia* of Peter, another one of Silas and again another one of Timothy; but by whatever terms the *ousia* of Paul is shown, these same will fit the others as well. And those are *homoousioi* to each other, who are described by the same formula of being (λόγος τῆς οὐσίας).[17]

This reconstruction of Cappadocian ontology is not altogether wrong, but it is one-sided. It overlooks that next to this abstract dimension with its emphasis on shared and incommunicable properties, the Cappadocian ontology equally rests on a concrete notion of being, existing in and through hypostases. Looking again at the so-called *Epistle 38* and its semantic theory, it is noticeable that the difference between universal and proper names is introduced as a difference of precision in the terms' reference.[18] The universal term, it is said, has an "imprecise" or "vague" meaning (ἀόριστος σημασία), whereas the proper name permits the unequivocal identification of the individual.[19] This suggests that the universal *physis* is the concrete whole containing all its individuals.[20] In this perspective, the Cappadocian theory aims much more at continuity between the universal and the particular. Both are one and the same reality, seen either in its universal coherence or in its individual particularity:

> This, then, is *hypostasis*. It is not the indefinite notion of *ousia*, which finds no stability (στάσις) on account of the community of what is signified. It is that notion which sets before the mind a circumscription in one thing (πρᾶγμα) of what is common and uncircumscribed by means of such properties as are seen with it (ἐπιφαίνομαι).[21]

This ontological vision of unity and distinction in universal being tallies perfectly with the doctrinal needs of the Trinitarian controversy. God is both one and three; his being (οὐσία) is one and the same in all three Persons, but it is also possible to draw a clear distinction by emphasizing either the level of commonality or the level of particularity as expressed through sets of properties. Crucially, there is no *ousia* that exists in separation from the three *hypostases*, but the common *being* of the three is realized solely through their hypostatic existence.

The Cappadocian ontology thus has two dimensions. One of them may be called concrete; it perceives being as a unity-in-plurality unfolding by means of a dynamic process. It assumes that being is universal, but only exists in individuals. In this perspective, the terminological and conceptual differentiation between *physis/ousia* and *hypostasis* is not crucial, as can be seen from the fact that it is absent from Gregory of Nyssa's cosmology, which rests on exactly the same ontological foundation.[22]

The second dimension of Cappadocian ontology can be called abstract; it perceives being through properties that are shared by a larger or smaller number of individuals, or are unique to only one in particular. In this perspective, therefore, the distinction between universal or particular becomes crucial, and so does the terminological differentiation of *ousia/physis* and *hypostasis*.

It is important to see that there is little indication that Gregory of Nyssa, who offers the most elaborate development of this ontology, saw these two perspectives as mutually exclusive or even in tension with one another. For him, the abstract perspective was just another way of explaining why the same being was both universal and existing only in particulars. The concrete perspective, on the other hand, somehow implied that the transition from the universal level of being to the individual level of existence was achieved by means of properties.

It is, however, arguable that these two elements could only be held together in the Cappadocian synthesis because the focal point of their ontology was, *pace* Zizioulas, the universal and not the particular.[23] This becomes evident once we consider that the main objection against the Cappadocians was their alleged tritheism. In order to refute this claim, Gregory of Nyssa finessed (but did not alter) their theory by clarifying that individuation of the *ousia* does not break it up into individual substances (οὐσίαι μερικαί), but the one *ousia* merely exists in a multitude of hypostatic individuals.[24] This answer was as good as any in the Trinitarian context, but only because the "individuality" of the three Persons was not really an issue beyond the need for the common substance somehow to subsist in three hypostases. The moment the Cappadocian theory was tested in a context in which individuation truly mattered, its drawbacks became painfully evident.

Christology as the crisis of the Cappadocian model

If the "individuality" of the three divine Persons was not really an issue for Trinitarian theology, for Christology it was. The idea of the Incarnation, expressed summarily in John 1:14 (ὁ λόγος σάρξ ἐγένετο), necessitates the notion that the unity of the second Person of the Trinity with the human person of Jesus of Nazareth was also the union of God and man. Yet Cappadocian ontology and logic fails to account for this assumption. As we have seen, it only reckons with universal being and individual hypostases. In Gregory's model, therefore, we would either have to say that "God becomes human" is a universal statement, which is therefore equally predicated of all three Persons, or it is a statement affecting only the particular properties of the second Person.

It is perhaps fair to say that this systemic tension, which the Christological problem caused for the Cappadocian synthesis, was not recognized in the fifth century.[25] Instead, the trajectory that led to the solution of Chalcedon and beyond, was based on the assumption that the Cappadocian theory permitted, even required, the positing of two natures in the person of the savior. It was easy to substantiate this assumption with quotations from both Gregory of Nazianzus and Gregory of Nyssa, emphasizing the abstract element of their theory at the expense of its concrete side.[26] In such a perspective, divine and human natures are reduced to collections of properties, which are then said to coexist in one and the same person. One might call this an "essentialist" reading of the Cappadocian ontology, as it pretends that their *physis* is an immanent universal essence in which individuals participate.

No appreciation of the post-Chalcedonian debates is, however, possible without recognizing the deeply problematical nature of this one-sided reconstruction of Cappadocian ontology. The famous battle cry of the anti-Chalcedonian theologians, "no nature without hypostasis,"[27] is ultimately a protestation on behalf of the Cappadocian tradition. "Divine nature" for Basil and Gregory was not a free-floating essence in which individuals can participate almost at will, but a concrete universal that exists in precisely three hypostases. If, therefore, both so-called Nestorians and so-called monophysites agreed that to posit two natures in Christ implied the need for two hypostases as well, they merely demanded the full application of the Cappadocian theory.

This is important because the conflict over Chalcedon, especially from the sixth century onwards, has sometimes been characterized as a debate between the "Cappadocian" Chalcedonians and their opponents who, whatever they claimed, were evidently willing to abandon the framework of fourth-century ontology. Yet the truth, I believe, is more complicated. Christology was not ultimately compatible with the Cappadocian model; no side, however, simply gave up on it. Instead, all parties sought to develop Cappadocian insights further in order to permit a more fully worked-out explanation of the doctrine of Christ. This process was complex, tensional, often confusing, and sometimes confused. Yet its outcome was precisely the ontological revolution whose seeds were contained in Cappadocian thought.

Individuals in Severus of Antioch

At this point, it becomes possible to perceive the specific problem with the conventional understanding of miaphysite theology following the influential scholarship of Lebon. While it is true that among them there was an almost visceral opposition to the language of two natures, adopted by Chalcedon, and while it is also true that a Cyrilline emphasis on the unity of the incarnate Christ was of supreme significance for Severus and his followers, there was a deeper, philosophical intuition underlying their protest against the official religion of the Roman Empire.

This intuition can be expressed, somewhat roughly, by saying that for the miaphysites, the individual hypostasis was the uniquely privileged locus in and through which being can be known. Nature, therefore, was not rightly understood as an abstract universal essence, but signified the being of individual hypostases. Put simply, *physis* meant individuals *qua* being. Conversely, *hypostasis* meant nature insofar as it existed.

This is essentially a restatement of the "concrete" dimension of the Cappadocian theory as it was sketched above. Yet phrasing the miaphysite position in such a way also helps to understand how it could, wrongly, be seen as identifying *physis* and *hypostasis*. No *hypostasis* can be conceived that is not the concrete realization of a *physis*, while *physis* only exists in and through *hypostases*. This principle, it seemed, was compromised when Chalcedonians justified the coexistence of two natures in one *hypostasis* by referring exclusively to the abstract properties characteristic of each of them:

> We call him God, not a God, and we call him man, not a man. For he is God and man, and the [use of the] universal terms indicates that of which he is [composed] – not of particular hypostases but of universal substances.[28]

Severus's response to this line of arguing was dismissive. If this really *were* what *physis* meant in the Christological context, he urged, the consequence would be that all the divine Persons were incarnated into the whole of humanity.[29] This clearly is a *reductio ad absurdum* indicating that the philosophical model on which Chalcedonian theology is based must be false. Yet the underlying issue was far from trivial. Severus's challenge questioned the conceptual ability of his Chalcedonian opponents to explain the reality of the Incarnation in one individual person, Jesus Christ. In spite of their formula of two natures in one *hypostasis*, he alleged, the Chalcedonians have no answer to the question of how the Incarnation, understood along the lines of the conciliar formula, could have resulted in one single person of the God-man.

Significantly, the conceptual basis for Severus's charge is not the Apollinarian principle that "two perfect beings cannot become one" ($δύο\ τέλεια\ ἓν\ γενέσθαι\ οὐ\ δύναται$),[30] but the Cappadocian one that natures cannot be conceived in abstraction from individuals. It is for this reason that, according to the patriarch of Antioch, one must stipulate one nature of the incarnate, as only this assumption makes plausible the Cyrillian (and Chalcedonian) postulation of a single *hypostasis* in the incarnate Christ. One hypostasis, then, is possible only if there is also one single nature.

Any claim that the miaphysites contributed to the emergence of the concept of the person must be assessed in the context of this particular understanding of nature and *hypostasis*. At first sight, Severus's notion of *hypostasis* is very close to that of the Cappadocians. Consider the following passage from one of his homilies:

> The set of properties of Peter is one; the fact that he is from the little village of Beth-Saida, the son of John, the brother of Andrew, and the fisherman of skill, and after these things, an apostle, and because of the orthodoxy and firmness of his faith had been newly named "Rock" by Christ. But another is the set of properties of Paul, the fact that he is from Cilicia, that he used to be a Pharisee, that he was taught and learned the law of the fathers at the feet of Gamaliel, and that after having persecuted, he preached the Gospel [. . .] In the same way hypostasis does not deny genus or ousia or abolish it, but it sets apart and limits in particular icons the one who subsists. For in ousia and in genus Peter is a man as is Paul; but in propriety he is distinguished from Paul.[31]

Roberta Chesnut rightly gave prominence to this text in her elucidation of Severus's understanding of *hypostasis*, but failed to see that the text is almost literally a melange of allusions or even quotations from two celebrated Cappadocian works, Basil's *Adversus Eunomium* II 4[32] and the *Epistle 38*.[33] Parallels with the latter writing are also evident elsewhere in Severus,[34] and it is therefore arguable that this key Cappadocian text served as an important basis of Severus's understanding of hypostasis as the existential realization of natures.

It would nevertheless be mistaken to see Severus as simply replicating the Cappadocian position. Rather, one might say that he inverts it because of his need to employ their categories within the Christological context. The focal point of the Cappadocian theory was universal nature, even when considered as existing in a plurality of *hypostases*. For Severus, by contrast, the problem was how an individual was the full and genuine hypostatization of a nature; whether the latter was universal or not was of secondary importance. As a matter of fact, the single nature he postulated for the incarnate Christ would obviously only ever be realized in one single individual.

If, therefore, as Chesnut opined, Severus's "use of the word 'hypostasis' is key for understanding his Christology,"[35] it is crucial to see the close and inseparable link between hypostasis and nature in his thought. For Severus, all depends on the assumption that the one and only way natures exist – that is, occur in the realm of our experience – is in and through their concrete realizations as hypostases. While Severus takes this insight in principle from the Cappadocians, he, much more than they, makes it the central pillar of his philosophy. Thus far, Zizioulas's claim of an "ontological revolution," putting the individual at the center of the hierarchy of being, applies to Severus much more than to Basil and the two Gregories.

Things admittedly get more complicated once the precise technicalities of Christology come into play. Ultimately, Severus's conceptual difficulties explaining the union of the two natures before the Incarnation are not so different from those the Chalcedonians encountered with the hypostatic union. Be this, however, as it may, for the purpose of the present chapter, these further complications have to be left to one side here. More important are two other questions: first, is there evidence that Severus does not merely emphasize individuality but more specifically has an interest in persons? Second, what does his "inversion" of the Cappadocian position mean for universal nature?

From individual to person

If it seems beyond reasonable doubt that Severus subscribed to an ontology that put the individual at its center, can he also be seen as an early proponent of a theory of personality? Key to this will be the significance of his insistence on one "particular nature" for each individual hypostasis. The idea of *physis* as the dynamic, unifying principle of individual identity is a genuinely Christian notion, even though it resonates with much earlier Greek thought going back as far as the Presocratics.[36] It has its first elaborate proponent in Apollinarius of Laodicea, but the example of Cyril and his followers shows that it could be used without the heretical overtones it had in that fourth-century theologian. It seems immediately evident how this notion leads at the very least to a strong, ontologically rich notion of individual being and quite possibly to something akin to modern ideas of personality.

From a Western (and obviously Chalcedonian) perspective, this may, admittedly, sound counterintuitive. In the thirteenth century, discussion about the hypostatic union led to the juxtaposition of natural being (*esse naturale*: according to which the duality in Christ was emphasized) and moral being (*esse morale*) enabling the perception of Christ's personal unity.[37] This association of personality and the moral order was subsequently developed in a variety of contexts and evolved into the modern idea of personhood as a quality distinct from natural categories.[38] It might, therefore, seem that the logic underlying the miaphysite position, which builds individual existence on the unity and uniqueness of a nature, runs counter to the notion of personality, as it never reaches beyond the concept of a natural unity.

Yet if Severus was not a forerunner of the Western notion of the person, this may merely indicate that his concept of personality was different, not that he lacked one. In seeing *physis* as the carrier of rationality, free will, and overall activity and agency, he clearly followed a patristic tradition going back to Origen and Gregory of Nyssa.[39] It is, therefore, arguable that personality for Severus (as for his contemporary Boethius)[40] is not something that goes beyond nature, but the particular expression and outgrowth of a particular kind of nature – namely, rational nature. In other words, as for Severus *hypostases* possess unity of will and operation, his insistence on "one nature, one hypostasis, one prosopon" in Christ may be taken not only as a commitment to an ontologically rich individual but a concept of personality emphasizing the unity of organic, volitional, and energetic forces in the concrete existence of the individual.

John Philoponus and radical ontological particularism

Let me now turn to the latter of my above two questions. The consequences of Severus's ontology for universal being can be perceived most clearly by studying the sixth-century, philosopher-theologian John Philoponus.[41] Compared with Severus, Philoponus offers a much more philosophically reflected account of doctrinal topics; in fact, notable scholars have argued that his Aristotelianism offers the key for Philoponus's specific take on Christian doctrine.[42] Yet whatever the biographical evidence on this issue, Philoponus's theological stance *can* be fully explained as an attempt to take up Severus's mantle and develop miaphysite positions into a philosophically coherent form.[43] For the present purpose, the theological context is paramount.

Philoponus, first of all, subscribed to what I have called Severus's "inversion" of Cappadocian ontology. Natures can only exist in individuals, and any postulation of such entities detached from their instantiations must therefore be resisted. Philoponus further agreed with Severus that, for this reason, the formula of Chalcedon must be rejected. Where the Alexandrian thinker went beyond his Antiochene predecessor was in the conceptual justification he offered for that inversion.

We have seen Severus protest that the Chalcedonian claim that "divine nature" became incarnate in "human nature" would make the whole Trinity incarnate in the whole of humanity. For Philoponus, this problem was analogous to a well-known logical conundrum. Instead of saying "Socrates dies," we can say "a man dies," but this does not mean that this individual death somehow implies the death of the whole human race. Rather, it indicates that with the death of Socrates, the particular "humanity" that he incorporated has been done away with. Philosophers since Alexander of Aphrodisias had solved that difficulty by postulating "particular natures," and by the time of Philoponus, such entities were routinely accepted by the Aristotelian commentators. For Philoponus, it was therefore clear that the absurdities of the Chalcedonian position could only be avoided by introducing particular natures on both the divine and human side.[44]

While it is arguable that up to this point, Philoponus merely reconstructed Severus's argument in more explicitly philosophical lingo, he thereby nevertheless increased the tension with the Cappadocian theory. For Gregory of Nyssa's defense against tritheism was built on the rejection of particular natures. Severus, and arguably before him Cyril of Alexandria, reintroduced the latter in the Christological context but without drawing attention to the ensuing rift with the Cappadocian position, not to mention potentially devastating consequences for Trinitarian theology. Philoponus, by contrast, was not afraid of doing so, thus setting the stage for open conflict with the single most respected Christian philosophy across the entire East, accepted as classical by Chalcedonians as well their opponents.

Yet it is the next step of Philoponus's argument that fully takes him beyond Severus's position. In line with the philosophical consensus since Porphyry, Philoponus denied that individuated, "particular natures" are universal:

> Now, this common nature of man, in which no one differs from any other, when it is realised in any one of the individuals, then is particular to that one and is not common to any other individual [. . .]. Thus that rational animal that is in me is common to no other animal.[45]

Looked at dispassionately, this claim is by no means extravagant, outrageous, or even unexpected. Gregory of Nyssa rejected particular natures precisely because he wanted to avoid this particular consequence. Severus, on the other hand, worked with them in all but name in the interest of a coherent Christology. Philoponus merely drew the conclusions from the Christological development of the past century and, not least, from Severus's theology: the ontological primacy of the individual, so helpful for explaining the hypostatic union, made impossible the realistic universal Gregory of Nyssa stipulated in his Trinitarian writings.

Such a dispassionate assessment was, however, difficult to maintain given the radical doctrinal challenge emanating from Philoponus's reasoning. After all, Trinitarian doctrine was the one area of Christian theology on which a binding agreement had been reached after almost a century of controversy. The pivotal role the Cappadocians had played in this settlement surely was a major reason for the unique prestige of their thought among later Eastern thinkers. Philoponus put his contemporaries on notice that this settlement was about to unravel:

> For what should the one nature of the divinity be if not the common intelligible content of the divine nature seen on its own and separated in the conception (τῇ ἐπινοίᾳ) of the property of each hypostasis?[46]

For this outspoken and provocative position, Philoponus has been widely condemned as a tritheist, but as Dirk Krausmüller has shown, his thinking was far less idiosyncratic than heresiological accounts would suggest.[47] Whatever one's assessment of Philoponus's own contribution to the history of Christian thought – and any such assessment is marred by the fragmentary transmission of his works – his rigorous commitment to intellectual coherence serves to highlight the knock-on effect Severus's emphasis on the ontological dignity of the individual had on the ontological status of universal *physis*.

Conclusion

In this chapter, I have offered a rough sketch more than a detailed investigation of what is a complex and underexplored area of Eastern Christian thought in the first millennium. It should have become clear, however, that major miaphysite thinkers are serious contenders in the search for patristic origins of the notion of the person. Severus's "inversion" of Cappadocian ontology led him to an unprecedented emphasis on the unity and individuality of the hypostasis as the unique existential expression of being (*physis*). Individual human nature appears as the bearer of rational and volitional activity, and thus the foundation of personality.

As a result of this transformation, however, the Cappadocian claim that *physis* had ontological reality as a universal item lost plausibility, and the question of how individual persons are in reality united could no longer be answered. In Philoponus, this led to a radical form of particularism with wide-ranging, and deeply problematical, consequences for the entirety of Christian theology, not least the doctrine of the Trinity.

More generally, my argument points to Christology as a crucial doctrinal locus directing Greek Christian thinkers in late antiquity toward an emphasis on the particular and, ultimately, the person, for which there was no precedent in earlier Greek thought. It is in the context of the Christological debates following the Council of Chalcedon that these truly revolutionary ideas were first developed. Cappadocian ontology, as we have seen, played an important but also ambivalent role in this process. In order to gauge the intellectual effect of the Greek patristic tradition, it is therefore crucial to combine an emphasis on the foundational contribution of Basil of Caesarea and the two Gregories with a recognition of the significance of the subsequent transformation of their ideas in the search of an adequate understanding of the Incarnation.

One of the main features of this development is an increased investment in notions of individuality and indeed personality. Yet, as we have seen, the loss of a notion of universal being was a possible consequence of this novel concern for the individual even in the sixth century. It is tempting, but facile, to write Philoponus's views off as the opinions of a wayward, and heretical, individual. Rather, his well-argued case should be taken seriously as an indication of the difficulty anyone who seeks to defend the ontological (and theological) dignity of the universal or the community faces while equally claiming to do justice to the unique value of the individual person.

Notes

1 Barth (1955), pp. 374–80; Rahner (1962), pp. 131–2.
2 Barth (1955), pp. 379–80.
3 Zizioulas (2002), p. 36.
4 Lossky (2009).
5 Turcescu (2005).
6 Zizioulas (2002), pp. 36–9.
7 Kobusch (1997).
8 Lebon (1909). Cf. Lebon (1951).
9 Edwards (2009), pp. 137–8.
10 Allen and Haywood (2005), p. 34.
11 Cf. Gleede (2012), pp. 50–1.
12 For what follows cf. in more detail Zachhuber (2013), pp. 428–47.
13 Cf. Zachhuber (1999), pp. 21–42.
14 Cf. Athanasius., *Contra Arianos* I 14,1,1–3 (Werke 1/1, 123 Tetz) and Williams (1983), pp. 66–70.
15 On the question of authorship: Zachhuber (2003).
16 [Basil], *ep.* 38,2.
17 [Basil], *ep.* 38, 2, 19–26 (1, 82 Courtonne).
18 Zachhuber (2013), pp. 439–40.
19 [Basil], *ep.* 38, 3, 3 (1, 82 Courtonne).
20 Zachhuber (2005), pp. 75–98.
21 [Basil], *ep.* 38, 3, 8–12 (1, 82 f. Courtonne).
22 This theory is developed principally in Gregory's writing *In hexaëmeron*.
23 Thus far I agree with the "revisionist" account of Gregory of Nyssa's thought put forward by Coakley (2003).
24 Gregory of Nyssa, *ad Graecos* (23,4–13 Mueller).
25 Cf. Lebon (1909), p. 450.
26 Cf. Gregory of Nazianzus, *ep.* 101, 19: φύσεις μὲν γὰρ δύο Θεὸς καὶ ἄνθρωπος. Gregory of Nyssa, *Antirrheticus adversus Apollinarium* (151,14–20 Mueller). Cf. Zachhuber (2013), pp. 455–6.
27 References for this motto in: Lang (2001), p. 63.
28 Anastasius of Antioch, *Orationes* III (54, 15–18 Sakkos).
29 Cf. Severus of Antioch ap. John the Grammarian, *Apologia Concilii Chalcedonensis*, 14, 8 (72–5 Richard); Severus of Antioch, *Contra impium Grammaticum* II 22 (188 Lebon); III 23 (23 Lebon).
30 ps.-Athanasius, *De incarnatione contra Apollinarium* I, 2 (PG 26, 1096 B).
31 Severus of Antioch, *Homilia* CXXV (236 Brière); ET: Chesnut (1976), pp. 11–12.
32 Basil, *Adversus Eunomium* II 4,9–18 (II 20 Sesboüé).
33 [Basil], *ep.* 38, 3, 8–12 (1, 82 f. Courtonne).

34 Cf. the use of Job 1 in Severus of Antioch, *Contra impium grammitum* II, 1 (47 Lebon) and [Basil] *ep.* 38, 3, 12–30 (1, 83 Courtonne).
35 Chesnut (1976), p. 9.
36 Cf. Johannes Zachhuber, "Physis I" in *Realenzyklopädie für Antike und Christentum* (forthcoming).
37 Alexander of Hales (attributed), *Summa universalis theologica* III, inq. 1, tract. 1, quaest. 4, tit. 1–46; ed. Quarracchi, Rome (Collegium St. Bonaventurae) 1924–1948, vol. III, 70.
38 Kobusch (1997), pp. 23–36.
39 Cf. Origen, *de principiis* III 1; Gregory of Nyssa, *Contra Eunomium* III/6, 16–17. Cf. Frede (2012), ch. 7.
40 Boethius, *de persona et duabus naturis* III: "Persona est naturae rationalis individua substantia."
41 On Philoponus cf. Lang (2001); Erismann (2008).
42 Erismann (2014), pp. 143–59.
43 Zachhuber (2013), pp. 462–5, following Lang (2001).
44 Philoponus, *Arbiter* 7 = John of Damascus, *De haeresibus* 83 addit. (52, 55–65 Kotter).
45 Philoponus, *Arbiter* 7 = John of Damascus, *De haeresibus* 83 addit. (52,52–5 Kotter); ET: Erismann (2008), pp. 289–90.
46 Philoponus, *Arbiter* 7 = John of Damascus, *De haeresibus* 83 addit. (52,72–3 Kotter); ET Lang (2001), p. 62.
47 Krausmüller (2017).

Select bibliography

Allen, P. and Haywood, C. T. R. (2005), *Severus of Antioch*, London and New York.
Barth, K. (1955), *Die kirchliche Dogmatik I/1*, 7th ed., Zürich.
Chesnut, R. (1976), *Three Monophysite Christologies: Severus of Antioch, Philoxenus of Mabbug and Jacob of Sarug*, Oxford.
Coakley, S. (ed.) (2003), *Re-Thinking Gregory of Nyssa*, Oxford.
Edwards, M. (2009), *Catholicity and Heresy in the Early Church*, Farnham.
Erismann, C. (2008), "The Trinity, Universals, and Particular Substances: Philoponus and Roscelin," *Traditio* 53, pp. 277–305.
Erismann, C. (2014), "John Philoponus on Individuality and Particularity," in A. Torrance and J. Zachhuber, eds., *Individuality in Late Antiquity*, Farnham, pp. 143–59.
Frede, M. (2012), *A Free Will: Origins of the Notion in Ancient Thought*, ed. A. A. Long, Oakland.
Gleede, B. (2012), *The Development of the Term ἐνυπόστατος from Origen to John of Damascus*, Leiden.
Kobusch, T. (1997), *Die Entdeckung der Person: Metaphysik der Freiheit und modernes Menschenbild*, Darmstadt.
Krausmüller, D. (2017), "Under the Spell of John Philoponus: How Chalcedonian Theologians of the Late Patristic Period Attempted to Safeguard the Oneness of God," *The Journal of Theological Studies*, flx075, https://doi.org/10.1093/jts/flx075.
Lang, U. (2001), *John Philoponus and the Controversies Over Chalcedon in the Sixth Century*, Leuven.
Lebon, J. (1909), *Le monophysisme Sévérien: Étude historique, littéraire et théologique sur la résistance monophysite au concile de Chalcédoine jusqu'à la constitution de l'église jacobite*, Louvain.
Lebon, J. (1951), "La christologie du monophysisme syrien," in A. Grillmeier and H. Bacht, eds., *Das Konzil von Chalkedon: Geschichte und Gegenwart*, 3 vols., Würzburg, vol. 1, pp. 425–580.

Lossky, V. (2009), *Essai sur la théologie mystique de l'Église d'Orient*, Paris.
Rahner, K. (1962), "Bemerkungen zum dogmatischen Traktat 'De Trinitate,'" in K. Rahner (ed.), *Schriften zur Theologie*, 3rd ed., Zürich/Cologne, pp. 103–33.
Turcescu, L. (2005), *Gregory of Nyssa and the Concept of Divine Persons*, New York.
Williams, R. (1983), "The Logic of Arianism," *The Journal of Theological Studies* 34, pp. 56–81.
Zachhuber, J. (1999), *Human Nature in Gregory of Nyssa: Philosophical Background and Theological Significance*, Leiden.
Zachhuber, J. (2003), "Nochmals: Der '38. Brief' des Basilius von Caesarea als Werk des Gregor von Nyssa," *Zeitschrift für Antike und Christentum* 7, pp. 73–90.
Zachhuber, J. (2005), "Once Again: Gregory of Nyssa on Universals," *The Journal of Theological Studies* 56, pp. 75–98.
Zachhuber, J. (2013), "Universals in the Greek Church Fathers," in R. Chiaradonna and G. Galluzzo, eds., *Universals in Ancient Philosophy*, Pisa, pp. 425–70.
Zizioulas, J. D. (2002), *Being as Communion: Studies in Personhood and the Church*, New York.

Section II
Early to middle Byzantine

4 Hypostasis, person, and individual according to St. Maximus the Confessor, with reference to the Cappadocians and St. John of Damascus

Jean-Claude Larchet

Over the course of the last few decades, certain Orthodox theologians have developed, on the basis of modern personalism and existentialism, a particular conception of the person and the individual, and have then attempted to find a patristic basis and justification for this, especially in the Cappadocian Fathers (Basil of Caesarea, Gregory of Nazianzus and Gregory of Nyssa) and in Maximus the Confessor. It is not within the purview of the patrologist to challenge the freedom held by a philosopher or a theologian to develop a new theological or anthropological theory. It does, however, fall within the competency of the patrologist to pass judgment on the question of the agreement or disagreement of this theory with the patristic bases from which it seeks its backing.

A certain number of patrologists have long spoken out on the question of the relationship of personalism and existentialism (which we find particularly in C. Yannaras, J. Zizioulas, and the latter's disciples) with the thought of the Cappadocians, concluding that there exists a discordance between the two conceptions and noting the anachronistic character of an interpretation of the theology of the Cappadocian Fathers based on modern personalism.[1] Some patrologists have, more recently, come to the same conclusion with regard to the relationship between the same personalist and existentialist conception and the thought of St. Maximus the Confessor.[2] Since representatives of the personalist current have, during a recent colloquium devoted to Maximus the Confessor, restarted the debate[3] (with arguments which seem to this author to be marked by certain a priori notions and by insufficient reference to the sources),[4] it is an opportune moment to return to the total corpus of St. Maximus's writings to determine his precise position regarding the definition of, and relationship between, the concepts of hypostasis (ὑπόστασις), of person (πρόσωπον) and of individual (ἄτομον), all while highlighting in addition its relationship to the position of the Cappadocians and of St. John of Damascus.

Part one: the equivalence of the notions of person and hypostasis

In several passages in his writings, St. Maximus explicitly and unambiguously affirms the identity of the notions of hypostasis and person (generally expressed with the word ταὐτόν), or else their equivalence (denoted by the conjunctions ἤτοι, ἤγουν, τουτέστι or καί, or by the alternative and undifferentiated use of the two words).

a. In general definitions

He does this in a general way in the following well-known definition found in *Th. Pol.*, 14 (PG 91:152A): "*Hypostasis and person: the same thing* (ὑπόστασις καί πρόσωπον, ταυτόν); the two indeed have what is proper and particular, being circumscribed in themselves, without possessing by nature, however, their predication in plurality." This definition is similarly found in a passage in *Ep.* 15 (PG 91:549B) : "If [a hypothesis admitted by Maximus] *hypostasis and person are the same thing* (ταὐτόν δέ πρόσωπον καί ὑπόστασις)."

b. In various particular contexts

Maximus equally affirms the identity or equivalence of the two notions in particular contexts that relate to the Trinity, to Christ, to the angels, to men, but also to other natural beings. We can in particular mention the following passages:

- *Ep.* 12 (PG 91:468D): "The hypostasis, that is the person [τήν ὑπόστασιν, ἤτοι τό πρόσωπον]."
- *Ep.* 15 (PG 91:549BC): "If essence and nature are the same thing and similarly *hypostasis and person are the same thing* (ταὐτόν δέ πρόσωπον καί ὑπόστασις), it is evident that beings of the same nature and essence as one another are of a different hypostasis. And by both, the nature and the hypostasis, no being is the same as another. Thus, beings united according to one and the same nature, in other words beings of the same essence and nature, are never united according to *one and the same hypostasis, that is to say person* (κατά μίαν καί τήν αὐτήν ὑπόστασιν ἤγουν πρόσωπον), put otherwise they cannot have a *single person or hypostasis* (τουτέστιν ἕν πρόσωπον ἔχειν οὐ δυνήσεται καί μίαν ὑπόστασιν). And beings that are united according to *one and the same hypostasis, that is to say person* (τά κατά μίαν καί τήν αὐτήν ὑπόστασιν ἤγουν πρόσωπον ἡνωμένα), would be unable to combine themselves into one and the same essence or nature, that is to say would be unable to come from one and the same essence and nature. But beings united according to one and the same nature, that is to say essence, are distinguished one from the other by *the hypostases, that is to say the persons* (ταῖς ὑποστάσεσιν, ἤγουν προσώποις), as is the case with the angels, with men, or with all creatures considered in a genus or species."
- *Ep.* 15 (PG 91:552A): "Unbegottenness, Begotenness, and Procession, do not split the single nature and power of the ineffable divinity into three unequal or equal essences or natures. But these things, regarding the single divinity, that is the essence or nature, characterize *the persons, that is the hypostases* (πρόσωπα τουτέστιν ὑποστάσεις). But the [elements] that are united according

to *one and the same hypostasis, that is person* (*τά κατά μίαν καί τήν αὐτήν ὑπόστασιν, ἤγουν πρόσωπον ἠνωμένα*), are of one single hypostasis and constitute one person, differing by the *logos* of the essence or nature." We can note in this passage the reversible character of the equivalence: person-hypostasis, hypostasis-person.

- *Ep.* 15 (PG 91:552BC): "All those who are united according to one and the same essence, that is to say nature, are always of the same essence one with the other, but of a different hypostasis; [. . .] *they are of a different hypostasis by the logos of personal heterogeneity which distinguishes them by the characteristic properties of the hypostasis, according to which one is distinguished from the other and they do not come together by the characteristic properties of the hypostasis* (*ἑτεροϋπόστατα δέ, τῷ λόγῳ τῆς αὐτά διακρινούσης προσωπικῆς ἑτερότητος καθ' ὅν ἄλλος ἄλλου διακέκριται, μή συμβαίνοντες ἀλλήλοις τοῖς καθ' ὑπόστασιν χαρακτηριστικοῖς ἰδιώμασιν*). But each, by the coherence in it of its properties, carries the *logos* of its proper hypostasis which prevents it from being the same as those who are of the same nature and the same essence as it. Those things that are united according to *one and the same hypostasis, that is to say person* (*κατά μίαν καί τήν αὐτήν ὑπόστασιν ἤγουν πρόσωπον*), that is are completed in unity according to one and the same hypostasis, are of the same hypostasis but of a different essence."

- *Ep.* 15 (PG 91:553D): "The Word of God, perfect according to essence and nature, according to which he is the same as the Father and the Spirit and consubstantial with them, and *according to the person and hypostasis* (*κατά τε τό πρόσωπον καί τήν ὑπόστασιν*) different than the Father and the Spirit, preserving unconfusedly his *personal* difference (*τήν προσωπικήν διαφοράν*)."

- *Ep.* 15 (PG 91:556AB): "By reason on the one hand of the communion of the parts of which he is constituted according to essence, united to his Father and to his mother according to nature, [the incarnate Word] revealed himself as preserving the difference one from the other of the parts of which he is constituted. By reason on the other hand of the *identity of his proper parts according to hypostasis* (*τῷ δέ λόγῳ τῆς καθ' ὑπόστασιν τῶν οἰκείων μερῶν ἰδιότητος*), distinguishing himself from his 'extremes' – I mean his Father and his mother – he reveals himself in the unity of his proper hypostasis, absolutely without difference, united to the utmost degree by the *personal identity* (*προσωπικῇ ταυτότητι*) of his parts one with the other."

- *Ep.* 15 (PG 91:556D-557A): "By [the hypostasis of the Word], the extremes – which I define as his Father and his mother – unite in him without [constituting] the least difference, so that there is no complete disappearance of the *hypostatic identity* of the parts (*τῆς καθ' ὑπόστασιν τῶν μερῶν ταυτότητος*); for the coming to be of a hypostatic difference on account of the parts would *dissolve the hypostatic union into a duality of persons* (*εἰς δυάδα προσωπικήν διαλύουσα τήν καθ' ὑπόστασιν ἕνωσιν*), and could not then be seen to safeguard the *personal identity* of the parts one with the other (*τήν πρός ἄλληλα τῶν μερῶν προσωπικήν ταυτότητα*), having been divided *by the hypostatic difference into a duality of persons (τῇ καθ' ὑπόστασιν διαφορᾷ πρός δυάδα προσώπων μεριζομένην).*"

- *Ep.* 15 (PG 91:557C): "By the distinctive properties which differentiate him from those who are of the same essence, the Incarnate Word keeps, with regard to the combination by union, *the identity of the hypostasis preserved in the absolute singleness of the person (τήν καθ' ἕνωσιν φυλάττει ταυτότητα τῆς ὑποστάσεως, ἐν τῷ πάντη μοναδικῷ τοῦ προσώπου συντηρουμένην).*"

- *Ep.* 15 (PG 91:565D): "As for us, [. . .] it is in all piety that we affirm the same in Christ: by reason of the single hypostasis (τῷ λόγῳ τῆς μιᾶς ὑποστάσεως), we confess him by the identity of God the Word with the flesh, so that the glorious Trinity not become a tetrad by the addition of a person (προσθήκην προσωπικήν)."

- *Ep.* 15 (PG 91:568C): "Severus of Antioch, by saying with regard to the divine Incarnation that the essence and hypostasis or the nature and person are the same thing (ταυτόν κυρίως οὐσίαν καί ὑπόστασιν, φύσιν τε λέγων καί πρόσωπον), does not know union without confusion, even if he feigns to say it, nor difference without division, even if he boasts of doing the opposite."

- *Pyr.* (PG 91:289D–292A): "And here is what we shall find, according to you, with regard to the blessed Divinity that surpasses all essence and every good: because of its single will, it has only one *hypostasis*, as Sabellius says; because of the three *Persons*, it also has three wills, and, because of this, three natures, as Arius says, since, according to the definitions and canons of the Fathers, a distinction of wills entails also a distinction of natures."

- *Pyr.* (PG 91:336D): "You will be constrained by following your own rules [according to which the operation is referred to the person or hypostasis and not to the essence or nature] either, because of the single operation of the Holy Divinity, to speak of only one *person* in it, or because of its three hypostases to speak also of three operations (ἤ διά τήν μίαν ἐνέργειαν τῆς ἁγίας Θεότητος, καί ἕν λέγειν αὐτῆς πρόσωπον· ἤ διά τάς τρεῖς αὐτοῦ ὑποστάσεις, τρεῖς καί ἐνεργείας)."

- *Pyr.* (PG 91:340B): "Is it in a double manner, because of the duality of nature, that he operates, or is it in a single manner *because of the singularity of the hypostasis (διά τό μοναδικόν τῆς ὑποστάσεως)*? Well, if it is in a double manner, he who operates being himself one, this means that the number of energies is not linked to the number of operations. But if it is in a single manner, *because of the singularity of the person (διά τό μοναδικόν τοῦ προσώπου)*, the reasoned reflection on these things will demonstrate in this case similar absurdities [as those treated earlier]. For if the operation is hypostatic, multiplicity of hypostases and distinction of operations will have to be seen as going hand-in-hand."

- *Th. Pol.* 2 (PG 91:40C): "If [Severus] says that the union is of *the hypostases, that is to say the persons (ἐξ ὑποστάσεων ἤγουν προσώπων).*"

- *Th. Pol.* 5 (PG 91:64C): "The two natures concurring in *one hypostasis and one person (εἰς μίαν ὑπόστασιν καί ἕν πρόσωπον).*"

- En *Th. Pol.* 3 (PG 91:52C-56D): In a text too long to cite here, we observe the alternate and undifferentiated use of the notion of person (used 12 times) and the notion of hypostasis (used 10 times).
- *Th. Pol.* 13 (PG 91:145B-148A): "For the Holy Trinity, *there is identity of essence and difference of persons. For we confess one essence and three hypostases* (ταυτότης μέν ἐστιν οὐσίας· ἑτερότης δέ προσώπων μίαν γάρ οὐσίαν ὁμολογοῦμεν· τρεῖς δέ ὑποστάσεις). And for man, the *identity of person* and the difference of essences (ταυτότης μέν ἐστι προσώπου· ἑτερότης δέ οὐσιῶν), for man is one, but of one essence, the soul, and of another one, the flesh. Similarly in our Master Christ, there is identity of person, and difference of essences (ταυτότης μέν ἐστι, προσώπου· ἑτερότης δέ, οὐσιῶν); for being *one person or truly one hypostasis* (ἑνός γάρ ὄντος προσώπου, ἤτοι ὑποστάσεως), the divinity is of one essence, the humanity of another."
- *Th. Pol.* 14 (PG 91:149C): "Something *enhypostatic* is also that which comes together in composition and coexistence with another different essence *in order to constitute one person and make one hypostasis* (ἐνυπόστατόν ἐστι, τό ἄλλῳ διαφόρῳ κατά τήν οὐσίαν εἰς ἑνός σύστασιν προσώπου καί μιᾶς γένεσιν ὑποστάσεως)."
- *Th. Pol.* 14 (PG 91:152A): "The union is thus hypostatic which links and brings different essences, or natures, *into one person and one and the same hypostasis* (ὑποστατική οὖν ἕνωσίς ἐστιν, ἡ τάς διαφόρους οὐσίας ἤγουν φύσεις εἰς ἕν πρόσωπον, καί μίαν καί τήν αὐτήν ὑπόστασιν συνάγουσά τε καί συνδέουσα)."
- *Th. Pol.* 16 (PG 91:192C): "[The gnomic will] constitutes a free impulse causing us to be pulled from both sides, and a distinctive mark determining not the nature but properly speaking *the person and hypostasis* (ἀλλά προσώπου κυρίως καί ὑποστάσεως)."
- *Th. Pol.* 16 (PG 91:201D-204A): The notions of "composite person" and "composite hypostasis" are used by Maximus as equivalents.
- *Th. Pol.* 19 (PG 91:225A): "If they are attached absolutely to *hypostatic, that is personal* [wills] (ὑποστατικά, τουτέστι προσωπικά) in beholding natural things with an evil eye, they introduce also the differentiation of the person and decree that which is not natural and is the shaming of essences."
- *Th. Pol.* 23 (PG 91:269CD): "I declare that the life-giving flesh of the Son of God has, in the Word of God, all that is supernatural from his proper [divine] nature, completing the two natures *in one person and one hypostasis* (εἰς ἕν πρόσωπον καί μίαν ὑπόστασιν) of the Word of God."

We can add to these two texts that were not written by Maximus but reflect his thoughts:

- *Dis. Byz.* 14 (CCSG 39:107): "It is thus clear that there is no operation according to hypostasis. Otherwise we would be constrained to attribute hypostatic energies to the Father and the Spirit in the same manner as to the Son and, according to you, the blessed Divinity would have four operations: three distinct – those *of the persons* which compose it – and one common to the three, indicating the natural communion of *the three hypostases (τρεῖς ἀφοριστικὰς τῶν ἐν οἷς ἐστι προσώπων, καί μίαν κοινήν σημαντικήν τῆς κατά φύσιν τῶν τριῶν ὑποστάσεων κοινότητος)*."

- *Ep. Cal.* (CCSG 39:166.18–22): "if diverse properties naturally characterize a composite of different essences, because the difference of the natures is in no wise suppressed by the union, but on the contrary, being maintained the property of each nature, it comes together *in one single person and one single hypostasis*."

In these various passages and in many others, we can observe the identity of these terms, their equivalence, and their reversibility (we could in every case use one of the terms instead of the other); the context does not give any connotation proper to one or to the other, which would allow us to distinguish one from the other.

c. Agreement with the Cappadocians

In affirming the equivalence of the concepts of hypostasis and person, Maximus explicitly bases himself on the Fathers who preceded him:

> Common, then, and universal or general, according to the Fathers, are essence and nature: they affirm that these things are equivalents. Proper and particular are hypostasis and person: we find that these expressions according to them mean the same thing.[5]

Two passages from Gregory of Nazianzus, cited *in extenso* by Maximus, neatly affirm the equivalence of the notions of hypostasis and person. The first is, "Since it must be held that there is one God and to confess *the three hypostases, that is to say* persons, and each with its property."[6] The second is as follws:

> When I say "God," be hit by the illumination of one single light and three lights: three in what concerns the properties or *the hypostases – if we wish to call them thus – or the persons (τρισὶ μὲν, κατὰ τὰς ἰδιότητας, εἴτουν ὑποστάσεις, εἴ τινι φίλον καλεῖν, εἴτε πρόσωπα)*, for we do not wage a war amongst ourselves over names, as long as the different syllables bring us to the same thought.[7]

After this, Maximus concludes,

> Such is the symphony which our inspired Fathers, Gregory and Basil, have passed down from the bright harmony of the divine dogmas: the identity of nature with essence, as corresponding to what is common and general; of

hypostasis with person, as corresponding to what is proper and particular (τῇ δέ ὑποστάσει τό πρόσωπον, ὡς ἰδικόν τε καί μερικόν).[8]

It must, however, be noted that in Gregory of Nazianzus, and even more in Basil, the use of the word *prosopon* is rare (it is revealing that Maximus cites the name of Basil, but not any of his texts that contains the word itself). These two Fathers preferred the word *hypostasis*, by reason of the associations the word *prosopon* still had in their day with Sabellian modalism as well as the risks of confusion the word's use could bring for certain readers. This reticence is also found in Gregory of Nyssa, except in his small Trinitarian treatises, in particular, *To the Greeks, Based on Common Notions*; he also considers the two terms synonymous but uses *hypostasis* more easily than *prosopon*.[9] The equivalence was somewhat officially and universally admitted at the Council of 381 where the Fathers call for belief "in one single essence of the Father, the Son, and the Holy Spirit [. . .] *in three perfect hypostases or three perfect persons*."[10]

d. Possible objections and replies to those objections

Two objections could be pitted against the affirmation of the equivalence of the two concepts or to their undifferentiated use by St. Maximus.

First, St. Maximus, in several passages, uses the two terms by linking them with "and" or with "or." For instance, "the natures concur in constituting one person *and* one hypostasis of the Son (πρός ἕν ἄμφω συντελεῖν πρόσωπον τοῦ Υἱοῦ καί μίαν ὑπόστασιν)";[11] "the two [natures] constitute one person of the Son *and* one hypostasis (πρός ἕν ἄμφω συντελοῦσι πρόσωπον τοῦ Υἱοῦ καί μίαν ὑπόστασιν)";[12] "beings of the same essence and nature [. . .] cannot have a single person and hypostasis (ἕν πρόσωπον ἔχειν οὐ δυνήσεται καί μίαν ὑπόστασιν)";[13] "the [elements] that are united according to one and the same hypostasis, that is to say person, that is are of one hypostasis and form one person (τουτέστι μιᾶς ὑποστάσεως ὄντα, καί ἑνός συμπληρωτικά προσώπου), differ by the *logos* of the essence or nature."[14] Is this not indicative of a difference between the two terms?

To the contrary, we should rather see this as a mark of insistence, precisely aiming to underline the equivalence. It serves at once to exclude all interpretation of a Sabellian modalist stripe (which was already the sense of the expression used by the Fathers of the Council in 381, cited above) as well as any Nestorian interpretation.

Second, John Zizioulas and his disciple D. Skliris assert that Maximus uses the word "hypostasis" for all beings, but avoids using the word "person" with reference to nonrational beings, reserving it for the three divine hypostases, for the angels, and for men.[15] For this position, they refer to Maximus's use of the concept in a theological context, in *Amb. Io.* 37, where he says,

It is according to the person when it [the word of Scripture] calls these angel, archangel, seraphim and other intelligible essences in the heavens or when Abraham, Isaac or Jacob are designated by name, or any other that Scripture praises or abhors.[16]

They conclude that the word "person" has a connotation for Maximus that the notion of hypostasis does not: it designates beings endowed with intelligence and freedom.

J. Zizioulas, targeting M. Törönen – who named one of the sections of his thesis on Maximus, "Can a mouse be a person?" (surely, in order to be a little provocative, but demonstrating in this section that for the Cappadocians and for Maximus an animal is considered a hypostasis and a person)[17] – considers that "a mouse, for example, cannot be called a person."[18] But what might appear strange from the point of view of modern usage was not the case at a time when the word *prosopon* still had a technical sense, and it is not methodologically correct to want to judge ancient usage from the perspective of modern usage.

Having supposed that Maximus had anticipated current modern usage that speaks of persons as beings endowed with reason and the capacity of self-determination (implying will and freedom), this would in no way lead to the confirmation of the personalist and existentialist theory, since [Maximus's position] would imply that persons are such by virtue of their nature (reason and the capacity of self-determination being common properties of the divine, angelic, and human natures).

It must, however, be noted that in Maximus, as in his predecessors, the concept of person, if it does not bear the spiritual and axiological connotations that modern religious personalism gives it, neither does it involve the idea, equally linked to modern personalism, that the person is characterized as a being endowed with spirit, intellect/reason, conscience, capacity of self-determination, or of will and freedom. For the Fathers, and even more so for Maximus (who became a fervent defender of the association of the will with nature), these faculties pertain to the nature, even if he considers that the hypostasis or person can make use of them in different ways.[19]

In contrast to the objection presented above, we can assert that Maximus, as we have just seen, comes down most explicitly and in a multitude of texts in favor of the equivalence of the two concepts of hypostasis and of person, uses them without differentiation, and, in any case, gives indication of no difference of connotation in the sense wished by Zizioulas and his disciple. The majority of the texts are situated in a Christological context, because the theological reflection of Maximus takes place largely in such a context. It is in conjunction with this central preoccupation and to resolve Christological problems posed by monophysitism, monoenergism, and monotheletism that St. Maximus appeals to Triadology and anthropology. It is not relevant for him to appeal to cosmology in a reflection on hypostasis or person in their relationship to essence or nature.

The passage in *Amb. Io.* 37 advanced by the two authors must itself be restored to its context, which is by no means exclusive. Thus several lines above, Maximus notes,

It is according to the genus when [the word of scripture] points to the angels or to what is in heaven among the ranks of intelligible essences, or the sun, the moon, the stars, the fire and what is in the air, the earth, the sea, animals, plants.[20]

He omits mentioning humanity, but this does not indicate that humanity does not belong to its own genus.

We can note that when Maximus defines, like the Cappadocians but also like Leontius of Byzantium and Leontius of Jerusalem, a person or a hypostasis by the particulars that properly characterize it in the framework of the common essence, or distinguish it from other beings of the same kind/genus, he does not mean that [the person] has to do with properties referring specially to the divine persons, to the angels, or to human persons, but he adopts a universal definition applicable to all beings. Thus in *Ep.* 15, he writes, "A hypostasis is that which exists in itself in a distinct manner since, we say, the hypostasis is an essence with properties distinguishing it in number from others of the same kind/genus,"[21] or again in *Th. Pol.* 23: "the hypostasis defines a person by the characteristic properties (ἡ μέν ὑπόστασις πρόσωπον ἀφορίζει τοῖς χαρακτηριστικοῖς ἰδιώμασι)."[22]

But the objection of Zizioulas and Skliris is definitively contradicted by two Maximian passages that they ignore, where he accepts the usage of the concept of person, assimilated once again to the concept of hypostasis, for beings other than the divine, angelic, and human previously mentioned.

Thus in a passage in *Ep.* 13, which belongs to Maximus's demonstration that Christ is not an individual, he rejects "the argument of the phoenix," which his opponents use against him by asserting that this latter, as a living being taking its place among the birds of the created world, is not singular as Christ is. We can observe here that Maximus does not hesitate to reflect on the comparison of the hypostasis of Christ with that of the phoenix and does not raise the objection that the word *prosopon* (person) is being used with reference to this bird.[23]

But another passage is even more determinative in showing that beings other than God, the angels, and humans can be, according to Maximus, termed persons as well as hypostases:

> Beings united according to one and the same nature, that is to say essence, are distinguished one from another *by the hypostases, that is to say the persons* (ταῖς ὑποστάσεσιν, ἤγουν προσώποις), as is the case with angels, men *or with all creatures found in their own kind/genus or species*. Angel is distinguished from angel, man from man, *ox from ox* by hypostasis but not by nature or essence.[24]

On this point, there are a number of patristic antecendents. Thus St. Gregory of Nyssa notes,

> One thing is distinguished from another either by essence, or by hypostasis, or by essence and hypostasis. Thus man is distinguished from a horse by essence, Peter is distinguished from Paul by hypostasis, and this hypostasis of man is distinguished from this hypostasis of horse by both essence and hypostasis.[25]

Gregory of Nyssa does not freely use the word person, but given that he considers it equivalent to the word hypostasis, he could just as easily say the same thing regarding person.

This is something done without hesitation by St. John of Damascus, who not only follows Maximus very closely but also offers a synthesis of patristic knowledge from the preceding centuries: for him, not only do the concepts of hypostasis and person seem altogether synonymous, but apply, one as well as the other, to all beings, including the animals.[26] He notably affirms,

> The holy Fathers have called [. . .] person [. . .] that which exists of itself having its own proper solidity, which is made up of essence and accidents, is distinct by number and designates something determined, for example Peter, Paul, this horse.[27]

Part two: the equivalence of the concepts of hypostasis, person, and individual

Maximus similarly affirms in an explicit manner the equivalence of the concepts of "hypostasis" and "individual" or their derivatives.

Sometimes the equivalence of the two concepts – as is the case also for the notions of hypostasis and person – is presented with the conjunction τουτέστι, thus in *Th. Pol.* 18 (PG 91:213A), cited next.

Also, on occasion, Maximus uses the concept of the "individual" where one could use the concept of "person." Thus,

- *Ep.* 12 (PG 91:484B), where Maximus writes against Nestorius, "It cannot be that two particular hypostases, separated by their proper *logos* into particular individuals, become one hypostasis (ἐκ δύο γάρ ὑποστάσεων ἰδικῶν τῶν πρός τά ὁμοειδῆ ἄτομα ἰδικῷ λόγῳ μεμερισμένων, μίαν γενέσθαι ὑπόστασιν, ἀμήχανον)."
- *Ep.* 12 (PG 91:513B), where he evokes "the particularity of individuals of a similar genus distinguished by their accidents." One can compare this passage to *Dis . Byz.* 14 (CCSG 39:105): "Hypostatic traits, such as an aquiline or snub nose, blue eyes, baldness and things of this kind, are individuating accidents of beings different from one another by number." It appears that the accidents belonging to individuals correspond to what is mentioned here as being distinguishing hypostatic traits, which indicates that what distinguishes hypostases is also what distinguishes individuals and vice versa.
- *Ep.* 13 (PG 91:528AB), where we can note that Maximus defines hypostasis and individual in a similar way – namely, an essence or nature with *idiomata* – that is to say, with particulars or particularities: "Just as we say, to define a hypostasis in simple terms, that a hypostasis is an essence with particulars, or else that an essence takes hold of all the particulars taken one by one in each individual (ὑπόστασίς ἐστιν οὐσία τις μετά ἰδιωμάτων, ἤ, οὐσία τις τῶν καθ' ἕκαστα περιληπτική τῶν ἐν τῷ οἰκείῳ ἀτόμῳ πάντων ἰδιωμάτων), we say also, in defining [the hypostasis] specifically and not simply, that a composite hypostasis is a composite essence with particulars, or else that a composite essence takes hold of all the particulars taken one by one in each individual (ὑπόστασς σύνθετός ἐστι, οὐσία τις σύνθετος μετά ἰδιωμάτων· ἡ οὐσία

τις σύνθετος τῶν καθ' ἕκαστα περιληπτική τῶν ἐν τῷ οἰκείῳ ἀτόμῳ πάντων ἰδιωμάτων)." In PG 91:528C, he combines the two notions when speaking of "an individual hypostasis with the particulars properly characterizing it (τῷ ἀτόμῳ τῆς ὑποστάσεως συνεξέφηνε μετά τῶν αὐτήν ἰδικῶς χαρακτηριζόντων ἰδιωμάτων)."

- *Dis. Byz.* 22 (CCSG 39:123–5), where Maximus underlines that the operations/energies refer to the nature and not to the hypostasis or person, and we can observe that he considers the notions of hypostasis (and thus person) and individual equivalent, notions here applied to human beings and angels: "No one operates as someone *qua* hypostasis but as something *qua* nature. For example, Peter and Paul have one operation/energy, not as Peter and Paul but as human beings; for both are human beings by nature, given the common principle that defines the nature and not hypostatically in view of their particular quality. Similarly, Michael and Gabriel operate, not insofar as they are Michael or Gabriel, but insofar as they are angels, for both are angels. And thus we discern in every nature that contains many [individuals] one common but not individual operation/energy. To speak then of a hypostatic energy implies that nature itself, which is one, is rendered infinite in number by the operations/energies, and different from itself according to the multitude of individuals it contains."
- *Th. Pol.* 23 (PG 91:264C): "A composite hypostasis is a certain composite essence, taking hold of all the particulars of each of the beings in a specific individual (ὑπόστασις σύνθετός ἐστιν, οὐσία τις σύνθετος, τῶν καθ' ἕκαστα περιληπτική τῶν ὄντων ἐν τῷ οἰκείῳ ἀτόμῳ πάντων ἰδιωμάτων)."

One of the texts in which the equivalence of the concepts of hypostasis and individual is most clearly affirmed is the following definition from *Th. Pol.* 18: "Union according to essence is said with regard to hypostases, that is to say individuals (Ἡ κατ' οὐσίαν ἕνωσις, ἐπί τῶν ὑποστάσεων, τουτέστι τῶν ἀτόμων)."[28]

It is interesting to note that this equivalence holds also for animals, to whom the notion of hypostasis is explicitly applied in *Th. Pol.* 21:

> With regard to the divine Fathers, their brief and concise explanation does not result from one subject, that is from one essence or nature, but from what we consider in the essence and, of course, the hypostasis. They thus say that a quality is, on the one hand, essential, like the reasoning of a man or the neighing of a horse and, on the other hand, hypostatic, like the button- or Roman nose of a man or the dappled or chestnut coat of a horse. It is thus for all other created essences or hypostases, considered in beings [by quality] as common or as particular, as general that is or as part, and by which the difference of forms and individuals from one another is recognized, discerning the reality of things (οὕτω δέ καί ἐπί τῶν ἄλλων ἔχει γενητῶν ἁπάντων οὐσιῶν καί ὑποστάσεων, κοινῶς τε καί ἰδικῶς, ἤγουν καθολικῶς τε καί μερικῶς τοῖς οὖσιν ἐνθεωρουμένην, καθ' ἥν καί πρός ἄλληλα διαφορά τῶν τε εἰδῶν καί ἀτόμων γνωρίζεται, διευκρινοῦσα τήν τῶν πράγματων ἀλήθειαν).[29]

Most of these references indicate an equivalence of the notions of hypostasis and individual, and only indirectly refer to the notion of person (by way of the equivalence hypostasis-person), but sometimes Maximus suggests in an explicit manner the equivalence of the notions of individual and person. Thus in *Th. Pol.* 16:

> To whom is it not evident that we are unable to observe in the same essence and nature a difference of existence or natural operation? For none differs from itself, which is in any case impossible. That said, it is always and everywhere the case in *an individual and a person* (ἐν ἀτόμῳ δέ καί προσώπῳ), if they are composed.[30]

We likewise see the equivalence in the following text from *Th. Pol.* 26:

> An essence for the philosophers is a reality founded in itself without owing it to another. For the Fathers, it is a natural entity predicated of many and different hypostases. An individual for the philosophers is a collection of properties whose combination cannot be found in any other. For the Fathers, it is Peter and Paul or a certain man defined by his personal properties (προσωπικοῖς ἰδιώμασι), distinct from other men. A hypostasis for the philosophers is an essence with properties. For the Fathers, it is each man in particular, personally (προσωπικῶς) separated from other men.[31]

a. Possible objections and replies to those objections

First, it could be objected that in the preceding texts, the equivalence of the notions of "hypostasis" and "individual" appear frequently but that of the notions of "person" and "individual" do not. But we can reply that the equivalence being established between the notions of hypostasis and person, the equivalence of the notions of "person" and "individual" follows from that, by virtue of the logical principal whereby if $A = B$ and $A = C$, then $B = C$.

Second, the argument has been advanced that the concept of the individual is of a different nature to that of hypostasis or person: while the latter two concepts are ontological categories, the notion of the individual belongs rather to a logical category, having its place in a system of classification (of Aristotelian origin lightly modified by the Neoplatonic disciples of Aristotle, particularly Porphyry), taking its meaning only in relation to the categories of essence, of nature, and, more particularly, of genus, designating at the heart of this the smallest element (that which remains indivisible: this being the proper sense of *atomon*) resulting from its division; the concept of individual would thus be linked to that of number and also to that of division, and so to the concept of separation.[32]

This appears particularly in *Th. Pol.* 16 where Maximus shows that Christ, as composite hypostasis or composite person, cannot be considered an individual:

> I refrain from saying that the composite person of Christ is properly speaking an individual, for it has no relationship with the division descending from

the most general genus via the subordinate species towards the most specific/individuated form, which circumscribes in the latter its proper process. Accordingly, according to the wise Cyril, for this reason, the name of Christ has no value of definition, for it is not a form predicated of entities differentiated by number, nor certainly does it designate the essence of something. Nor is it an individual reducible to a species or a genus, neither is it easily defined by them according to essence; but a composite hypostasis "identifying" in itself, "at its height," the natural separation of extremes, bringing them into unity by the union of its proper parts.[33]

It is thus not possible to deduce from this text a difference and an *a fortiori* opposition between the concepts of hypostasis or person and the concept of the individual: what is at stake is the *composite hypostasis* of Christ, which constitutes a unique case of a hypostasis that unites two natures. As the God-man, Christ is not a member of an essence or a nature, nor yet of a unique genus that is made of a multitude of individuals.

Maximus notes this in *Ep.* 12:

> The name "Christ" is not there to signify *an essence, that is to say a nature as a genus of a series of multiple individuals differentiated by hypostasis*, as the blessed Cyril said in his scholia: "This name of Christ does not have a value of definition nor does it show the essence of a certain [kind]; it is [the name] of the hypostasis of the Word understood as having assumed a noetic soul." Neither does the human being have a single nature [made] of a soul and a body; it is the name of a specific genus in relation to the others by the difference of constitution separating him and likewise affirmed of the individuals it encompasses.[34]

He says it again in *Ep.* 13, where he shows that Christ, as God-man, is not a generic nature:

> If Christ was a general nature, it would obviously be predicated by the number of different [individuals], and only in thought among those who owe him their existence, and it would not be known in a certain particular hypostasis, in Himself, without the accidents which are in the individuals it comprises. Such is the definition and the reason for every general nature.[35]

See also his remarks in *Ep.* 13:

> May they show us that the composite hypostasis of Christ depends upon a composite nature, thereby sanctioning some contemporary factions, and may they reproach then [our error] with good reason. As long as they cannot do this, they build their opinions on shifting sands. For he who endeavors to subject Christ to these absurdities because he is a composite hypostasis – something we too recognize with piety – errs greatly from the path leading to

the truth, or to put it better, from truth itself. For this is the great and venerable mystery of Christ. He does not, like an individual, have a general nature, like a species; nor, certainly, is he this genus himself or the species for the individuals naturally emerging from him. Just as he does not fit into any of these rules mentioned, so too the coming together [of parts] in the case of composite [beings] is in no wise comparable or similar to the coming together of the Word of God with the flesh.[36]

In other words, Maximus, who went so far as to establish, in *Th. Pol.* 16, an equivalence between the concepts of the composite person and the composite individual, wants less to show in what immediately follows that Christ is not an individual, but more that he is not an individual within a genus. *A fortiori*, he has no intention of establishing any kind of opposition between the concepts of person or hypostasis and the concept of the individual.[37]

It is true that Maximus relates, in several texts, individuals to the genus and sometimes links them with the concept of number: see *Ep.* 13 (PG 91:513B) and *Ep.* 15 (PG 91:564BC, 565D-568A); the clearest texts on this subject can be found in *Ep.* 13 (PG 91:528B) and *Th. Pol.* 23 (PG 91:264C).

Yet Maximus is far from considering the concept of the individual to be inseparable from that of genus. We find in a certain number of texts that he mentions individuals as included under nature, or as related to an essence, for instance in these passages from the *Dialogue with Pyrrhus*:

- *Pyr.* (PG 91, 304D): "If the will is found in all human beings and not in some but not others, and if what we perceive as a common element in all is *a character of the nature in the individuals who are under this common element*, it is thus by nature that the human being is endowed with will."
- *Pyr.* (PG 91:336BC): "The unity of man according to species and the unity of the soul and body according to essence are not identical. For the unity of man according to species designates the perfect similitude that reigns between *all the individuals under the nature*."
- *Pyr.* (PG 91:345BC): "With regard to the living operation/energy [of his human nature], [Christ] showed this by breathing, speaking, seeing, hearing, touching, smelling, eating and drinking, moving his hands, walking, and doing the other things which, in *all the individuals under the nature*, show identity of operation/energy according to nature."

The most precise statements on this subject are found in *Ep.* 13 and *Th. Pol.*:

- *Ep.* 13 (PG 91:528B): "The particularities considered in common within the individuals of the same genus principally characterize what is generic in the essence or nature in the individuals under it. What is compound is common to *all the individuals who are under a composite genus*; thus what is composite principally characterizes *a composite nature in the individuals under it*, but not a hypostasis."

- *Th. Pol.* (PG 91:264C): "*What we consider to be common in the individuals under the same genus is what characterizes the essence or nature*, principally in the individuals under it, and generally what is common of all the individuals under a composite genus."

Besides, it can be observed that it is not only the individual that Maximus relates to genus but also hypostasis or person, as can be seen in this passage from *Ep.* 15 (PG 91:549C):

> Those who are united under one and the same essence or nature are distinguished one from the other by the hypostases or persons, as is the case with the angels, human beings and every creature counted among a species or genus.

If we take into account the texts cited above as a whole, the following comments can be made:

a) Maximus mentions individuals several times as being "under a genus," but he also presents them as being under an essence, and often as being under a nature. He thus does not have a strictly scholastic use of the concept, placing it exclusively under genus in an abstract system of classification where the concept of the individual has an exclusively numerical sense.

b) What is said regarding the individual as included by a nature or an essence can similarly be said for hypostasis or person. And, inversely, what is said regarding hypostasis or person can similarly be said for the individual, with the exception of the particular and unique case of the composite hypostasis of Christ, precisely because it is composite.

In what follows the passage cited above from *Ep.* 13, where Maximus forcefully relates the individual to genus, it can be noted that the concept of the individual and hypostasis remain equivalents and comprise only one concept since Maximus even speaks of an "individual hypostasis":

> Every definition that falls within that which is common to the individuals is completed under it. And all those who depend on [that which is common] take by nature their descriptive principle from these generalities; for it is clear that that which defines is that which properly and principally is. If this is true, and it is, it is evident that whoever speaks of a composite hypostasis taken under one nature, indicates that which exists generally by what is common in the essence in one individual hypostasis (τῷ ἀτόμῳ τῆς ὑποστάσεως) with the particularities properly characterizing it. Such that, he who speaks of a composite hypostasis completed by one nature says nothing other than one nature, or one essence, composed with particularities. If then, as we have shown, every composite nature is but a non-deliberative coming together, without the proper choice of its parts, it acquires the parts at the same time,

contemporaneously, and completes the entirety of what we consider in beings, each a whole in its genus. Also, each hypostasis has its own invariable constitution in its genus and species.[38]

In *Th. Pol.* 14, it can be observed that the concept of hypostasis is used as an equivalent to individual even when the context has to do with indicating a specimen belonging to a genus:

> A hypostatic difference is a *logos* according to which the difference of the assembly of the particularities, considered as belonging to what is common to the essence, which makes the quantity of individuals by dividing them one from the other according to number (ὑποστατική δέ διαφορά, τυγχάνει λόγος, καθ' ὅν ἡ κατά τό ἄθροισμα τῶν ἐνθεωρουμένων ἰδιωμάτων τῷ κοινῷ τῆς οὐσίας ἑτερότης, τέμνουσα κατ' ἀριθμόν ἄλλον ἀπ' ἄλλου, τήν τῶν ἀτόμων ποιεῖται πληθύν).[39]

The same is true later in *Th. Pol.* 14, where one can note in addition that the concept of hypostasis is connected to that of essence, whereas the concept of the individual is connected to that of existence (something that completely subverts the categories of modern personalism-existentialism):

> The property of the *enhypostasized* is either to be recognized with another different according to essence in one indissoluble hypostasis, or that which is found naturally in individuals according to existence (ἐνυποστάτου ἴδιόν ἐστι, ἤ τό μετ' ἄλλου διαφόρου κατά τήν οὐσίαν ἐν ὑποστάσει γνωρίζεσθαι καθ' ἕνωσιν ἄλυτον· ἤ τό ἐν ἀτόμοις φυσικῶς τυγχάνειν καθ' ὕπαρξιν).[40]

In *Th. Pol.* 16, one also sees that the concept of the individual is used in a context were the concept of hypostasis or that of person could equally have been used: "I hasten to say that none of the natural traits are to be brought back primordially to the individual, but to its nature and essence."[41]

c) The numerical distinction does not only call upon the concept of the individual but also can be expressed with the concept of hypostasis, as is shown in this passage from *Th. Pol.* 14: "The property of the hypostasis is the fact of being seen in oneself and being distinguished numerically from others of the same genus."[42]

b. The person is not more relational than the individual is divisive

The idea that the individual is separable or divisible, while the person or hypostasis is not (an idea dear to modern personalism, founded in large part on the opposition of person to individual) supported by the thought of Maximus.

First, Maximus considers hypostasis to be that which distinguishes beings of the same nature and particularizes in each what is common of the essence or the nature:

- *Ep.* 15 (PG 91:557D): "What is proper to the hypostasis is the fact of being considered in itself and being *numerically distinct* from others of the same genus."[43]
- *Th. Pol.* 14 (PG 91:152D): "A hypostasis is that which establishes and circumscribes in a particular manner, in something, what is common and uncircumscribed. A hypostasis is something that has together with the universal something singular."
- *Th. Pol.* 26 (PG 91:276B): "According to the Fathers, the hypostasis is each human being in particular, *personally separated* from other human beings."

In other words, the hypostasis – or the person – is rather that which sets apart beings belonging to the same nature one from the other, or that distinguishes and even separates one being from another of the same essence, and thus assures to each being belonging to the same essence or nature an independence or autonomy with regard to the others.

Maximus follows here an ancient tradition that will continue after him. Very early in Christian literature (notably in Origen), the *hypostasis* designates an individual existence, concrete and distinct, and goes together with the notion of particularity (ἰδιότης).[44] Theodoret of Cyrrhus notes, "Following the teaching of the Fathers, there is the same difference between essence and hypostasis as between the general and particular."[45] St. Basil of Caesarea similarly writes that the relationship that exists between essence and hypostasis is the same as that which exists between the general and particular.[46] St. Gregory of Nyssa proves to be more precise by noting that

> when we name someone, we do not name him according to his nature, thereby preventing the general character of the name from causing error, [. . .] but [. . .] we use the term that applies properly to him – I mean that which signifies the subject – and we separate him from the multitude.[47]

Leontius of Jerusalem, who is one of the authors who contributed most to clarifying the notion of hypostasis in the context of the Christological controversies, but who also greatly inspired Maximus's choice of vocabulary, proves to be very precise in this conception of hypostasis. He underlines that it applies just as much to the person, going so far as to speak not only of separation but also of distance:

> The hypostasis, as well as being composed [of several particular properties] and manifesting the individual subject (τὸ ὑποκείμενον ἄτομον) as separated from all those of the same species and of other species by its distinct, particular mark, is also of itself a "something," a distancing from (ἀπόστασις)[48]

and distinction (διορισμός) of indistinct substances in order to number each of them, person by person; this is why the Fathers called the hypostasis "person."[49]

We later find the same idea in St. John of Damascus, who notes that the name of the hypostasis "signifies the existence in itself and its self-subsisting and, according to this definition, it designates the individual distinct in number."[50]

Second, it must nonetheless be noted that distinction and even separation and "distancing" between beings (in the opposite sense of indistinctiveness and confusion) does not mean division, let alone opposition.

Third, it can be seen that individuals remain united among themselves despite their "distinguishing" – and in a certain sense separating – property, by the *logoi* of the genus or the nature to which they belong (which comes from the general principle according to which there is in nature a unity on each level realized by the superior level, the general *logoi* playing a unifying role as compared with the particular *logoi*, as is indicated in *Amb. Io.* 41).[51]

Fourth, that which, according to the thought of Maximus, establishes a true division and opposition between beings is the *gnomē*, which arises from a particular disposition of the human hypostasis or person.[52] Such a division is not related to a logical or ontological category, as is the concept of the individual. Inversely, hypostases or persons are not, simply by virtue of their reality – or "ontologically" to take up the language of personalist/existentialist philosophy – unifying, but the unity that is accomplished between them occurs as the result of a positive orientation of the same *gnomē*.

We can say that Maximus does not perceive any difference between person and individual on an ontological level: the fact that the individual can appear in certain contexts as a logical category does not exclude the possibility that it might also have an ontological character.

Similarly, it can be noted that as regards the concept of person, there is for Maximus no relational connotation, nor any particularly positive ethical connotation, nor any ontological connotation, contrary to what we find in the concept of person held by modern personalism/existentialism.

Conclusion: the flexibility of Maximian vocabulary

In conclusion, we can observe that, in Maximus, the concepts of hypostasis, person, and individual are actually equivalent, and that each of them is used with a certain flexibility. They seem, in some contexts, to have particular connotations, but they lose these in others and appear generally interchangeable.

The notion of hypostasis is used, in Maximus as well as his predecessors, far more often than that of person or individual, which is why its meaning seems broader than that of the other two. It mostly serves to designate a concrete existent being, which, in the framework of a common nature, distinguishes itself from other concrete existent beings by the particular properties it synthesizes/sums up. The hypostasis thus seems to have a role at once of distinction (even of separation, which does not mean division) and of synthesis/summing up, one or the other of these aspects being brought to the fore depending on the context. The "composite hypostasis" of Christ constitutes a particular case. Beyond this particular case, the concepts of person and individual can have the same connotations as that of hypostasis. The three concepts, in any case, cannot be distinguished using strictly scholastic categories and the particular connotations that, in an anachronistic manner, are ascribed to them by modern existentialist personalism.

Notes

1 See Panagopoulos (1985); Halleux (1986); Wilks (1995); Turcescu (1997); Turcescu (2002); Turcescu (2005); Harrison (1989); Harrison (1998); Loudovikos (2009); Larchet (2011), pp. 244–75 *(passim)*.
2 See Törönen (2007), pp. 244–75 *(passim)*.
3 See Zizioulas (2013); Skliris (2013), pp. 444–9.
4 See my review of Vasiljević (ed.) (2013) in *Revue d'Histoire Ecclésiastique* 109, 1–2, 2014, pp. 283–96, and its expanded version in *Crkvene Studije / Church Studies* 11, 2014, pp. 705–19.
5 Ep. 15 (PG 91:545A): Κοινόν μέν οὖν ἐστι καί καθολικόν, ἤγουν γενικόν, κατά τούς Πατέρας, ἡ οὐσία καί ἡ φύσις· ταυτόν γάρ ἀλλήλαις ταύτας ὑπάρχειν φασίν. Ἴδιον δέ καί μερικόν, ἡ ὑπόστασις καί τό πρόσωπον· ταυτόν γάρ ἀλλήλοις κατ' αὐτούς ταῦτα τυγχάνουσιν.
6 Gregory of Nazianzus, *Discourse* 20.6 (SC 270:70.25–7) cited in Maximus, *Ep.* 15 (PG 91:548B): ἐπειδὴ χρὴ καὶ τὸν ἕνα Θεὸν τηρεῖν, καὶ τὰς τρεῖς ὑποστάσεις ὁμολογεῖν, εἴτ' οὖν τρία πρόσωπα, καὶ ἑκάστην μετὰ τῆς ἰδιότητος.
7 Gregory of Nazianzus, *Discourse* 39.11 (SC 358:170–2), cited in Maximus, *Ep.* 15 (PG 91:548CD).
8 Maximus, *Ep.* 15 (PG 91:548D).
9 For Gregory of Nazianzus, see the note by P. Gallay in SC 358:171. For the three Cappadocians, see Bonnet (2006). It is worth noting that in *Letter* 210, St. Basil tolerates the usage of the word prosopon on condition that it be associated with *hypostasis* in order to avoid any confusion with Sabellianism, which proposes according to him "a fiction of persons without hypostases." "It is insufficient to count differences of person (*prosopon*), one must also confess that each person (*prosopon*) exists in a true *hypostasis*" (*Letter* 210.5.37 – ed. Courtonne 2:96). We are far from the ontological character that Zizioulas intends to attribute in an absolute and exclusive manner to the person, claiming as his basis the Cappadocians and particularly St. Basil.
10 Theodoret of Cyrrhus, *Ecclesiastical History* 5.9.13.
11 Maximus, *Ep.* 12 (PG 91:469D).
12 Maximus, *Ep.* 12 (PG 91:492C).
13 Maximus, *Ep.* 15 (PG 91:549C).
14 Maximus, *Ep.* 15 (PG 91:552A).
15 Zizioulas (2013), p. 88. See also Skliris (2013), p. 443.
16 Maximus, *Amb. Io.* 37 (PG 91:1293D).
17 Törönen (2007), pp. 55–9.
18 Zizioulas (2013), p. 88.
19 On this topic, see the perceptive remarks in Törönen (2007), pp. 52–9.
20 Maximus, *Amb. Io.* 37 (PG 91:1293D).
21 Maximus, *Ep.* 15 (PG 91:557D).
22 Maximus, *Th. Pol.* 23 (PG 91:261B).
23 See Maximus, *Ep.* 13 (PG 91:517D).
24 Maximus, *Ep.* 15 (PG 91:549C).

25 Gregory of Nyssa, *To the Greeks, based on common notions* 16 (GNO III-1:29).
26 See Louth (2002), pp. 50–3, who underlines the discrepancy between Zizioulas's conception and that of St. John Damascene.
27 John of Damascus, *Dialectica* 44 (PTS 7:109).
28 Maximus, *Th. Pol.* 18 (PG 91:213A). This text also figures in the critical edition by Deun (2000), p. 145.
29 Maximus, *Th. Pol.* 21 (PG 91:248B-249A).
30 Maximus, *Th. Pol.* 16 (PG 91:201C).
31 Maximus, *Th. Pol.* 26 (PG 91:276AB).
32 Cf. Zizioulas (2013), p. 91: "Ἄτομον remains for Maximus a category *in the realm of essences* [. . .] Ἄτομον differs, therefore, fundamentally from hypostasis and πρόσωπον because it falls under the category of nature. It may be used as equivalent to hypostasis only in so far as it indicates particularity and indivisibility. If it is identified with hypostasis/person it leads to a total confusion between nature and hypostasis." Cf. also and especially Skliris (2013), pp. 438–44.
33 Maximus, *Th. Pol.* 16 (PG 91:201D-204A).
34 Maximus, *Ep.* 12 (PG 91:488AB).
35 Maximus, *Ep.* 13 (PG 91:517D).
36 Maximus *Ep.* 13 (PG 91:528D-529A).
37 See *Th. Pol.* 16 (PG 91, 201C-204A).
38 Maximus, *Ep.* 13 (PG 91:528BD).
39 Maximus, *Th. Pol.* 14 (PG 91:152B).
40 Maximus, *Th. Pol.* 14 (PG 91:152D – 153A).
41 Maximus, *Th. Pol.* 16 (PG 91:197BC).
42 Maximus, *Th. Pol.* 14 (PG 91:152D).
43 Leontius of Byzantium, *Contra Nestorianos et Eutychianos* I (PG 86–1:1280): "The hypostasis is defined thus: those who are the same by nature and different in number." We see that enumeration is not proper to individuality as Yannaras and Zizioulas affirm, following on from Berdiaev (in the sense in which they understand the notion of indivduality).
44 See Meunier (ed.) (2006), pp. 172–3; Törönen (2007), pp. 53–5.
45 Thedoret of Cyrrhus, *Eraniste I*, ed. Ettlinger 64; cf. 65.
46 Basil of Caesarea, *Letter* 214.4, ed. Courtonne 2:205.
47 Gregory of Nyssa, *Ad Ablabium*, GNO III, p. 40.
48 *Against the Nestorians*, II, 1 (PG 86–1:1529D). We see that this characteristic is not proper to individuality as Zizioulas affirms (with the meaning he ascribes to this latter term).
49 Leontius of Jerusalem, *Against the Nestorians* 2.1 (PG 86–1:1529D).
50 John of Damascus, *Dialectica* 43, PTS 1, p. 108.
51 See Maximus, *Amb. Io.* 41 (PG 91:1312CD).
52 See, among others, Maximus, *Ep.* 2 (PG 91:396CD, 400CD).

Select bibliography

Bonnet, M. (2006), "*Hupostasis* et *prosôpon* chez les Cappadociens au ive siècle," in Meunier (ed.) (2006), pp. 179–207.

Deun, P. van (2000), "L'*Unionum definitiones* (CPG 7697, 18) attribué à Maxime le Confesseur: étude et édition," *Revue des études byzantines* 58, pp. 123–47.

Halleux, A. de (1986), "Personnalisme ou essentialisme trinitaire chez les Cappadociens? Une mauvaise controverse," *Revue théologique de Louvain* 17, pp. 132–55.

Harrison, V. (1989), "Yannaras on Person and Nature," *St. Vladimir's Theological Quarterly* 33, pp. 287–98.

Harrison, V. (1998), "Zizioulas on Communion and Otherness," *St. Vladimir's Theological Quarterly* 42, pp. 273–300.
Larchet, J.-C. (2011), *Personne et nature*, Paris.
Loudovikos, N. (2009), "Person Instead of Grace and Dictated Otherness: John Zizioulas's Final Theological Position," *Heythrop Journal* 52.4, pp. 684–99.
Louth, A. (2002), *John Damascene: Tradition and Originality in Byzantine Theology*, Oxford.
Meunier, B. (ed.) (2006), *La Personne et le christianisme ancien*, Paris.
Panagopoulos, I. (1985), " Ὀντολογία ἤ θεολογία τοῦ προσώπου. Ἡ συμβολή τῆς πατερικῆς Τριαδολογίας στήν κατανόηση τοῦ ἀνθρωπίνου προσώπου," *Synaxē* 13, pp. 63–79; 14, pp. 37–47.
Skliris, D. (2013), " 'Hypostasis,' 'Person,' 'Individual,' 'Mode': A Comparison Between the Terms that Denote Concrete Being in St Maximus's Theology," in Vasiljević (2013), pp. 437–50.
Törönen, M. (2007), *Union and Distinction in the Thought of St Maximus the Confessor*, Oxford.
Turcescu, L. (1997), "Prosopon and Hypostasis in Basil of Caesarea's Against Eunomius and the Epistles," *Vigiliae Christianae* 51, pp. 375–95.
Turcescu, L. (2002), " 'Person' Versus 'Individual,' and Other Modern Misreadings of Gregory of Nyssa," *Modern Theology* 18, pp. 527–39.
Turcescu, L. (2005), *Gregory of Nyssa and the Concept of Divine Persons*, Oxford and New York.
Vasiljević, M. (ed.) (2013), *Knowing the Purpose of Everything through the Resurrection: Proceedings of the Symposium on St Maximus the Confessor, Belgrade, October, 18–21, 2012*, Alhambra CA and Belgrade.
Wilks, J. G. F. (1995), "The Trinitarian Ontology of John Zizioulas," *Vox evangelica* 25, pp. 63–88.
Zizioulas, J. D. (2013), "Person and Nature in the Theology of St. Maximus the Confessor," in Vasiljević (ed.) (2013), pp. 85–113.

5 Mary, the mother of God, in dialogue

The drama of personal encounter in the Byzantine liturgical tradition

Mary B. Cunningham

Janet Soskice, citing the philosophical works of Iris Murdoch and Charles Taylor, informs us that personhood, or the state of being "fully human and moral" consists in reacting "to that which demands or compels our response – the *other* attended to with love. It is this loving which both draws us out of ourselves and constitutes us fully as selves."[1] Such a sense of personhood, as a relational state of existence (as opposed to the idea of a disengaged individual who is defined by his or her rational awareness of an inner "self"), has dominated the work of modern Orthodox theologians such as Metropolitan John Zizioulas and Christos Yannaras.[2] The approach of the present book, which brings together the papers delivered at a recent conference on personhood,[3] is to depart from previous dogmatic or philosophical discussions of the topic and instead to explore liturgical, hagiographic, homiletic, ascetic, and other expressions of what it means to exist as a relational hypostasis – whether divine, human, or (in the case of Jesus Christ) both. This chapter focuses on the Virgin Mary, Mother of God, as an example of a human person who exists in a unique relationship both with God and with the rest of humanity.[4] It is my hope that this will provide a different perspective on the issue of personhood as a state of loving reciprocity and personal growth.

I shall focus primarily on Byzantine liturgical texts, mainly homilies and hymns, which celebrate Mary, the Mother of God.[5] These works (some of which continue to be employed in Orthodox liturgical services) both celebrate the Virgin Mary as a human person who was holy enough to conceive and give birth to Christ, the Word of God, and develop in a dramatic way her physical and emotional involvement in this mystery. Liturgical reflection on the Mother of God, especially from about the sixth century onward, also deals with her response to later events in the life of Christ. Mary's grief at the foot of the cross, for example, which George of Nicomedia describes as being like "searing flames of fire that penetrate her womb,"[6] reveals her close connection with her Son, which – as in the case of any mother – causes her to suffer with him as he hangs from the cross.[7] The extent to which involvement with "the other" in a relationship causes the subject to undergo personal transformation and growth is frequently demonstrated by means of imaginative exegesis and dramatic narrative in Byzantine liturgical texts.[8] Mary, the Mother of God, is one of the biblical figures who receives extensive treatment in this context. I shall therefore demonstrate how she represents an ideal example of "personhood," not only as the Theotokos in whose womb the divine and human natures were joined hypostatically in Christ but also as a sentient, rational, and fully human person in her own right.

For reasons of space, it is necessary to set aside some Byzantine literary genres that deal with this holy figure, including hagiographical works,[9] miracle stories,[10] and the interesting *Apocalypse of the Theotokos*, which has been dated to the ninth or tenth century.[11] Such works explore the Virgin Mary's character in various ways that sometimes diverge from more standard liturgical treatments.[12] They are based not only on the New Testament narratives but also on various apocryphal traditions that were circulating in the Eastern Christian world from about the middle of the second century onward.[13] Although it is convenient to divide such texts into separate literary genres on the basis both of their structure and didactic purpose, it is also important to emphasize that they overlap in many ways with the Marian sermons and hymns. For example, John Geometres' *Life of the Virgin*, which is described in catalogues as a hagiographical work,[14] in fact represents a series of meditative orations on the events in her life that are celebrated in the Byzantine liturgical calendar.[15]

Before examining in detail the ways in which homilies and hymns treat the personhood of Mary, the Mother of God, we should remind ourselves of some distinctive qualities with regard to their performance. First, it is important to recognize the paradoxical timelessness and immediacy of liturgical celebration in the Eastern Christian tradition.[16] When a feast such as the Nativity or Dormition of the Theotokos takes place, the congregation – led by its bishop or priest – participates fully in that historical, but also eternally significant, event. The preacher, whether delivering his oration (or orations) during the festal all-night vigil or Divine Liturgy, draws on a repertoire of rhetorical devices that is outlined in Late Antique school handbooks in order to promote the spiritual and emotional involvement of his congregation in the event that is being reenacted. *Enargeia*, or the translation of lived experience into language, is assisted by *ekphrasis* (description), *exclamatio* (exclamation), *ethopoiia* (monologue or dialogue), and many other tropes.[17] Such methods enable Christian listeners to sympathize, and thereby partially to understand, the motivations and actions of biblical personages including not only the Virgin Mary but also even Christ himself. If true personhood involves awareness of another (as we saw earlier), then we see this process unfolding in a multitude of ways in Byzantine sermons and hymns. Not only do the relationships between biblical or apocryphal characters develop in the course of liturgical narratives but also, presumably, the congregation's relationship with these figures changes in response to the sermon, not to mention that of the preacher both with his biblical subjects and with his listeners.[18] This is a complex picture, which I can only begin to explore in the context of this chapter. It should be possible on the basis of a few examples, however, to illustrate briefly the dynamic nature of the liturgical treatment of the Mother of God in the Byzantine Church. The following discussion is divided into two parts: first, I propose to treat briefly the typological and metaphorical understanding of Mary as the meeting-place of the divine and human realms; second, we shall explore her entirely human response to the mysteries of the Incarnation and the Passion of Christ.

Turning first to Mary, the Theotokos, as the person in whom the divine and human natures were joined at the moment of Christ's conception as the incarnate God, it is noticeable that liturgical writers from the early fifth century onward resort to metaphor or typology in order to express this mystery in words.[19] Proclus of Constantinople describes her in his famous first homily, delivered on the feast in honor of the Virgin that was celebrated in association with Christ's Nativity as the "workshop for the union of natures; market-place of the contract of salvation; the bridal chamber in which the Word took the flesh in marriage," and many other metaphors.[20] Later, Byzantine preachers and hymnographers continued this tradition, adding to a large repertoire of types and images associated with the Mother of God. The *Akathistos Hymn*, written sometime between the fifth and early seventh centuries,[21] represents one of the richest sources of Marian imagery in its stanzas known as the *chairetismoi*, which are based on the archangel Gabriel's greeting to the Virgin in Luke 1:28. The eighth-century preacher Germanos of Constantinople provides a string of such acclamations in his homily on the Annunciation, calling the Theotokos the "ark of the sanctuary," "tabernacle," "table," "jar of manna," "throne of the Creator," and many other typological epithets.[22] It is noticeable that many such types are associated with the tabernacle or the temple of Old Testament Judaism. Mary is understood in the Christian context as the living fulfillment of these holy places in which God chose to manifest himself.[23] John of Damascus writes in his homily on the Nativity of the Theotokos as follows:

> [The Theotokos is] the living and rational tabernacle of God. For she was the receptacle not just of the activity of God, but essentially of the hypostasis of the Son of God. Let a tabernacle that was entirely covered with gold recognize that it cannot compare with her, along with a golden jar which contained manna, a lampstand, a table, and all the other objects from long ago. For they have been honoured as her types, as shadows of a true archetype.[24]

Types and metaphors that are used for the Mother of God in Byzantine liturgical texts express her role in the Incarnation of Christ in various ways. To categorize them roughly into three groups, we may identify those that indicate the Virgin Mary's role as container (for example, the "temple," "tabernacle," or "jar"), as bridge or link between the divine and created realms (for example, "Jacob's ladder" or "gate of the temple"), or as sign of God's immanence in creation (such as the "burning bush," "Gideon's fleece," and others).[25] It is worth noting that many Byzantine liturgical writers stress the significance of the Virgin Mary's link with creation in their use of metaphor and typology. Germanos of Constantinople, for example, addresses the Theotokos as follows in his first homily on the entrance into the temple:

> O wholly unblemished and all-praised and entirely august one, preeminent offering for God of all created things, untilled earth, unplowed field, luxuriant

vine, most cheering chalice, gushing fountain, Virgin who gives birth and Mother with no knowledge of a man, vessel of purity and ornament of piety [. . .] steer us into a harbour without waves, that is, one that is entirely free of [. . .] heresies and scandals.[26]

The Mother of God is a liminal figure because she bridges the gap between the divine and created states of being. As Andrew of Crete puts it, she "mediates between the height of divinity and the humility of flesh,"[27] or, as John of Damascus pictures her, she is "a living ladder whose base has been set on earth and whose top reaches to heaven itself."[28]

What then does such imagery convey about the *person* of the Mother of God in Eastern Christian tradition? According to the liturgical texts that have just been cited, Mary, the Theotokos, is a figure who plays an essential part in God's immanence in creation, both before and after his Incarnation as Jesus Christ. Mary is the "living heaven, vaster than the immensity of all the heavens,"[29] because she contained the One who is greater than all of these. Types or metaphors such as these may appear to convey an abstract idea of the Mother of God, describing her more as an inanimate object than as a living human being. However, each of these images is intrinsically relational, whether it represents a container, a bridge, or a sign of God's immanence, biblical types of the Theotokos reveal her role as the means whereby God entered creation and assumed human nature. She is thus the meeting-place of the divine and created worlds, where Christ, the coeternal Son and Word of God, took flesh and became man.

To take up the second aspect of Mary's relational nature, which has more to do with her human qualities, it is striking that liturgical writers throughout the Byzantine period emphasize both her rational and emotional responses to the events that are described in biblical and apocryphal sources. She experiences the tender feelings of motherhood, combined with premonitory fears concerning the activities of her divine Son, Jesus Christ. Mary also suffers the agony of a woman who is forced to witness the torture and execution of her only son. Byzantine liturgical texts frequently interpret Symeon's prophecy that a sword would pierce the Virgin's soul (Luke 2:35) as referring to the Passion of Christ.[30] Byzantine icons, whether depicting her holding the Christ child or in a narrative scene, portray the Virgin Mary as a serious and sorrowing mother who fully participates in the self-emptying acts of her Son.[31] It is clear, on the basis both of texts and iconography, especially after about the middle of the ninth century,[32] that Mary, the Mother of God, began to be portrayed in the Byzantine liturgical tradition as a fully human example of responsive personhood.

Such literary treatment of the Virgin Mary began even earlier in the Syriac and Greek liturgical traditions, however. One of the most vivid portrayals of Mary's response to the birth of her Son, Jesus Christ, appears in Romanos the Melodist's famous kontakion on the Nativity.[33] Romanos is apparently the earliest hymnographer – at least in the Greek-speaking Christian world – to explore the Virgin's character by means of monologue and dialogue (thus employing the rhetorical device of *ethopoiia*).[34] He uses this method ostensibly in order to teach the congregation the theological meaning of the Incarnation by means of Mary's hesitant questioning of the Christ child himself. However, the device also serves to reveal her emotional perplexity as she contemplates the newborn baby, as we see in the following stanza:

> When Mary heard these amazing words,
> she bowed low and worshipped the offspring of her womb
> and with tears, she said, "Great, my Child,
> great is all that you have done for me in my poverty;
> for see, magi are outside seeking you."[35]

Even more significant for our purposes, however, is the emphasis that Romanos places on the Virgin's role as mediator, or intercessor, between Christ and the rest of humanity, which he again conveys by means of dramatic dialogue. The Mother of God addresses her Son as follows:

> For I am not simply your mother, compassionate Saviour;
> it is not in vain that I suckle the giver of milk,
> but for the sake of all I implore you.
> You have made me the mouth and the boast of all my race,
> and your world has me
> as a mighty protection, a wall, and a buttress.
> They look to me, those who were cast out
> of the Paradise of pleasure, for I bring them back.[36]

Later Byzantine hymns composed for the forefeast and feast of the Nativity of Christ pick up the themes of the Virgin's amazement, doubt, and role as intercessor between God and humanity. She is a figure who not only plays a central role in the event that is being liturgically reenacted but also interprets its meaning, by means of direct speech, to the Christian faithful. This mediating role demonstrates the active, relational aspect of personhood; the subject may not understand the full implications of loving openness to divine transformation, but she is transformed by her willingness to be involved.

Such responsiveness is revealed even more clearly in the scene of the Annunciation. Byzantine liturgical writers again employ dialogue in order to engage their audiences in Mary's gradual acceptance of God's will when she is greeted by the archangel Gabriel in the first chapter of Luke's Gospel. The evangelist himself records a dialogue between Gabriel and the young virgin, but preachers and hymnographers elaborated this exchange in imaginative ways from about the fifth century onward.[37] Some homilies, such as the highly literary oration that is attributed to Proclus of Constantinople but may, according to Roberto Caro, in fact date (at least in parts) to a later period,[38] employ a dialogue form that is unencumbered with commentary. In fact, such dramatic treatment of the story, which may have its origins in the Syriac dialogue poetic form known as the *soghyatha*,[39] continued to be used in later Byzantine sermons and hymns on the Annunciation. Romanos the Melodist,⁴⁰ Sophronios of Jerusalem,⁴¹ Andrew of Crete,⁴² and Germanos of Constantinople⁴³ all followed this tradition in the texts that they composed for the feast, developing in different ways – but always dramatically – the momentous encounter between Gabriel and the Virgin Mary. While the focus may shift in the hands of these writers from the archangel's quandary about how to gain access to the Virgin and convey his message, to the latter's initial fear, doubt, and eventual acceptance of the Incarnation, these liturgical writers are preoccupied above all with the *encounter* in which this process takes place. Above all, the Mother of God is affected, both emotionally and rationally, by the experience and, after uttering the words, "Let it be unto me according to your word" (Luke 1:38), enters into a state of mingled joy and awe in which she continues to reflect on the mystery of the Incarnation. Germanos has her ask, for example, "As one who is made of matter and who experienced an earthly birth, how shall I contain Christ, the Light of the world?"⁴⁴

I have speculated elsewhere about the possible ways in which dialogic sermons, such as that of Germanos on the Annunciation, might have been delivered either by the preacher himself or subsequently as a liturgical reading.⁴⁵ It is difficult to imagine the orator alternating between the voices of the two protagonists (or, in the second half of many homilies, between the Virgin Mary and Joseph), but the literary and liturgical purpose of such dialogue nevertheless seems clear. Such dramatic treatment of the scene allows the congregation to relive the encounter between these biblical characters and to understand – and perhaps even to share – their emotional turmoil. The performance to this day of the dialogic canon by John the Monk, which may be performed antiphonally by separate choirs in the office of Matins, should – if understood by its audience – have the same effect.⁴⁶ The liturgical texts that deal with the Annunciation thus illustrate, by dramatic means, the Virgin Mary's humanity, which is revealed in her initial lack of understanding, fear, and even suspicion of her angelic interlocutor, but also her willingness to listen and learn about a mystery that is beyond human comprehension.

Let us turn finally to the liturgical texts that concern the scene in which the Mother of God stands at the foot of the cross, weeping for her Son and attempting to comprehend the reason for his Passion. The extent to which preachers and hymnographers developed imaginatively the brief mention of Mary at Golgotha that appears only in the Gospel of John (19:25–7) is remarkable, especially in liturgical texts that date from the second half of the ninth century onward. However, we find premonitions of the affective handling of the Virgin's sorrow that appears in the sermons of George of Nicomedia and in the short hymns known as the *stavrotheotokia* (usually sung in the Wednesday and Friday offices of the Byzantine Church) in Romanos the Melodist's kontakion, "On Mary at the Cross," composed in the sixth century.⁴⁷

Byzantine liturgical writers use the scene at the foot of the cross to demonstrate several important truths about Mary, the Mother of God. First, she is entirely human, grieving as any mother would at the sight of her Son being led to his place of execution and nailed to the cross in order to die in excruciating pain. Romanos has Mary cry out "from her deep grief and great sorrow" in protest at this "unjust slaughter."[48] George of Nicomedia develops the theme of the Virgin's pain even further, as we saw above, describing it as a "burning fire" that affected her innermost being.[49] Mary's humanity, as in the case of the Annunciation and Nativity scenes, is also manifested in her lack of understanding about the purpose and outcome of Christ's *kenosis*; he meanwhile reassures her, thereby allowing the preacher an opportunity for theological instruction on the meaning of the Passion. Second, and even more importantly, the scene illustrates an important aspect of the Virgin's role in Christ's Incarnation. As Father Maximos Constas has recently argued, the Mother of God was involved in Christ's self-emptying life, death, and resurrection from the moment that she conceived him.[50] The intimate association of her person (in both physical and spiritual terms) with that of Christ is revealed in every icon or text that depicts her attentive (and often sorrowful) focus on her Son.

Paradox, liminal meeting-place between God and creation, and bridge between the old and the new covenants, Mary, the holy Virgin and Theotokos, might seem to assume a more symbolic than historical role in Eastern Christian theology. However, one of the extraordinary achievements of Byzantine liturgical writers is that they manage to hold all of her various qualities in balance. Even within one hymn or sermon that is intended for a particular Marian feast day, we frequently find historical, moral, and allegorical aspects of the Virgin Mary's person interwoven in relation to this event. She remains a distinctly human figure, as she is pictured listening, pondering, and responding to each phase of Christ's life, Passion, and resurrection. However, the preachers and hymnographers also continually remind us of Mary's cosmic importance in God's creation and dispensation.

In conclusion, it is worth citing one other, somewhat unusual, treatment of the Mother of God – this time in one of Symeon the New Theologian's mystical hymns. Symeon devotes most of his attention in these poetic works to Christ, who represents the sole object of his contemplative desire. However, in *Hymn 20*, the tenth-century mystic subtly identifies himself with the Mother of God, speaking in the first person but employing the types and epithets that are commonly associated with Mary:

> And thus you rendered me a throne of your divine divinity,
> and a home of your unapproachable glory and Kingdom,
> and an earthen jar bearing manna,
> manna of immortality
> and a lamp holding divine and unquenchable light within,
> and truly a wooden box for the beautiful pearl (Mt 13:45),
> and a field in which was hidden the treasure of the world (Mt 13:44),
> a fountain from which those who drink shall no longer thirst,
> the fountain that bubbles up abundant water tenfold,
> and it renders immortal everyone who drinks in faith,
> A paradise that has a new tree of life in its middle,
> And a land that covers all round the One who is uncontainable to all.[51]

There can be no doubt that Symeon is alluding to Mary, the Mother of God, in this passage; however, he deliberately chooses not to name her, implying that he himself is acting as container, or receptacle, of the Word. This serves to reinforce an underlying premise that the Virgin Mary is fully human. Indeed, we can each identify ourselves with her as we open ourselves fully to the presence and love of God that surrounds us, thus becoming like her, "Bearers of God." That there is a patristic basis for such an understanding is borne out in a passage ascribed to the late fourth- and early fifth-century preacher, Severian of Gabala:

> When you take the word of Christ and shape it in your mind and transform it in your thought as if in a womb, you are called his mother.[52]

Notes

1 Soskice (2007), p. 8 [the italics are my own]; cf. Murdoch (2001); Taylor (1989).
2 See, for example, Zizioulas (1985); Zizioulas (2006); Yannaras (1984); Yannaras (2007).
3 "*Understanding Persons: Ancient, Medieval, and Modern Perspectives from the Christian East,*" May 14–16, 2014, Thessaloniki, Greece.
4 I would like here to express my gratitude to Dr. Alexis Torrance, who invited me to the conference and encouraged me to submit my paper to the proceedings, which are published in this volume.
5 For introductory approaches to this field, see Graef (2009); Pelikan (1996); Vassilaki (ed.) (2005); Brubaker and Cunningham (eds.) (2011).
6 George of Nicomedia, *Oratio* 8, *PG* 100, 1480B; cf. Fr Maximos Constas (of Simonopetra), "And a Sword Shall Pierce Your Own Soul (Lk 2:35): The Kenosis of Christ and the Mother of God," unpublished paper delivered at the SS Mary and Martha Sisterhood Lenten Women's Retreat on March 23, 2013, the Holy Resurrection Orthodox Church, Allston, Massachusetts, p. 29.
7 For a full overview of Byzantine liturgical treatment of Mary's lament at the foot of the cross, see Tsironis (1998). See also Tsironis (1997); Ševčenko (2011).
8 See Cunningham (2003). For the background in Syriac liturgical texts, see Brock (1991).
9 See Cunningham (2016). The *Lives* include that which is ascribed to Maximus the Confessor and survives only in Georgian, recently reedited and translated in Shoemaker (2012); the *Life* by Epiphanios of Kallistratou, PG 120:186–216; the unedited *Life of the Virgin* by John Geometres, although the final section of this text is edited and translated in Wenger (1955), pp. 364–415; and a Metaphrastic *Life*, ed. Latyshev (ed.) (1912), pp. 345–82.
10 An easily accessible collection of such miracle stories (a group that is associated with the shrine of the *pege* ["spring"] of the Theotokos in Constantinople) can now be found in Talbot and Johnson (trans.) (2012), pp. 205–97.
11 Tischendorf (ed.) (1866), pp. 391–400.
12 For an excellent discussion of this subject, see Baun (2004).
13 Patlagean (1991).
14 For example, Halkin (1984), no. 1102g, 304.
15 As stated earlier, the *Life* (or set of orations) remains unpublished except for the final section of the text, which concerns the Dormition of the Virgin Mary. See note 9. A critical edition is currently underway, however, under the direction of Fr. Maximos Constas (of Simonopetra).

16 Schmemann (1966), pp. 33–6; Calivas (2003), pp. 37–48; Olkinuora (2015), pp. 139–43.
17 Kennedy (1983), p. 176.
18 On the various levels of discourse that may occur within a homily or hymn (including "intertextual" and "extratextual"), see Cunningham (2003), pp. 102–3. For a new definition and terminology, cf. Eriksen (2013), p. 102.
19 See Cunningham (2004), pp. 52–62.
20 Constas (ed. and trans.) (2003), p. 137.
21 The date and authorship of this important early hymn, which is still sung on the fifth Saturday of Lent in Orthodox churches, remains a subject of debate. Leena Mari Peltomaa has recently defended an early date on theological grounds, suggesting that it was composed at some time between the councils of Ephesus and Chalcedon (AD 431 and 451, respectively), whereas earlier scholars suggested a sixth- or even early seventh-century context for its composition. Peltomaa (2001), pp. 49–114; Wellesz (1957); Matons (1977), pp. 32–6.
22 Germanos of Constantinople, *Homilia in annuntiationem s. deiparae*, ed. Fecioru (1946), p. 71; trans. Cunningham (2008), p. 226.
23 For an excellent study of this typology, see Theokritoff (2005), pp. 81–3.
24 John of Damascus, *Homilia in nativitatem b.v. Mariae* 6, ed. B. Kotter, *Die Schriften des Johannes von Damaskos*, Berlin and New York, 1988, vol. 5, p. 176; trans. Cunningham (2008), p. 62.
25 For a full discussion of the meaning of the various Marian types and of their placement in liturgical texts for the feasts, see Ladouceur (2006).
26 Germanos of Constantinople, *Homilia I in praesentationem s. Deiparae*, PG 98, 308; trans. Cunningham (2008), pp. 161–62.
27 Andrew of Crete, *Homilia I in nativitatem b. Mariae*, PG 97:808; trans. Cunningham (2008), p. 73.
28 John of Damascus, *Homilia in nativitatem b.v. Mariae* 3, ed. Kotter, *Die Schriften*, vol. 5, 171; trans. Cunningham (2008), p. 57.
29 Ibid. 2, Kotter, *Die Shriften*, vol. 5, 170; trans. Cunningham (2008), p. 55.
30 See, for example, the kanon (attributed to Kosmas the Melodist) for the feast of the Meeting of our Lord (*Hypapante*), celebrated on February 2, Ode 7: "'And a sword will pierce your heart, O All Pure-Virgin,' Symeon foretold to the Theotokos, 'when you will see your Son upon the Cross to whom we cry aloud: O God of our fathers, you are blessed.'" See Mary and Ware (trans.) (1969), p. 424 (with adjustments).
31 Baltoyanni (2000), esp. pp. 147–52.
32 Kalavrezou (1990); Tsironis (2000).
33 Romanos, *Kontakion on the Nativity of Christ*, ed. P. Maas and C.A. Trypanis, *Sancti Romani Melodi Cantica: Cantica Genuina*, Oxford, 1963, pp. 1–9; trans. Lash (1994), pp. 3–12.
34 Two recent studies of Romanos the Melodist's work provide new insights in this area; see Arentzen (2017); Gador-Whyte (2017). See also Frank (2005), pp. 163–79.
35 Romanos, *Kontakion on the Nativity of Christ*, Stanza 6, Maas and Trypanis, *Sancti Romani Melodi Cantica*, 3; Lash (1994), p. 5.
36 Ibid., Stanza 23, Maas and Trypanis, *Sancti Romani Melodi Cantica*, 8; Lash, *St Romanos*, 11.
37 For an overview of these homilies, see Allen (2011), esp. pp. 72–8.
38 Caro (1971–73), vol. 2, pp. 308–44. See also Leroy (1967), pp. 298–324.
39 Brock (1994), pp. 12–13.
40 Romanos the Melodist, *Kontakia I and II on the Annunciation*, ed. Maas and Trypanis, *Sancti Romani Melodi Cantica*, pp. 280–93.
41 Sophronios of Jerusalem, *Homilia in annuntiationem*, PG 87:3217–88.
42 Andrew of Crete, *Homilia in annuntiationem*, PG 97:881–913; trans. Cunningham (2008), pp. 197–219.

43 Germanos of Constantinople, *Homilia in annuntiationem*, ed. Fecioru (1946); trans. Cunningham (2008), pp. 221–46.
44 Germanos, *In Annuntiationem*, ed. Fecioru, 'Un nou gen de predica', 87; trans. (with adjustments), Cunningham (2008), p. 233.
45 Cunningham (2003), pp. 111–13.
46 See Mary and Ware (trans.) (1969), pp. 448–58.
47 Maas and Trypanis, *Sancti Romani Melodi Cantica*, 142–49; Lash (1994), pp. 141–50. For discussion of the short troparia known as "stavrotheotokia," see Wellesz (1961), p. 243.
48 Maas and Trypanis, *Sancti Romani Melodi Cantica*, Stanzas 3–4, 143; Lash (1994), pp. 144.
49 George of Nicomedia, *Oratio in illud: "Stabant autem juxta crucem Jesu Mater ejus,"* PG 100:1468B, 1480B, etc.
50 Father Maximos of Simonopetra writes provocatively on the antinomy between Mary's virginity and her grief at the foot of the cross, as follows: "Mary, both virgin and mother, is a paradoxical figure. In a single moment, in the very form of her being, she embodies all the inviolability of virginity and all the pain of motherhood. In her virginity, she is a "sealed book that no man may open" (cf. Isaiah 29: 11–12). Yet in the experience of mourning for her lost son, the seals of her being are torn apart, rent like the veil of the temple, for this is her real childbirth, in which her hair is loose, her eyes leak, and midwives anxiously attend to her. In her pain she is one with the wounded Christ: she is porous, poured out, kenotic." See Constas (2014), pp. 127–28.
51 Symeon the New Theologian, *Hymn 20*, trans. Griggs (2010), pp. 200–10.
52 Severian of Gabala, *De caeco et Zacchaeo*, PG 59:605.

Select bibliography

Allen, P. (2011), "Portrayals of Mary in Greek Homiletic Literature," in Cunningham and Brubaker (eds.) (2011), pp. 68–89.

Arentzen, T. (2017), *The Virgin in Song. Mary and the Poetry of Romanos the Melodist*, Philadelphia, PA.

Baltoyanni, C. (2000), "The Mother of God in Portable Icons," in Vassilaki (ed.) (2000), pp. 139–53.

Baun, J. (2004), "Discussing Mary's Humanity in Medieval Byzantium," in Swanson (ed.) (2004), pp. 63–72.

Baun, J. (2007), *Tales From Another Byzantium: Celestial Journey and Local Community in the Medieval Greek Apocrypha*, Cambridge.

Brock, S. (1991), "Dramatic Dialogue Poems," in G. J. Reininck and H. L. J. Vanstiphout, eds., *Dispute Poems and Dialogues in the Ancient and Mediaevel Near East*, Leuven, pp. 91–108.

Brock, S. (1994), *Bride of Light, Moran 'Eth'o* 6, Kottayam, India.

Brubaker, L. and Cunningham, M. B. (eds.) (2011), *The Cult of the Mother of God in Byzantium: Texts and Images*, Farnham and Burlington VT.

Calivas, A. C. (2003), *Essays in Theology and Liturgy, vol. 3: Aspects of Orthodox Worship*, Brookline MA.

Caro, R. (1971–73), *La homiletica Mariana griega en el siglo* V, 3 vols., Dayton OH.

Constas, M. (2014), *The Art of Seeing: Paradox and Perception in Orthodox Iconography*, Alhambra, CA: Sebastian Press.

Constas, N. (ed. and trans.) (2003), *Proclus of Constantinople and the Cult of the Virgin in Late Antiquity*, Leiden and Boston.

Cunningham, M. B. (2003), "Dramatic Device or Didactic Tool? The Function of Dialogue in Byzantine Preaching," in E. Jeffreys (ed.), *Rhetoric in Byzantium*, SPBS Publications 11, Aldershot and Burlington VT, pp. 101–13.

Cunningham, M. B. (2004), "The Meeting of the Old and the New: The Typology of Mary the Theotokos in Byzantine Homilies and Hymns," in Swanson (ed.) (2004), pp. 52–62.

Cunningham, M. B. (2008), *Wider Than Heaven. Eighth-Century Homilies on the Mother of God*, Crestwood NY.

Cunningham, M. B. (2016), "The Life of the Virgin Mary According to Middle Byzantine Preachers and Hagiographers: Changing Contexts and Perspectives," *Apocrypha* 17, pp. 137–59.

Eriksen, U. H. (2013), *Drama in the Kontakia of Romanos the Melodist: A Narratological Analysis of Four Kontakia*, published PhD thesis, Aarhus University.

Fecioru, D. (1946), "Un nou gen de predica in omiletica ortodoxa," *Biserica Ortodoxa Romana* 64, pp. 65–91, 180–92, 386–96.

Frank, G. (2005), "Dialogue and Deliberation: The Sensory Self in the Hymns of Romanos the Melodist," in D. Brakke et al., eds., *Religion and the Self in Antiquity*, Bloomington and Indianapolis, pp. 163–79.

Gador-Whyte, S. (2017), *Theology and Poetry in Early Byzantium. The Kontakia of Romanos the Melodist*, Cambridge.

Graef, H. (2009), *Mary: A History of Doctrine and Devotion*, rev. ed., Notre Dame IN.

Griggs, D. K. (2010), *Divine Eros. Hymns of St Symeon the New Theologian*, Crestwood NY.

Halkin, F. (ed.) (1984), *Bibliothecae hagiographicae graecae: novum auctorium*, Subsidia hagiographica 65, Brussels.

Kalavrezou, I. (1990), "Images of the Mother: When the Virgin Mary Became the Meter Theou," *Dumbarton Oaks Papers* 44, pp. 165–72.

Kennedy, G. A. (1983), *Greek Rhetoric Under Christian Emperors*, Princeton NJ.

Ladouceur, P. (2006), "Old Testament Prefigurations of the Mother of God," *St Vladimir's Theological Quarterly* 50, nos. 1–2, pp. 5–57.

Lash, E. (trans.) (1994), *St Romanos: Kontakia on the Life of Christ. Chanted Sermons by the Great Sixth-Century Poet and Singer*, New York.

Latyshev, B. (ed.) (1912), *Menologii anonymi byzantini saeculi X quae supersunt*, vol. 2, St Petersburg.

Leroy, J. (1967), *L'homilétique de Proclus*, Rome.

Mary, M. and Ware, K. (trans.) (1969), *The Festal Menaion*, London.

Matons, J. G. de (1977), *Romanos le Mélode et les origines de la poésie religieuse à Byzance*, Paris.

Murdoch, I. (2001), *The Sovereignty of Good*, London.

Olkinuora, J. (2015), *Byzantine Hymnography for the Feast of the Entrance of the Theotokos*, Studia Patristica Fennica 4, published PhD thesis, University of East Finland.

Patlagean, E. (1991), "Remarques sur la production et la diffusion des apocryphes dans le monde byzantin," *Apocrypha* 2, pp. 155–64.

Pelikan, J. (1996), *Mary Through the Centuries: Her Place in the History of Culture*, New Haven CT and London.

Peltomaa, L. M. (2001), *The Image of the Virgin Mary in the Akathistos Hymn*, Leiden, Boston, and Cologne.

Schmemann, A. (1966), *Introduction to Liturgical Theology*, trans. A. E. Moorhouse, Crestwood NY.

Ševčenko, N. P. (2011), "The Service of the Virgin's Lament Revisited," in Brubaker and Cunningham (eds.) (2011), pp. 247–62.
Shoemaker, S. J. (2012), *Maximus the Confessor: The Life of the Virgin*, New Haven CT.
Soskice, J. (2007), *The Kindness of God. Metaphor, Gender, and Religious Language*, Oxford.
Swanson, R. N. (ed.) (2004), *The Church and Mary*, Studies in Church History 39, Woodbridge, Suffolk.
Talbot, A.-M. and Johnson, S. F. (trans.) (2012), *Miracle Tales from Byzantium*, Cambridge MA and London.
Taylor, C. (1989), *Sources of the Self: The Making of the Modern Identity*, Cambridge.
Theokritoff, E. (2005), "Praying the Scriptures in Orthodox Worship," in S. T. Kimbrough, Jr. (ed.), *Orthodox and Wesleyan Scriptural Understanding and Practice*, Crestwood NY, pp. 83–6.
Tischendorf, K. (ed.) (1866), *Apocalypses apocryphae*, Leipzig.
Tsironis, N. (1997), "George of Nicomedia: Convention and Originality in the Homily on Good Friday," *Studia Patristica* 33, pp. 573–77.
Tsironis, N. (1998), *The Lament of the Virgin Mary From Romanos the Melode to George of Nicomedia: An Aspect of the Development of the Marian Cult*, unpubl. PhD thesis, The University of London.
Tsironis, N. (2000), "The Mother of God in the Iconoclastic Controversy," in Vassilaki (ed.) (2000), pp. 27–39.
Vassilaki, M. (ed.) (2000), *Mother of God. Representations of the Virgin in Byzantine Art*, Athens and Milan.
Vassilaki, M. (ed.) (2005), *Images of the Mother of God. Perceptions of the Theotokos in Byzantium*, Aldershot and Burlington VT.
Webb, R. (2009), *Ekphrasis, Imagination and Persuasion in Ancient Rhetorical Theory and Practice*, Farnham and Burlington VT.
Wellesz, E. (1957), *The Akathistos Hymn*, Copenhagen.
Wellesz, E. (1961), *A History of Byzantine Music and Hymnography*, rev. ed., Oxford.
Wenger, A. (1955), *L'assomption de la très sainte Vierge dans la tradition Byzantine du Vie au Xe siècle*, Paris.
Yannaras, C. (1984), *Freedom and Morality*, trans. E. Briere, Crestwood NY.
Yannaras, C. (2007), *Person and Eros*, trans. N. Russell, Brookline MA.
Zizioulas, J. (1985), *Being as Communion: Studies in Personhood and the Church*, Crestwood NY.
Zizioulas, J. (2006), *Communion and Otherness: Further Studies in Personhood and the Church*, ed. P. McPartlan, London.

6 Personification in Byzantine hymnography
Kontakia and canons

Damaskinos (Olkinuora) of Xenophontos

The rich corpus of Byzantine liturgical hymns and homilies composed for religious celebrations is impressive for both its quantity and quality. These compositions, built on the rhetorical ideals of ancient Greek eloquence, existed in a tight intertextual connection not only with the scriptures (which one would expect) but also with earlier Greek literary traditions. In addition, Syrian liturgical poetry brought strong Semitic influences – to hymnography, most notably, especially from the remarkable sixth-century hymnographer Romanos the Melodist onwards – partly obscuring the differences between the two literary genres, resulting in poetical homilies[1] and sung sermons.[2]

One of the elements inherited from all three traditions – scripture, Greek literature, and Syrian poetry – is the use of rhetorical personification. Before continuing, however, it would be helpful to delineate the various uses of this term. Sometimes, personification is seen merely as a synonym of the Greek rhetorical term *prosopopoeia*, but in scholarship, much broader semantics have been introduced. Personification generally refers to the representation of nonsubstantial qualities as persons.[3] In his intriguing study on the use of personification in Wisdom and Romans, Joseph Dodson provides an extensive discussion on the different uses of the term. He divides the use of personification into roughly three categories ranging from what he calls "casual personifications" (a term referring to giving humanlike metaphors to inanimate objects, such as "time who marches on," used also in everyday language) to "general personifications" (referring to something inanimate being compared to a person, such as "rejoicing, the sun races to finish the line"), and, finally, "representative personifications" (which, according to Dodson's definition, "represents an attribute, passion or a part of a person or suprahuman power and is ontologically the same as or part of that being").[4] As we shall see during the course of this chapter, all these forms of personification appear in Byzantine hymnography. Later in his study, Dodson suggests the following purposes for the use of personification: it can "decorate or amplify," "educate or clarify," "motivate or manipulate," "expose the cause of something," "provide new insight," or "deflect attention away from difficult topics."[5] Later in this chapter, we shall reflect on whether or not these suggestions apply in our case studies.

Prosopopoeia has been a confusing term since antiquity – though often translated as "personification";[6] it represents only a few of the different types of personification mentioned previously. In ancient Greco-Roman rhetorical theory, *prosopopoeia* normally refers to a figure of speech where a nonhuman being comes alive and is capable of speaking and conducting other human activities.[7] Dodson makes a distinction between *prosopopoeia* and personification, meaning by the former the voicing of humans or gods, while personification refers, according to his definition, to inanimate objects acquiring humanlike characteristics;[8] I have decided to include *prosopopoeia* as a category of personification, but as a special term for a rhetorical device where a nonhuman or inanimate subject speaks, while I refer to the voicing of humans, angels, or gods as *ethopoeia*.

Personification is not merely a phenomenon of Greco-Roman rhetoric. In Judeo-Christian literature, the tradition of personifications is, again, prominent. In the Old Testament, both in Proverbs and the Book of Wisdom, we read of personified Wisdom – a topic that has received a great deal of attention in scholarship.[9] This Wisdom has been identified, among others, as a relic of the female goddess of early Hebrew polytheism,[10] a Stoic Logos,[11] Christ,[12] or, more lately in late nineteenth- and early twentieth-century Russian theology and philosophy, Sophia, a female aspect of the divinity.[13] In his recent study, Dodson explores the personifications of Death, Hades, Creation, Logos, Wrath, and Wisdom, among others, in the Book of Wisdom. He surmises that the purpose of these personifications is primarily related to soteriology and theodicy. Sophia, Dike, and Dynamis are represented as counterpowers of Hades, Death, and Destruction: the believer's task is to avoid divine punishment by joining the former.[14]

But one should not omit the tradition of Greek religion from consideration, either; indeed, the apparent link between scriptural and ancient Greek traditions is the Christianized personifications of ancient deities. Two of the most important ones – Hades, who marks also a toponym, and his companion Death – make their way to Christianity also through the New Testament:[15] Hades is mentioned in Revelation 6:8, where he accompanies the fourth Horseman of the Apocalypse, Death. The confusion between toponymity and personification appears, with both names, in Revelation 1:18: "I am alive for evermore, Amen; and have the keys of hell and of death." Death is also mentioned in Romans (which is rich in other personifications, as well): 5:14 ("nevertheless death reigned"), 17 ("for if by one man's offence death reigneth by one"), 6:9 ("death hath no more dominion over him"), and 1 Corinthians 15:26 ("the last enemy that shall be destroyed is death").[16]

One should remember that Death does not merely remain a personification of an abstract phenomenon: in ancient Greek religion, a deity called Death (Θάνατος) was regarded as the son of Night (Νύξ) and Darkness ("Ερεβος), and the twin brother of Sleep ("Υπνος). He is, thus, not only a personification of bodily corruption but also an identifiable divinity, like Hades.[17] As we shall see, these two infernal characters also became popular in hymnography, in contrast to the Judeo-Hellenistic Sophia, who does not have a significant hymnographic afterlife. We shall also reflect briefly on the relations between paganism and Christianity with regard to these terms.

Personifications made their way from earlier literary traditions to hymnography as stowaways. From the sixth century onward, Byzantine hymnography and homiletics experienced a major change. The exegetical and dogmatic sermons and brief strophic hymns of the fourth and fifth centuries were replaced by festal homilies and flourishing, extensive new hymnographic genres: the *kontakion* and the canon. At the same time, these texts were adorned with dramatic rhetorical devices in order to vivify the narrative and make it more personal for the audience, triggering emotional response. The use of personification falls into this category, and it was not restricted only to literature: in Byzantine iconography, personification became a prominent means for illustrating these literary figures.[18] Because of this fundamental change in the sixth century, I have decided to extend my survey from Romanos the Melodist to the ninth century, which marks the end of the flourishing tradition of canons: the influence Romanos had on later poetry and homilies is so remarkable, especially in the use of dramatic language, that it should not be omitted, as we will soon see. After the ninth century, Byzantine hymnography mainly followed old patterns, and no new hymnographic forms or major feasts were introduced.

The use of literary personification in Greek Antiquity has received a good amount of scholarly attention: similarly, dialogical *ethopoeia* (an invented dialogue between two characters in a narrative), either in its intra- or extratextual form,[19] has equally received much scholarly attention in the context of Byzantine hymnography. However, the use of personification specifically in hymnography has not been adequately dealt with,[20] and a more general investigation of this rhetorical mode or figure[21] has, thus far, remained a *desideratum*. In his study on the relationship between Byzantine hymnography and rhetoric, Korakides contents himself by stating that the use of *prosopopoeia* in hymnography is frequent; it is a daring rhetorical figure, and it is often found in conjunction with supernatural events, together with providing a few examples mainly from the hymnography of Holy Week.[22] Therefore, the present chapter is the first attempt at a broader survey and aims at providing a preliminary study of four different types of personification in liturgical material found in the repertoire of the sixth to the ninth centuries, discussing their functions and exploring their literary context.

Nature and places personified

Perhaps the most frequent use of personification in hymnography is related to nature, though these references are arguably the least daring too. Personified natural allusions appear both in pagan antiquity and in the scriptures. In the Psalms, there are numerous general personifications of nature ("Praise Him, sun and moon; praise Him, all ye stars and light. Praise him, ye heavens of heavens, and the water that is above the heavens. Let them praise the name of the Lord." [Ps 147:3–5 LXX]).[23] This group also demonstrates a wide range of personification types, from casual to representative, with general personifications dominating the repertoire.

The functions of natural personification range from a mere decoration of speech to more elevated meanings. Sometimes, the use of natural personification exists in conjunction with typology (which will be examined later in this chapter). Most often, nature is described as celebrating together with the gathered faithful, which seems to be a simple rhetorical trope used to embellish a hymn: a standard formula commands heaven and earth to rejoice together with believers on the feast day.[24] A subcategory of such exhortations to celebration is the use of toponyms: in Nativity hymns, for instance, Bethlehem is addressed,[25] and in the canon of Pascha, Zion is told to rejoice.[26]

On the other hand, nature also takes part in the sorrow of humanity: the most striking case is, naturally, the compassion Creation feels toward the Passion of its Creator, following the testimony of the Gospels: "Now from the sixth hour there was darkness over all the land unto the ninth hour [. . .] and the earth did quake, and the rocks rent" (Matt 27:45, 51). In iconography of the Crucifixion, this personification is attested to by the depiction of the sun and moon with human faces.[27] Canon poetry for the Passion is not particularly prominent – in contemporary liturgical tradition, there is only a *triodion*, a three-canticled canon, for Holy Friday. However, Romanos's *Kontakion On the Passion* begins with personifications of natural elements, especially the sun and moon. The first *prooimion* states,

Σήμερον ἐταράττετο τῆς γῆς τὰ θεμέλια,	Today the earth's foundations trembled,
ὁ ἥλιος ἠλλιοῦτο μὴ στέγων θεωρῆσαι	and the sun changed its looks since it could not bear seeing
ἐν σταυρῷ γὰρ περιέκειτο ὁ πάντων ζωοδότης[28]	the Life-giver of all hanging on the cross

In the first strophe, the poet addresses the entirety of creation:

Ἔκστηθι σήμερον, οὐρανέ· δῦνον εἰς χάος, ὦ γῆ·	[Be astonished today], O heaven! Descend to chaos, O earth!
μὴ τολμήσῃς, ἥλιε, σὸν δεσπότην κατιδεῖν ἐπὶ τοῦ ξύλου βουλήσει κρεμάμενον·	Sun, do not dare to look down on your Ruler, as He willingly hangs upon the cross!
ῥαγήτωσαν πέτραι,	Let rocks be rent,
ἡ γὰρ πέτρα τῆς ζωῆς νῦν τοῖς ἥλοις τιτρώσκεται·	for the Rock of Life is now wounded with nails;
σχισχθήτω τοῦ ναοῦ τὸ καταπέτασμα, σώματος δεσποτικοῦ λόγχῃ νυσσομένου ὑπὸ ἀνόμων·	may the veil of the temple be rent in twain, when the body of the Ruler is pierced with a spear by lawless men;
ἁπλῶς πᾶσα ἡ κτίσις τοῦ κτίστου τὸ πάθος φρίξῃ, στενάξῃ· μόνος χορεύει ὁ Ἀδάμ.[29]	let all of Creation be horrified by the passion of its Creator, may it groan – only Adam dances for joy.

Another scriptural personification that finds its continuation in hymnography is related to the feast of Theophany. The liturgical texts of the feast employ Psalm verses that personify the river Jordan and the sea: "The waters saw thee, O God, the waters saw thee, and feared; and the depths were troubled" (Ps 76:15 LXX), and "What ailed thee, O sea, that thou fleddest? and thou Jordan, that thou wast turned back?" (Ps 113:3 LXX).[30] These personifications are apparent in the iconography of Theophany, where they are depicted as humanoid figures riding fish.[31] Nevertheless, personifications of the river Jordan do not, perhaps surprisingly so, appear in Romanos's two *kontakia* composed for Theophany,[32] but are abundant in canon poetry. In an anonymous canon for the forefeast of Theophany (not in liturgical use today), the poet addresses the river Jordan:

Ἰορδάνη, ἀγάλλου ποταμέ· ἰδοὺ γὰρ ἐπὶ σοὶ παραγίνεται Χριστὸς τοῦ ἐκτελέσαι δικαιοσύνην, ἥνπερ ἀπ' αἰῶνος προώρισεν.[33]	Rejoice, O river Jordan! Behold, Christ comes to you in order to fulfil the righteousness that He had planned before the ages.

This humanlike emotion of joy is a rather frequent, general personification that appears in natural allusions. There are no hymns in which the Jordan is dealt with through actual *prosopopoeia* – i.e., giving voice to him as a character – but he is described in terms that imply possession of bodily senses. John the Baptist describes the Jordan's sight in his ethopoietic passage to Christ:

Σὺ παρ' ἐμοῦ καθάρσιον ὁ καθαίρων τὸν κόσμον αἰτῆσαι παρεγένου, ἐγὼ δὲ δέδοικα, Χριστέ· ὁ Ἰορδάνης τρόμῳ ἰδών σε στραφήσεται καὶ κωλύσει ὄντως τῇ ἐγχειρήσει τῇ ἐμῇ· σὺ οὖν με βάπτισον σὺν παντὶ τῷ ὄχλῳ, τὸν δοῦλον ὁ δεσπότης.[34]	Christ, You who cleanse The world, have come to me in order to ask for cleansing, and I have given it to You. The Jordan, having seen You, turns its flow in terror and truly hinders itself so that I can put my hands on You. Therefore, as Ruler, baptize me Your servant, together with all the people.

Another corporeal image is provided in the canon of the forefeast of Theophany, composed according to the model of the canon of Holy Saturday and sung at Compline on the eve of the feast:

Ἥπλωσεν Ἰορδάνης τὰ ὕδατα ὡς νῶτα μετὰ τρόμου, τοῦ δέξασθαι τὸν Κτίστην σωματικῶς βαπτιζόμενον, τὸν πάντας ἁγιάζοντα, Οὐκ ἔστιν ἅγιος πλήν σου, Κύριε, κραυγάζοντας.[35]	The Jordan, trembling with fear, spread out its waters like a back in order to receive the Creator, who is baptized bodily, and sanctifies all those who cry to Him: There is none Holy as You, O Lord.

In all of these examples from Theophany, the *troparia* that employ personification are few and dispersed. Personification can hardly be seen in them as a rhetorical mode, but more as a figure of speech whose function is not only to decorate the hymn but also to emphasize the meeting of material water and the prefiguration of baptism with God.

Hades and death revisited

A prominent tradition in the apocryphal literature is the descent into Hades by both Christ and Lazarus. These narratives have their antecedents in such ancient Greek legends as Orfeus and Heracles descending into Hades (among many others, including Odysseus's seeking advice from the blind oracle, Teiresias, at Hades's entrance). Already in mythology, Hades marks both a toponym and a personal deity; in Christianity, the term did not naturally refer to a god, only to a place, but his personification remained: the literary device of Hades's dialogues with other characters appears frequently in Christian literature. In the third-century Syriac/Aramaic *Odes of Solomon*, Sheol and Death react in a hostile way to Christ's descent into Hades.[36] Perhaps the most influential version of this event is preserved in the apocryphal gospel of pseudo-Nicodemus, dating from the fifth century: here, Satan (as an explicit personification of Death?) negotiates with Hades what to do before Christ descends there. Eventually, even Hades turns, together with the saints, against Satan.[37]

Not surprisingly, the personifications of Death and Hades became prominent in hymnography as well, something that has received considerable scholarly attention.[38] Particularly, much has been written on Romanos the Melodist's *kontakia*, especially on a hymn titled *On the Victory of the Cross*. Uffe Holmsgaard Eriksen, in his narratological study of Romanos's *kontakia*, emphasizes the importance of the personifications of the Devil, Hades, and Death as vehicles for their ridicule. In a quote from another *kontakion*, *On the Man Possessed with Devils*, Romanos presents this mockery through theatrical metaphors:

Τί δὲ τούτους τιτρώσκειν ἐγνώκαμεν,	We know how to injure them [i.e., the demons]:
ὅταν τὴν πτῶσιν αὐτῶν κωμῳδοῦμεν γηθόμενοι·	it is when we make a comedy of their fall.
ὄντως πενθεῖ ὁ διά[βολος],	Certainly, the Devil mourns
ὅταν δαιμόνων τὸν θρίαμβον	when the triumph of the demons
ἐν ἐκκλησίαις τρ[αγῳ]δῶμεν.[39]	is made into a tragedy by us in the churches.[40]

In the *kontakia*, which include episodes featuring Hades or the Devil, the mocking is rendered though ironic vocabulary,[41] most notably through the image of food poisoning. Georgia Frank suggests that the idea of Hades vomiting men, or Christ piercing Hades's insatiable belly with the cross,[42] could also be an allusion to the tradition of Roman satire, where gluttons were mocked.[43] Extending the satire further, Christ is depicted as bait on a fishing hook that deceives Hades and causes its belly to be torn into pieces:[44] fish, in the end, are very often the cause of food poisoning. Moreover, in a Christian context, overeating and then vomiting – a brutal description of gluttony's consequences, as if in a Greek orgy – is a counterimage for fasting, which is considered a fundamental virtue for every believer.

Even though much attention has been given to the representations of Hades and Death in the *kontakion* repertoire, the canons have been almost completely ignored, though not without reason: they are less striking and emotionally involved than the *kontakia*, but they are an important testimony for the continuation of the themes of *kontakia* in liturgical use up to the present day.⁴⁵ A canon attributed to Andrew of Crete, sung on the eve of Lazarus Saturday, follows the earlier tradition of *kontakia* and includes dialogical passages between not only Death and Hades but also Hades and Lazarus.

The sources of the canon are clear: as has been shown by Mary B. Cunningham, among others, Romanos's work particularly influenced Andrew of Crete.⁴⁶ In Romanos's first *kontakion* on the raising of Lazarus, the hymnographer speaks first to Death and exhorts him to calm down and receive Christ as a friend, for He will raise Lazarus from the dead. Upset, Death exhorts Hades to control his insatiable stomach and, later on, to vomit Lazarus in order to be relieved.⁴⁷ Unlike in some other of Romanos's hymns, the prosopopoetic passage here is not particularly extensive and does not fill the whole *kontakion*. Moreover, Romanos's *kontakia* do not give voice to Lazarus, unlike Andrew's canon.

In the canon, however, these "dialogues" are rather one-sided: Death and Lazarus are only presented as listeners, and they do not utter a word. The canon also seems to be a synthesis of all the personified themes found in Romanos's *kontakia* dealing with Christ's descent to Hades or Lazarus's rising, not exclusively hymns on Lazarus: the image of Christ piercing Hades's belly, found in the hymn *On the Victory of the Cross*, as we noted earlier, is present also here. The prosopopoetic passages are dispersed throughout the text, and they do not form a narrative continuation:

Οἴμοι! ὄντως νῦν ἀπόλωλα, / ἐκβοῶν ὁ ᾅδης οὕτω προσεφώνει / τῷ θανάτῳ λέγων· / Ἰδοὺ ὁ Ναζαραῖος τὰ κάτω συνέσεισε, / καὶ τὴν γαστέρα μου τεμών, / ἄπνουν νεκρόν, / φωνήσας ἤγειρε.⁴⁸

"Woe is me! Now am I destroyed utterly," / hell cried out, and thus / he spoke to death: / "See, the man from Nazareth has shaken the / lower world, and cutting open my belly / He has called a lifeless corpse / and raised it up."⁴⁹

[. . .]

Τοῦ πάθους τὰ σύμβολα, / καὶ τοῦ σταυροῦ σου γνωρίσαι βουληθείς, / ἀγαθέ, τοῦ ᾅδου τὴν ἄπληστον γαστέρα / ῥήξας, / ἀνέστησας ὡς Θεὸς τὸν τετραήμερον.⁵⁰

Wishing, O Good One, to reveal the meaning of Your Passion and Your Cross, You have broken open the insatiable belly of hell, and as God You have raised up the man four days dead.

[. . .]

Παρακαλῶ σε Λάζαρε, φησὶν, ἀνάστηθι, ἔξελθε τῶν κλείθρων μου ταχὺ, ἄπιθι οὖν· καλόν μοι γὰρ ἕνα θρηνῆσαι, πικρῶς ἀφαιρούμενον, παρὰ πάντας οὕς πρὶν, πεινῶν κατέπιον.	"I implore you, Lazarus," said hell, "rise up, depart quickly from my bonds and be gone. It is better for me to lament bitterly for the loss of one, rather than of all those whom I swallowed in my hunger."
Καὶ τί βραδύνεις, Λάζαρε, φησίν· ὁ φίλος σου, "Δεῦρο ἔξω" κράζει· ἑστηκὼς ἔξελθε οὖν, ἵνα κἀγὼ ἄνεσιν λάβω· ἀφ' οὗ γάρ σε ἔφαγον, εἰς ἔμετον ἡ τροφὴ ἀντικατέστη μοι.	"Why do you delay, Lazarus?" cried hell. "Your friend stands calling to you: 'Come out.' Go, then, and I too shall feel relief. For since I swallowed you, all other food is loathsome to me."
Τί οὐκ ἐγείρῃ, Λάζαρε, ταχύ; ἀνέκραζε κάτωθεν ὁ ἅδης θρηνωδῶν· τί οὐκ εὐθὺς ἐξαναστὰς, τρέχεις τῶν ὧδε, ἵνα μὴ καὶ ἄλλους μοι αἰχμαλωτίσῃ Χριστὸς, ἐξαναστήσας σε;[51]	"O Lazarus, why do you not rise up swiftly?" cried hell below lamenting. "Why do you not run straightway from this place? Lest Christ take prisoner the others, after raising you."

It should be clear by now that the figures of Death and Hades form perhaps the most prominent examples of personification in Byzantine hymnography, reaching from scriptural references to both major genres of hymnography. In previous studies, nevertheless, not much attention has been given to the fact that both Hades and Death represent personified deities of the pagan past. I do not think it is arbitrary that these characters continue their literary existence in a Christian context: in a way, Hades and Death, apart from representing death and corruption, become through their personification concrete scapegoats of the pagan past. The destruction of these persons exposes the fundamental change in the fate of humanity through Christ's salvific work.

Female virtues

Both in Greek antiquity and in the scriptures, it is common to present virtues as female personifications (as we saw earlier in the case of Wisdom). In hymnography, such personifications remain infrequent, but a remarkable exception exists: Romanos brings to the stage a fair number of personified characters in his *kontakion* on the temptation of the patriarch Joseph.[52] Uffe Holmsgaard Eriksen, in his narratological analysis of drama in Romanos's poetry, has characterized this *kontakion* as a "metaphorical athletic wrestling contest."[53] When the Egyptian woman, Potiphar's wife, tries to persuade Joseph to have intercourse with her (by using the euphemism ἐμοὶ συνομίλησον, "commune with me"), the spiritual battle is observed and assisted by a host of characters. In the eleventh strophe of the poem, the arena of a spiritual fight is set. The wrestlers, Joseph and Potiphar's wife, enter the scene, accompanied by their judges: the (rhyming!) personifications of Chastity (Ἁγνεία) and Lust (Λαγνεία). Angels and demons become spectators of this spiritual battle,[54] and God himself, who rewards Joseph for his endurance in the fight, takes the place of the emperor:

Φθεγγομένης τοιαῦτα τῆς μαινάδος ἐκείνης καὶ καταθωπευσούσης τὸν νέον, εἰς τὰ σκάμματα τῶν πειρασμῶν Ἰωσὴφ ὁ μέγας ἀθλητὴς ἔρχεται, πολύμορφον ἀντίπαλον βουλόμενος ἀντιπαλαῖσαι καὶ βραβευταὶ συνεισῆλθον δύο καὶ παρειστήκεισαν ἀμφοτέροις· τῷ μὲν Ἰωσὴφ ἡ ἁγνεία συνίστατο, τῇ δὲ γυναικὶ ἡ λαγνεία προΐστατο, μέσον τούτων ἠγωνίζετο ὁ φιλοσώφρων ἀνήρ, πρὸς αὐτὸν ἀντηγωνίζετο ἡ δολιόφρων γυνή· ἔθελγε μὲν ἐκείνη πρὸς μοιχείαν καλοῦσα, ἤθελε δὲ νικῆσαι τὴν αἰσχρὰν ὁ γενναῖος· τῷ Ἰωσὴφ συνέπραττον ἄγγελοι, τῇ γυναικὶ συνέτρεχον δαίμονες· ἄνωθεν δὲ θεωρῶν ὁ δεσπότης, τὸν νικητὴν ἔστεφε τοῖς ἐπαίνοις, ὅτι πάντα ἐφορᾷ τὸ ἀκοίμητον ὄμμα.[55]	When that mad woman had said these things and flirted with the young man, Joseph, the great athlete, came to the wrestling ground of temptations willing to fight against his adversary, who takes many forms. And two judges arrived, standing by both of them: Chastity with Joseph, Lust supporting the woman, and between them battled the moderation-loving man against the deceitful woman. She tried to attract him, enticing him to adultery, but the noble man wanted to win over the shameful woman. Angels assisted Joseph, demons raced in company with the woman. The Ruler, observing [the battle] from above crowned the winner with praises, for the sleepless eye watches over all.

The climax of the battle is the final attempt of the Egyptian woman to seduce Joseph: as she drags Joseph toward her, a countermovement is created by the female virtue of Grace (Χάρις). But then the devil himself takes a hold of Joseph, and the situation is solved by Moderation (Σωφροσύνη), who allows bodily sufferings to Joseph but guards him from spiritual harm:

"Ἐπάκουσόν μου, φίλτατε, καὶ δεῦρο, συνομίλησόν μοι." Ἔνθεν καθεῖλκεν ἡ Αἰγυπτία, πάλιν ἡ Χάρις ἀνθεῖλκε τοῦτον· αὕτη μὲν ἐβόα· "Ἐμοὶ συγκοιμήθητι," ἄνωθεν ἡ Χάρις· "Ἐμοὶ συγγρηγόρησον." Μετ' ἐκείνης ὁ διάβολος ἠγωνίζετο πικρῶς καὶ χερσὶ σφοδρῶς κατέσφιγγε τὸν γενναῖον ἀθλητήν· πάλιν ἡ Σωφροσύνη ἐκινεῖτο πρὸς πάλην, λῦσαι ἐπειγομένη τὰ κρατήματα τούτων ἔλεγε δέ· "Ραγῇ τὸ ἱμάτιον,	"My dearest one, listen to me and come, commune with me!" Then the Egyptian woman dragged him, but again Grace pulled him in the opposite direction: The former cried out: "Sleep with me!" while Grace uttered from above: "Stay vigilant with me!" The devil bitterly fought to support the former, and with his hands violently took hold of the noble athlete.

καὶ μὴ φθαρῇ τὸ σῶμα τοῦ σώφρονος·　　　Then Chastity moved to enter the fray,
λήψεται γὰρ παρὰ τοῦ ἀθλοθέτου,　　　　hastening to release the devil's grip.
ὡς νικητής, ἔνδυμα ἀφθαρσίας,　　　　　　She said: "May his tunic be ripped,
ὅτι πάντα ἐφορᾷ τὸ ἀκοίμητον ὄμμα."[56]　　but may the body of the chaste one remain incorrupt,
　　　　　　　　　　　　　　　　　　　　because he, as victor, will receive
　　　　　　　　　　　　　　　　　　　　the clothing of incorruptibility from the judge of this battle,
　　　　　　　　　　　　　　　　　　　　for the sleepless eye watches over all."

Such an abundant and vivid use of personified virtues is, to my knowledge, unique in the corpus of Byzantine hymnography: the rarity of this case makes it an even more striking rhetorical mode.

A less obvious case for personification of virtues could be made in the *vita* of the martyr Sophia and her three daughters, Faith, Hope, and Love (Πίστις, Ἐλπίς, and Ἀγάπη). There exists a canon composed in their honor, attributed to Theophanes.[57] The canon as such cannot be considered personification, but, rather, a standard presentation of the martyrs' qualities and struggles. That said, the Pauline triad of virtues, collected together by Wisdom – a virtue or power that has various interpretations, as we saw earlier – cannot but tempt the modern reader to see these four saints as personifications. In any case, it is not our task here to evaluate the historicity of these saints or the origins of their names.[58] In the end, personification has little to do with historical accuracy: *nomen est omen*, as the Romans said. Even today, names with etymological roots in virtues are widely in use, and the hymnographic material for these saints does not provide much inspiration for seeing them as personifications.[59]

In the introductory part of this chapter, we saw how in the scriptural tradition female virtues, such as Sophia or Dike, are often presented in juxtaposition with the personifications of evil, most prominently Hades and Death. But how is this to be seen relative to their prominence in the pagan past? The function of the vivid personifications of Hades and Death seems more straightforward: the destruction of their persons is associated with not only Christ's triumph over evil but also with the fall of the corrupt ancient religion. With virtues (who are supposed to represent the good), the situation becomes much more complicated when their idolatrous background in antiquity is considered, at least from a theological standpoint. How is the (by definition) corrupt, outdated, and even evil pagan past to be reconciled with the new ideal of Christian virtues?

Virtues, indeed, have a strong history in pagan antiquity: personified virtues appear in Greek literature, including, among others, Moderation.[60] Moreover, in the religion of the ancient Greeks, worship of personified virtues was a widespread practice.[61] Even though I am extremely reluctant to see the personification of virtues or the Christian "adaptation" of these ancient deities as a reconciliation with a polytheistic past, as a literary device, they prove useful for demonstrating an ideal Christian lifestyle: the living tradition of ancient literature in Byzantium must have aided in this process. Nevertheless, the function of their literary presentations becomes different in the new Christian context. Marina Warner suggests,

> Monotheism accorded them a complex, vaguely defined, but most interesting supernatural life. They were perceived as personal forces indwelling in the individual soul, and at the same time acting upon human destiny from the outside to change it for the better, as they had sometimes done as gods and goddesses; but a rich ambivalence marked their existence as beings at all.[62]

In the case of Joseph, virtues are presented as a counterpoint to temptation: they are simultaneously markers of Joseph's own qualities, such as Chastity and, especially, Moderation (since a common epithet for Joseph is σώφρων), and divine intervention. They could also be seen as symbolic of the soul's "good" passions,[63] inverse powers to the typical destructive passions: this is also suggested by the lexical similarity of Ἁγνεία and Λαγνεία.[64] The personification of virtues, then, exposes the cause of virtuous action, which appears both as divine intervention and a personally cultivated virtuous life. However, their presentation as divine powers is far from Bulgakov's ideas about Sophia as the female aspect of the deity: their personifications serve purely a didactic and entertaining purpose.

Typology as personification?

The last group of personifications I discuss here is related to the exegetical method called typology, which refers to the mimetic relationship between a type and its antitype:[65] according to Charles Kannengiesser's definition, a type is "a person, an event or an institution with a lasting significance which enables that person, event or institution to signify someone or something in God's future acting in history."[66] Of course, some types have their own independent historical significance, but in a patristic context, the Old Testament is always read in the light of Christ, His Mother, and the Christian Church.

Together with the flourishing of rhetoric, Middle Byzantine homilies and hymns were richly filled with biblical typologies that became increasingly prominent from the sixth century onward, especially relating to the cult of the Virgin. She was revered as a special protector of the capital, Constantinople (particularly through the important relics, her veil and belt, that were kept there), and the calendar became rich with feasts (and therefore also hymnography) dedicated to her.[67] Most Marian typologies refer to objects rather than persons: she is seen as the burning bush, the living temple, Aaron's rod, the bright cloud, and the Red Sea, to mention only a few. Typologies do not, naturally, fall into the traditional category of personification, but one cannot ignore the strong association these types acquire when they are comprehended by believers, guided by liturgical texts, as personified apparitions of the Theotokos. In a later period, the same idea is repeated in the famous frescoes of the Peribleptos church in Ochrid, dating to the twelfth century, where each of the Marian typological depictions of the Old Testament is illustrated with a mandorla, including a depiction of the Theotokos.[68]

Old Testament typologies appear throughout the repertory of Marian hymnography, but examples are particularly abundant in the liturgical texts for the feast of the Entrance of the Theotokos into the Temple of Jerusalem, celebrated in the Byzantine liturgical calendar on November 21. The event of Mary entering the Temple as a three-year-old child was included in apocryphal texts as early as the second century in the influential Protoevangelium of James,[69] and even though the origins of the liturgical feast remain somewhat obscure (it was most probably widely established only in the ninth century and thus among the last major celebrations of the Theotokos to be introduced), it quickly became one of the most important Marian commemorations.

In most typological cases concerning the Theotokos, she and her foreshadowings are separated by several centuries, in narrative time. During the events of the Entrance, however, Mary encounters the objects of her own foreshadowings: in the liturgical texts of the feast, she is described as the living temple, the ark of the covenant, and the Holy of Holies while physically present among them. In a canon assigned to the forefeast of the Entrance (attributed to a hymnographer of unknown identity called George, which has fallen out of contemporary liturgical use), particular emphasis is given to this encounter.[70] Through the personification of the temple with humanlike attributes, the poet creates a dynamic image of the meeting of the ambassadors of the Old and New covenants – the lifeless building meets Mary, the living temple:

Πύλας καὶ εἰσόδους ὁ ναὸς,	Having opened the gates and entrances,
ἀναπετάσας τὴν πύλην εἰσδέχεται,	the temple receives the gate
τοῦ παμβασιλέως καὶ Θεοῦ,	of God the King of all,
καὶ κοσμεῖ τὰ ἐνδότερα,	and adorns the inner parts.
ἧς ἐν τῇ εἰσόδῳ,	At her entrance
καταφαιδρύνεται χάρισιν.	the temple is illuminated with grace.[71]
Ὡς ὄντως,	Today the temple receives you
ὡραίαν σε καὶ δόξῃ τῇ κρείττονι,	as a pure and truly beautiful bride
κεκοσμημένην ὁ ναός,	adorned with great glory
νύμφην δεξάμενος ἁγνὴν,	and introduces the symbols
τὰ σύμβολα σήμερον τῆς μυστικῆς,	of your mystical marriage to God,
Θεῷ προσάγει νυμφεύσεως,	arraying you in bridal finery,
νυμφοστολῶν σε τὴν μόνην ἀμίαντον.	O only undefiled one.[72]
Σὲ φωτεινὸν Θεοτόκε ὄχημα,	When the divine temple of the law
τοῦ βασιλέως καὶ Θεοῦ,	was about to receive you, O Theotokos,
ὁ τοῦ νόμου θεῖος ναὸς,	the shining carriage of God and King,
μέλλων ὑποδέχεσθαι,	it rejoiced at being so adorned
ἔχαιρε κοσμούμενος,	and cried out unto Him
καὶ τῷ ἐκλεξαμένῳ σε ἔκραζεν,	who chose you:
ὁ αἰνετὸς τῶν πατέρων ἡμῶν,	O supremely glorious God,
Θεὸς καὶ ὑπερένδοξος.	praised by our fathers![73]

Similar personifications of the temple of Jerusalem can be found in the hymnography for the feast of the Presentation of the Lord. In a canon attributed to

Andrew, the first ode refers to the gates of the temple that should receive the infant Christ (preceded by a standard exhortation for creation to rejoice):

Ἀγαλλιάσθω καὶ χορευέτω, ἡ κτίσις,	May creation rejoice and dance
τὰ τοῦ ναοῦ προπύλαια, ἐξανοιγέσθω,	and the gates of the temple open
καὶ δεχέσθω τὸν ἱερέα καὶ ἀμνόν,	and receive the priest and lamb
τὸν τοῦ Μωσέως σαρκὶ πληροῦντα νόμον.[74]	who fulfills the Law of Moses in flesh.

Moreover, an unpublished canon of the Entrance broadens the meeting of Mary with the objects of her foreshadowings to include her types as a whole, which the author describes as recognizing and making space for her:

Ἴδον καινὸν τοῦ ναοῦ σε θέαμα,	The archaic types beheld you
οἱ παλαιοὶ τύποι ἁγνὴ,	as a new vision of the temple
εἰσαχθείσης σου ἐν αὐτῷ,	when you entered it
καὶ ὡς ἀληθείας τε πλήρωμα ἐδέξαντο,	and accepted you as the fullness of truth,
καὶ τῷ Δεσπότῃ πάντων ἐβόησαν,	crying out to the Ruler of all,
ὁ αἰνετὸς τῶν πατέρων,	O supremely glorious God,
Θεὸς καὶ ὑπερένδοξος	praised by our fathers![75]

Based on these examples, I would suggest that typology forms a special category within the discussion of personification, because types exist only in fulfillment through figures who have an actual existence. Here the type is not merely an artistic device, a decorative or entertaining addition to the substance of a literary work, but has a "prophetic" grounding in anticipating a real person-to-come; the type's foreshadowing is neither fictitious nor imaginary. Typology does not correspond explicitly to Stephen Barney's characterization of personifications, which, he claims, "merge the abstract (and real) and the concrete (and fictional)."[76] In typologies, the categories of abstract and concrete – both representing reality – overlap: the timelessness of the divine reality is presented in a form comprehensible to men, perhaps creating shadows of reality, but the type itself never departs down the road of fiction or rhetorical device.

Another characteristic peculiar to typological personification, as opposed to the other flavors described earlier, is the ambiguity of identity between the two or more figures and/or objects. John Breck has described typology as a "*double movement: from past to future, but also from the future to the past. That is, within the type the antitype or archetype is already proleptically present, present by anticipation.*"[77] However, seeing the type-antitype relation as a merely historical process does not represent the full richness inherent in typology. Frances Young asserts,

> Typology does not simply operate in the linear-eschatological time-frame, nor should we be tempted to bring back the historicity of events [. . .] The particularities of the earthly realm, whether those of nature or scripture, become luminous in a hidden eternal reality.[78]

Returning to our case study of the temple, a singular/simple or linear idea of typology does not, indeed, apply here: the historical temple of Jerusalem is a type

Personification in Byzantine hymnography 93

both of the Theotokos, the "living temple," and Christ, whose humanity becomes a temple for divinity.[79] Moreover, every Christian is called to become a temple of the Spirit, an exegesis that might be described more as a moral allegory (tropology) than typological. The personification of the temple in hymnography serves to mark this manifold exegetical structure. It proclaims the end of a spiritual death and resurrection through the person of Christ, enacted in each Christian who imitates Him.

* * *

The present survey has, perhaps, been somewhat selective and scattershot in its approach, but such is the problem of a first survey in any field. Moreover, the brevity of this chapter does not allow an exhaustive list of all the different personifications in the Middle Byzantine repertoire to be drawn up. The reader might wonder why I have not discussed angels, often presented with anthropomorphisms (which, as we saw, are not synonymous with personification), or the cross, addressed frequently in hymns. The reason is that they are actually not personifications. If personification is a rhetorical literary representation of a nonsubstantial entity as a person, angels as existent, bodiless persons clearly do not belong in this category. As for the cross, there are numerous hymns that indeed address the cross seemingly as a person, but they never surpass the level of casual personification (if they even reach it): never does the reader encounter *prosopopoeia* in this context.

Even though this chapter provides a first step, more research is needed on hymnographic personification. Here our examples have been drawn from *kontakia* and canons exclusively; in the future, a broader examination taking other hymnographic genres also into consideration should be conducted.[80] It is not surprising, even basing this observation on such a small survey, that personification is more prominent in the *kontakion* repertoire: the rhetoric, dramatic vocabulary, and strong Syrian influences of the *kontakia* brought personifications easily to a liturgical environment. We should be ready, nevertheless, to look for the afterlife of *kontakion*-like influence in canons, as was the case in the Canon on Lazarus, nor should we categorize canons as being completely nondramatic in their character, as we saw in the cases of the Theophany canons and the Canon on the Entrance. Another task for future scholarship is to explore the use of personification in the homiletic repertoire, in which it also appears with some frequency,[81] and the cross-fertilization between these literary genres and linguistic areas, most importantly Syriac poetry. In any case, personification serves primarily an educational, but also an entertaining, purpose: for believers, the defeat of concrete persons, such as Hades and Death, or the victory of others, such as Moderation and Chastity, through didactically effective figures of speech underlines the substantial message of each narrative.

Notes

1 Numerous Middle Byzantine homilies include metrical passages or imitate the language of hymnography. An excellent, even though exceptional, example is Germanos of Constantinople's homily on the Annunciation, where he includes two long,

dialogical passages: one between Mary and archangel Gabriel, and another between Mary and Joseph. Both of these are composed in a strophic metre and include an acrostic; see Germanos's *In sanctissimae Dei Genitricis annuntiationem* (PG 98:320–37).
2 This is a characterization that emerges often in scholarly literature in conjunction with *kontakia*.
3 See Paxson (1994), p. 42.
4 Dodson (2008), pp. 31–2; see also pp. 27–40 for his exhaustive examination on the definition on the term, together with its abundant bibliography.
5 Dodson (2008), p. 41.
6 For example, Quintilian (*Inst.* 9.2.36) refers to Prodicus's personified Pleasure and Virtue as *prosopopoeia*, but later, Erasmus of Rotterdam sees *prosopopoeia* as giving voice to a fictive person, which is commonly, in today's scholarship, referred to as *ethopoeia*. Erasmus uses the term *prosopographia* for the voicing of anything non-human. See *De Copia* in C. R. Thompson (ed.), *Collected Works of Erasmus: Literary and Educational Writings 2 De Copia/De Ratione Studii,* Toronto, 1978, pp. 17–28.
7 For example, Rowe (1997), p. 144 sees the term as giving voice to anything nonhuman.
8 Dodson (2008), p. 37.
9 Wisdom is not the only personification in the Book of Wisdom: also Justice, Power, Death, and Creation enter the scene.
10 Margaret Barker, in her thought-provoking study on the history of the Marian cult, suggests the character of Wisdom has its root in ancient Hebrew female deities; see Barker (2012).
11 This is particularly prominent in Philo's thought; see, for example, *De fuga et inventione* 50–2, where he discusses the antithesis of a masculine Logos and female Sophia.
12 For example, the Church of Hagia Sophia (Holy Wisdom) was dedicated to Christ, and its patronal feast day was December 25, the day of the Nativity of Christ; see Janin (1953), p. 471.
13 Sophia as the female personification of wisdom was particularly prominent in the thought of the renown nineteenth-century Russian philosopher, Vladimir Solovyov, who encountered an entity named Sophia three times during his life, and archpriest Sergey Bulgakov, whose sophiological teaching on the Wisdom as a feminine aspect of God, coexistent with the Holy Trinity, was proclaimed heretic by a synod of the Russian Orthodox Church Abroad in 1935: see Kornblatt (ed. and trans.) (2009), Bulgakov (1993), as well as Powell (2007).
14 Dodson (2008), pp. 115–18.
15 Hades is often translated into English as "Hell" or, more infrequently, as the Hebrew equivalent "Sheol." However, I have retained the original Greek word that marks also a personified deity of the ancient religion: moreover, Hades is considered an intermediate state of the afterlife, while "hell" most often is associated with eternal damnation.
16 Dodson concludes his survey on personifications in Romans by describing, again, antithetical personifications of evil and virtues: Dodson (2008), pp. 178–81.
17 See Hesiod's *Theogony,* verses 211–55.
18 An important collection on essays that combines not only ancient Greek and Byzantine thought but also different art forms, including art and literature, is Herrin and Stafford (eds.) (2005).
19 These terms were coined by Inge Lunde in her study on the homiletics of a twelfth-century preacher Cyril of Turov. By "extra-textual" dialogues she means a dialogue between the homilist and a person of the narrative, while "intra-textual" dialogues are discussions between two persons of the narrative, described by the homilist; see Lund (1999), pp. 84–101.
20 The most significant work on hymnographic personification has been published by Georgia Frank in her studies on the personification of Hades and Death; see Frank (2009) and Frank (2010).
21 A distinction between personification being a rhetorical mode or a mere figure of speech needs to be drawn. As Paxson suggests, there can be a distinction on

anthropomorphisms remaining as figures of speech, or if they form a whole narrative: Paxson (1994), p. 35. Frank adds that in the narrative personification, "the corporeal being is endowed with feelings, thought, and language." (Frank [2010], p. 59). Concerning the use of terminology here, Dodson (*Powers*, p. 36) warns of equalling anthropomorphism with personification: in its most narrow sense, anthropomorphism relates only to representation of divine entities in human shape. Dodson includes, in the Christian context, only human representations of God in this category, but perhaps, in some cases I think, angels could fit in the same category as bodiless powers.
22 Κορακίδης (2006), pp. 301–2.
23 Recently, Steve Wiggins published a "meteorotheological" survey on the use of weather images in the Hebrew book of Psalms; see Wiggins (2014). This work does not consider the use of personification, but may still provide inspiration for understanding the semantics of weather imagery in the psalms.
24 See, for example, the canon on the Presentation of the Lord in the Temple (Hypapante), attributed to Cosmas the Poet: Συνέσει ταθέντες οὐρανοὶ εὐφράνθητε, ἀγάλλου δὲ ἡ γῆ . . . (first ode, third *troparion; Μηναῖα τοῦ ὅλου ἐνιαυτοῦ, τόμος Γ" περιέχων τὴν ἀκολουθίαν τῶν Ἰανουαρίου καὶ Φεβρουαρίου μηνῶν* (Rome, 1896), p. 482).
25 Βηθλεὲμ, εὐφραίνου, Ἡγεμόνων Ἰούδα βασίλεια . . . (first canon of the Nativity, third ode, third troparion; *Μηναῖα τοῦ ὅλου ἐνιαυτοῦ, τόμος Β' περιέχων τὴν ἀκολουθίαν τῶν Νοεμβρίου καὶ Δεκεμβρίου μηνῶν* (Rome, 1889), p. 663).
26 Χόρευε νῦν καὶ ἀγάλλου Σιών . . . (ninth ode, *heirmos; Πεντηκοστάριον χαρμόσυνον* (Rome, 1883), p. 11).
27 For a brief interpretation of the Crucifixion icon, see Ouspensky and Lossky (1982), pp. 180–84.
28 *On the Passion;* SC 128:202. The English translations of this hymn are my own.
29 *On the Passion;* SC 128:204.
30 An allusion to this verse can be seen, for example, in the third *troparion* of the fourth ode of the first canon of Theophany: φυγοῦσα δὲ θάλασσα διχῇ, καὶ Ἰορδάνης οὗτος στραφείς (*Canon XII In profestum Epiphaniae*, first ode, third *troparion; Analecta Hymnica Graeca* 5, p. 148).
31 For a brief interpretation of the Theophany icon, see Ouspensky and Lossky (1982), pp. 164–67.
32 See *On Epiphany* I and II; SC 110:229–93.
33 *Canon XII In profestum Epiphaniae*, first ode, third *troparion; Analecta Hymnica Graeca* 5, 104. The English translations of this canon are my own.
34 *Canon XII In profestum Epiphaniae*, seventh ode, third *troparion; Analecta Hymnica Graeca* 5, 110–11.
35 Third ode, second *troparion: Μηναῖα, τόμος Γ'*, p. 79. The English translation is my own.
36 *Odes Sol.* 42:11–13. For an English translation, see Charlesworth (1985), pp. 21–71.
37 For important scholarly contributions on this work, see Izydorczyk (ed.) (1997), especially Izydorczyk and Dubois (1997).
38 See Frank (2009) and (2010), together with their rich bibliographies on the personifications of these "deities" in a wider context; and Eriksen (2013), pp. 206–46. Intriguing work on the personifications of Hades in Psalter illustrations has been done by Fanar (2006).
39 Second strophe; SC 114:56.
40 The English translation is from Eriksen (2013), p. 239.
41 However, one should be cautious of exaggerated readings of Romanos's texts: Frank (2010), pp. 74–5 suggests that the verb θρηνῶ, used in Romanos's poetry for Hades' lament, has a female connotation and is, therefore, a mocking word: Eriksen (2013), p. 240 is of the same opinion and calls it "the most ridiculing statement Romanos gives." I cannot support this idea. Romanos uses, as Frank notes, the same verb for Peter's repentance in a nonmocking way. Moreover, in a wider liturgical context as well as in the later tradition of canon poetry, the same word appears in Adam's laments

(sung on Cheesefare Sunday before Great Lent; see Τριῴδιον, pp. 99–109) as well as in the Great Canon of Andrew of Crete (*Magnus canon* [PG 97:1329–85]), with no particular reference to female lamentations.

42 As Frank (2010), p. 66 notes, both of these images appear in the *kontakion On the Victory of the Cross*, first strophe (SC 128:286): Ξυλίνῃ με λόγχῃ ἐκέντησεν ἄφνω καὶ διαρρήσσομαι· / τὰ ἔνδον πονῶ, τὴν κοιλίαν μου ἀλγῶ· / τὰ αἰσθητήριά μου· μαιμάσσει τὸ πνεῦμά μου, / καὶ ἀναγκάζομαι ἐξερεύξασθαι / τὸν Ἀδὰμ καὶ τοὺς Ἀδὰμ ξύλῳ δοθέντας μοι.

43 Frank (2009), pp. 223–24. See also the relevant discussion in Eriksen (2013),pp. 242–46, where he also summarizes the earlier patristic tradition of this image, including Cyril of Jerusalems's *Catechetical Lectures* (14:17) and Ephrem's *Hymn on the Unleavened Bread*, eleventh to fourteenth stanzas. The image of Hades being pierced by Christ's descent is inherited by later hymnography as well: it is presented antithetically with the piercing of Christ's side also in the canon of Holy Saturday, attributed to Cosmas: Τέτρωται ᾅδης ἐν τῇ καρδίᾳ, δεξάμενος τὸν τρωθέντα λόγχῃ τὴν πλεύραν (Τριῴδιον, p. 732).

44 As Eriksen (2013), p. 244 notes, this idea appears in Romanos's poem *On the Resurrection V*, seventh strophe (SC 128:558): καταπίνει [ὁ Ἅιδης] ὡς δέλος τὸν οὐράνιον ἄρτων, / τιτρώσκεται ἀγκίστρῳ θεότητος. / Ὁ Ἅιδης δὲ ὀδυνηρὰς ἀνεβόησε φωνάς· / Κεντῶμαι τὴν κοιλίαν, ὃν κατέπιον οὐ πέπτω.

45 *Kontakia* were, in their liturgical use, gradually reduced to the present-way practice of performing only the two first strophes; however, full canons are performed even today; for a history of the liturgical history of the *kontakion*, see Lingas (1995).

46 Cunningham (2008), pp. 251–60.

47 *On the Raising of Lazarus* II, ninth to eleventh strophes; SC 114:166–68.

48 Third ode, fifth *troparion*; *Canon in Lazarum* (PG 99:1389B).

49 The English translation of the canon can be found in Mary and Ware (trans.) (1978), pp. 466–75; the version here is slightly modified from Mary and Ware's translation.

50 Fourth ode, fifth *troparion*; *Canon in Lazarum* (PG 99:1392A).

51 Seventh ode, fourth to sixth *troparia*; *Canon in Lazarum* (PG 99:1396AB). Hades and Death are also referred to in the ninth ode of the canon.

52 *On Joseph's Temptation;* SC 99:247–93.

53 Eriksen (2013), p. 195.

54 As Eriksen (2013), pp. 174–75, 196 summarizes, the theme of angels and demons being present in this fight appears already in Basil of Seleucia's and pseudo-Chrysostom's homilies on the temptation of Joseph (that might, however, be later reworkings of the *kontakion*, rather than its sources), but the personification of virtues is unique to the *kontakion*.

55 *On Joseph's Temptation*, strophe 11; SC 99:276–8. The English translation is my own.

56 *On Joseph's Temptation*, strophe 18; SC 99:286–8.

57 See Μηναῖα τοῦ ὅλου ἐνιαυτοῦ, τόμος Αʹ περιέχων τὴν ἀκολουθίαν τῶν Σεπτεμβρίου καὶ Ὀκτωβρίου μηνῶν (Rome, 1888), pp. 190–95.

58 A survey on the history of this legend can be found in Esbroeck (1981).

59 One could also expect that the hymns on the dedication of Hagia Sophia (December 23) would include personification, but this is not the case, at least when based on a *kontakion* composed for the second inauguration of the church in 562; see Trypanis (1968), pp. 139–47.

60 See, for example, a Greek tomb epigram dating from the end of fifth century BC: πότνια Σωφροσύνη, θύγατερ μεγαλόφρονος Αἰδὸς, πλεῖστα σὲ τιμήσας εὐπόλεμόν τε Ἀρετήν Κλείδημος Μελιτεὺς Κελιδνημίδο ἐνθάδε κεῖται, ζῆλος πατρί ποτ' ὤγ, μητ[έρι νῦν ὀ]δύ[νη] (*GVI*, 1564).

61 See Stafford (2000), where she explores the vague borderline between a religionized personification and a merely aesthetic rhetorical figure, as well as Hamdorf (1964).

62 Warner (1985), p. 82.

63 Especially Maximus the Confessor, reinterpreting the Evagrian ascetical tradition, describes good passions as the counter-energies of passions that lead toward sin; see *Capita de caritate* (CPG 7693) 3:67, 71.
64 It must be noted that in the Western hymnographic tradition the personification of virtues becomes more prominent than in the Greek East: a highpoint of this is Hildegard von Bingen's *Ordo virtutum*, a precursor of morality plays dating from the twelfth century, where altogether 17 personified virtues assist a soul in her battle against devil. For a scholarly account of the work, see Davidson (ed.) (1992).
65 See Young (1997), pp. 152–3, where she challenges the idea of a strong historical connection between the type and its antitype and proposes instead that the essential link between a type and its antitype is their mimetic similarity.
66 Kannengiesser (2006), p. 230. See also Olkinuora (2015), pp. 131–38 for a discussion on the use of typology in hymnography, and Hannick (2005).
67 A complete, critical history of the development of Marian feasts, together with an interpretation with their theological message, still is to be done. In the meantime, one can consult Ledit (1976).
68 For the frescoes of the Peribleptos church, see Olkinuora (2015), pp. 137–38.
69 The most recent study on the feast of the Entrance is by the author of this chapter; see Olkinuora (2015), especially pp. 24–38 for the history of the feast and its textual sources.
70 The canon is not in use in the contemporary liturgical books, but has been published in two editions: *Analecta hymnica graeca* 3 (pp. 465–77) includes an edition of the MSS *Paris. gr.* 1570, *Mess. gr.* 138, and *Paris. gr.* 259; my own work includes an edition of the text as it appears in Sinait. gr. 570, without integrated troparia to the celebrated saint of that day, Gregory of Dekapolis, that appear in other manuscripts. The edition quoted here is from Sinait. gr. 570, and the English translation is my own.
71 First ode, first *troparion*; Olkinuora (2015), p. 281.
72 Fourth ode, third *troparion*; Olkinuora (2015), p. 283.
73 Seventh ode, second *troparion*: Olkinuora (2015), p. 285. The translation here is slightly modified from the published version in order to mark clearly the use of *prosopopoeia*.
74 *Canon I In Hypapantem Domini*, first ode, second *troparion*; *Analecta Hymnica Graeca* 6, p. 2.
75 Seventh ode, second *troparion*: Olkinuora (2015), p. 285.
76 Barney (1979), p. 24.
77 Breck (2001), p. 23.
78 Young (1997), p. 156.
79 This is an ancient tradition that precedes the celebrations of the Entrance; see, for example, Gregory of Nazianzos's poem *Ad Nemesium*, where he describes how Mary was a temple for Christ, who, in turn, was a temple for the Logos (Μήτηρ γὰρ Χριστοῖο ναός, Χριστὸς δὲ Λόγοιο; PG 37, 1565A).
80 For instance, the *stichera kekragaria* of the Holy Saturday Vespers include *prosopopoeia* of Hades; see Τριῴδιον, p. 737.
81 A good example is (pseudo-)John of Damascus's homily on the Nativity of the Theotokos (*In Nativitatem sanctae Dei Genitricis Mariae*, BHG 1087; CPG 8060 *spuria*; Bonifatius Kotter, *Die Schriften von Johannes von Damaskos V: Opera homiletica et hagiographica*, Berlin, 1988, pp. 147–82), where the author personifies centuries: Ἡμιλλῶντο οἱ αἰῶνες, ποῖος τῇ σῇ ἐγκαυχήσονται γεννήσει, ἀλλ' ἐνίκα τῶν αἰώνων τὴν ἅμιλλαν ἡ προωρισμένη βουλὴ τοῦ θεοῦ τοῦ τοὺς αἰῶνας ποιήσαντος καὶ γεγόνασιν οἱ ἔσχατοι πρῶτοι τὴν σὴν εὐμοιρήσαντες γέννησιν (p. 177:22–5).

Select bibliography

Barker, M. (2012), *The Mother of the Lord, Volume 1: The Lady in the Temple*, London.
Barney, S. A. (1979), *Allegories of History, Allegories of Love*, Hamden CT.
Breck, J. (2001), *Scripture in Tradition: The Bible and Its Interpretation in the Orthodox Church*, Crestwood NY.
Bulgakov, S. (1993), *Sophia, the Wisdom of God: An Outline of Sophiology*, Hudson NY.
Charlesworth, J. (1985), *The Old Testament Pseudepigrapha*, 2 vols., Garden City NY.
Cunningham, M. B. (2008), "The Reception of Romanos in Middle Byzantine Homiletics and Hymnography," *Dumbarton Oaks Papers* 62, pp. 251–60.
Davidson, A. E. (ed.) (1992), *The Ordo Virtutum of Hildegard von Bingen: Critical Studies*, Kalamazoo MI.
Dodson, J. R. (2008), *The 'Powers' of Personification: Rhetorical Purpose in the Book of Wisdom and the Letter to the Romans*, Berlin and New York.
Eriksen, U. H. (2013), *Drama in the Kontakia of Romanos the Melodist: A Narratological Analysis of Four Kontakia*, doctoral dissertation, Aarhus University.
Esbroeck, M. van (1981), "Le saint comme symbole," in Sergei Hackel (ed.), *The Byzantine Saint*, Chester, pp. 128–40.
Fanar, E. M. (2006), "Visiting Hades: A Transformation of the Ancient God in the Ninth-Century Byzantine Psalters," *Byzantinische Zeitschrift* 99/1, pp. 93–108.
Frank, G. (2009), "Christ's Descent to the Underworld in Ancient Ritual and Legend," in Robert. J. Daly (ed.), *Apocalyptic Thought in Christianity*, Cambridge MA, pp. 211–26.
Frank, G. (2010), "Death in the Flesh: Picturing Death's Body and Abode in Late Antiquity," in Colum Hourihane (ed.), *Looking Beyond: Visions, Dreams, and Insights in Medieval Art & History*, Princeton NJ, pp. 58–74.
Hamdorf, F. (1964), *Griechische Kultpersonifikationen der vorhellenistischen Zeit*, Mainz.
Hannick, C. (2005), "The Theotokos in Byzantine Hymnography: Typology and Allegory," in M. Vassilaki (ed.), *Images of the Mother of God: Perceptions of the Theotokos in Byzantium*, Aldershot, pp. 69–76.
Herrin and Stafford (eds.) (2005), *Personification in the Greek World: From Antiquity to Byzantium*, Aldershot.
Izydorczyk, Z. (ed.) (1997), *The Medieval Gospel of Nicodemus: Texts, Intertexts, and Contexts in Western Europe*, Tempe AZ.
Izydorczyk, Z. and Dubois, J.-D. (1997), "Nicodemus' Gospel Before and Beyond the Medieval West," in Izydorczyk, Z. (ed.) (1997), pp. 21–41.
Janin, R. (1953), *La Géographie Ecclésiastique de l'Empire Byzantine. 1ère partie: Le Siége de Constantinople et le Patriarcat Oecuménique, 3ème volume, Les Églises et les Monastéres*, Paris.
Kannengiesser, C. (2006), *Handbook of Patristic Exegesis: The Bible in Ancient Christianity*, Leiden.
Κορακίδης, Α. (2006), *Βυζαντινὴ ὑμνογραφία, τόμος Α΄: Ὑμνογραφία καὶ ῥητορική*, Athens.
Kornblatt, J. D. (ed. and trans.) (2009), *Divine Sophia: The Wisdom Writings of Vladimir Solovyov*, Ithaca NY.
Ledit, J. (1976), *Marie dans la liturgie de Byzance*, Paris.
Lingas, A. (1995), "The Liturgical Place of the Kontakion in Constantinople," in Constantine Akentiev (ed.), *Liturgy, Architecture, and Art in the Byzantine World: Papers of the XVIII International Byzantine Congress (Moscow, 8–15 August 1991) and Other Essays Dedicated to the Memory of Fr. John Meyendorff*, Saint Petersburg, pp. 50–7.

Lund, I. (1999), *Dialogue and Rhetoric: Communication Strategies in Russian Text and Theory*, Bergen.
Mary, M. and Ware, K. (trans.) (1978), *The Lenten Triodion*, Oxford.
Olkinuora, J. (2015), *Byzantine Hymnography for the Entrance of the Theotokos: An Intermedial Approach*, Helsinki.
Ouspensky, L. and Lossky, V. (1982), *The Meaning of Icons*, Crestwood NY.
Paxson, J. J. (1994), *The Poetics of Personification*, Cambridge.
Powell, R. (2007), *The Sophia Teachings: The Emergence of the Divine Feminine in our Time*, Great Barrington MA.
Rowe, G. O. (1997), "Style," in Stanley E. Porter (ed.), *Handbook of Classical Rhetoric in the Hellenistic Period 330 B.C.–A.D. 400*, Leiden, pp. 121–57.
Stafford, E. (2000), *Worshipping Virtues: Personification and the Divine in Ancient Greece*, London.
Trypanis, C. (1968), *Fourteen Early Byzantine Cantica*, Vienna.
Warner, M. (1985), *Monuments and Maidens: The Allegory of the Female Form*, Berkeley, CA.
Wiggins, S. (2014), *Weathering the Psalms: A Meteorotheological Survey*, Eugene OR.
Young, F. (1997), *Biblical Exegesis and the Formation of Christian Culture*, Cambridge.

Section III
Late Byzantine

7 The exemplar of consubstantiality

St. Gregory Palamas's hesychast as an expression of a microcosmic approach to personhood

Demetrios Harper

An examination of St. Gregory Palamas's anthropological teaching, no matter how brief, inevitably and properly begins with the mention of one of his most prominent theological forebearers – namely, St. Maximus the Confessor. St. Maximus's microcosmic approach to the ontological structure of the human being is taken as axiomatic by nearly all serious scholars of his work, functioning as the inspiration for the title of Lars Thunberg's venerable monograph, *Microcosm and Mediator*. As the Confessor insists, human nature has an intrinsically "synthetic" character, composed of both psychic and somatic elements, being defined not by one or the other, but rather constituted by the coherence of their relationship, their σχέσις.[1] It is this synthetic quality that provides the human being with the unique capacity – the δύναμις – for a mediatorial role in relation to the rest of creation, possessed of the possibility of expressing in particular the divine purpose for the created world, by drawing together the disparate aspects of creation into a microcosmic unity.

Maximus's endorsement of a human "interior consubstantiality," as Nicholas Loudovikos defines it,[2] arguably marks the culmination of a lengthy process to understand and correct the problematic tendencies of Origenist anthropology,[3] providing a theological touchstone for subsequent generations of theologians and ecclesiastical writers. Despite many contemporary commentators' unwillingness to recognize or acknowledge it, among the recipients of this Maximian legacy stands St. Gregory Palamas (1296–1359). While indeed the noted defender of the mystical practice of hesychasm, a careful reading of Palamas's corpus reveals not what Hans Urs von Balthasar disparagingly refers to as the "reorientalizing" of Christian spirituality,[4] but rather the careful assimilation and appropriation of the theological criteria prized by Maximus himself. In what follows, this chapter shall attempt to provide evidence of St. Gregory's inherently Maximian approach to anthropology. Though difficult to prove conclusively in so brief a chapter, it aspires to show that the eschatological achievements of the practitioner of hesychia described by Palamas in the *Triads* constitutes the application of the Confessor's own internalized consubstantial approach to the human person.

The Maximian foundation

Before examining St. Gregory's views in greater detail, let us briefly survey the tools provided him by St. Maximus's expansive theological synthesis. As noted earlier, Maximus supports the notion of a synthetic human nature, a φύσις σύνθετος, a view that constitutes not only a departure from an earlier Origenistic dualism but also seems to function as a gentle corrective of later thinkers, such as Leontius of Byzantium.[5] This position is perhaps most strongly affirmed in his famous *Ambiguum* 7, where the Confessor asserts in Porphyrian terms that it is the "confluence" of the soul and body that constitutes the single human species or εἶδος.[6] Moreover, he declares it is only through the "careful discernment of mind" (ἐπινοίᾳ) that we are able to contemplate the substantive differences within the synthetic human hypostasis. As Thunberg argues, Maximus often uses the term σύνθεσις with reference to human nature in a way that suggests it can be used interchangeably with the term ὑπόστασις.[7] This symmetry between ὑπόστασις and synthetic nature is arguably suggested in *Opusculum* 23 when Maximus says, "Hypostasis cannot be conceived of apart from nature, neither can shape or color be thought of as separate from body," and "hypostasis is always present with nature, in the same way that shape is always present with the body."[8] Accordingly, we might say that the human hypostasis is a particular instance of synthetic human nature, as Melchisedec Törönen suggests,[9] and, therefore, an individual rendition of human microcosmic potentiality.

Maximus also includes the so-called lesser powers of the soul – the appetitive and the incensive faculties – as well as the physical senses themselves in humanity's microcosmic constitutionality and eschatological destiny.[10] Departing from the Origenist tendency to assign to incensiveness and desire a post-lapsarian character, the Confessor bestows on *passibility* a fundamental role in human development.[11] These aspects of human nature were not super-added to humanity's post-lapsarian nature or acquired as a result of the fall, nor do they fulfill a merely provisional purpose in the human agent's quest for his or her telos. Rather, they are provided to human nature from its inception with the intention that they co-energize and participate along with the intellect, proleptically analogizing and iconizing the perichoretic cooperation of the two natures in the hypostasis of the incarnate Logos.[12] A naturally (κατὰ φύσιν) functioning human being is one in whom there is a harmonious coordination of the powers of the soul and those of the body, as the bodily senses iconize and imitate the divinely directed soul, working in concordance with the natural hegemony of the intellect.[13] It is important to stress that the intellect leads because of its capacity to perceive God's intentions (λόγοι) for created nature, the collective totality of which, in Maximus's view, constitutes the natural law.[14] As Maximus explains in *Ad Thalassium* 54, a κατὰ φύσιν or natural state is facilitated when "the wisdom-loving intellect (ὁ φιλόσοφος νοῦς) enters into dialogue (διαλεχθεὶς) with the law of nature."[15] Nevertheless, the intellect's natural hegemony is not realized through the abrogation or suppression of the other human powers. Maximus asserts that our self-determining activity, our αὐτεξούσιον movement, is contingent on desire, on an *erotic* quest for the divine and the activation of passion that accords with nature's divinely inspired purpose.[16] He affirms this position explicitly in a passage from *Ambiguum* 48, arguing that God intentionally endowed human nature with the capacity for ἔρως and πόθος such that human beings might have the ability to desire communal kinship with the divine other and thereby possess fraternal love for the temporal other.[17]

It is this inclusion and celebration of the nonrational portions of human nature that provides the ultimate criterion for Maximus's microcosmic approach to humanity, giving each instance of humanity the opportunity to imitate the incarnate Logos' unification of natural divisions in himself.[18] This microcosmic μίμησις opens the way for the variously functioning "substances" to assume a single coherent identity. Indeed, as Maximus indicates in *Ambiguum* 41, it is through the voluntary maturation of each instance of humanity that the fragmented reality that is the totality of human nature is made whole. The macrocosmic divisions are traversed, the Confessor suggests, uniting the humblest animal elements with the noetic, bringing them all into communion with uncreated life.[19] In philosophical terms, we might describe human eschatological destiny as the transition from a multiplicity of Aristotelian "natures" to a single Stoic-style nature, albeit free from the necessity associated with the latter category. Conversely, unnatural (παρὰ φύσιν) movement and fall constitutes the voluntary violation of this consubstantial end, turning the human hypostasis into a battleground of conflicting urges and movements, which in turn facilitates the fragmentation and division of the created world as a whole.

The Palamite synthesis

With these Maximian criteria in mind, let us now turn to the texts of St. Gregory Palamas. At the outset, I would note that it is unfortunate that Palamas's anthropological suppositions have frequently been ignored within Anglophone circles, the scholarly focus being primarily on his teaching on the uncreated energies and the "mystical" aspects of his defense of the hesychasts. This incomplete analysis of St. Gregory's synthesis has worked to create many misimpressions, both among his critics and his defenders, which perhaps helps to explain von Balthasar's aforementioned ascription of an oriental "platonizing" to Palamas's theology. It is also unfortunate that John Meyendorff's groundbreaking study on Palamas,[20] a work that manifests an understanding of the continuity between Maximus and Palamas,[21] has also been unfairly reviewed.[22] It is often dismissed because of Meyendorff's use of contemporary terminology, which he deploys in an attempt to explain the nuances of Palamite thought. Critics have fixated on his use of terms such as "Christian materialism" or "existential theology,"[23] missing the fact that Meyendorff attempts to demonstrate that St. Gregory's spirituality is informed by a deeply world- and nature-affirming philosophy.

If we turn to Palamas's *Homily* 26, we find a vindication of John Meyendorff's effort and a description of the anthropological structure that could have been written by Maximus himself. Speaking at harvest time as the Bishop of Thessaloniki, St. Gregory provides a perfect articulation of the human being as a microcosm:

> God made man in a mysterious way, gathering together, so to speak, summing up all Creation in one small creature. That is why he was last to be created, belonging to both the visible and invisible worlds and adorning them both. In man God united mind and senses in an indescribable manner, using imagination, judgment, and reason to bind them truly together [. . .] Man and the world are both the work of the same Craftsman, and have much in common, but whereas the world is larger in size, man is more excellently constructed.[24]

The human being is unique in creation precisely because of his synthetic composition, because of his "mixed essence" (φύραμα), as Palamas suggests in *Homily* 8.[25] As he goes on to explain in *Homily* 26, the human intellect is created in the image of God *par excellence*, designed to seek and know God and lead the totality of the human being to a deified existence.[26] Palamas does not stop there, however, but also celebrates humankind's possession of a material and sensory dimension.[27] As he affirms, materiality and sense perception accord with the original divine purpose for creation, enabling human creatures to explore the movements and the phenomena of the created world, all of which laid the foundation for "scientific knowledge" (ταῖς κατὰ νοῦν ἐπιστήμαις τὴν ἀρχὴν [αἴσθησις ἀνθρώπινη] ἐχαρίσατο).[28] Consequently, the pursuit of the natural sciences and the exploration of the natural world functions as a proper and divinely ordered development of the human being's sensory powers. The development and use of the sensible world functions as the partial fulfillment of the human being's microcosmic and mediatorial role. This defense of the "scientific" or "rational" knowledge of the sensible on the part of Palamas may come as a surprise to those who are accustomed to interpretations that see him as one who is suspicious of all forms of scholastic knowledge. Already, we are far indeed from the icon of Palamas that von Balthasar presents in his *Cosmic Liturgy*. In addition to its affirmation of the microcosmic constitution of human being, *Homily* 26 also discloses Palamas's own belief in the proleptic quality of humanity's synthetic structure. Human nature was created in the way that it was, he tells us, in anticipation of the Incarnation of the Logos, because "God was going to clothe Himself in it."[29] This passage suggests an appropriation on the part of Palamas of both the notion of a predetermined Incarnation and a human hypostasis that analogizes the union of created and uncreated natures in Christ – ideas that are also most likely inherited from Maximus. Synthetic human nature is created from the beginning with the intention of not only uniting the disparate substances in creation but also with the goal of a deiform existence in Christ and the transformation of the lesser animal substances of the human being into a deified state. It is only through fallen or unnatural (παρὰ φύσιν) movement that antinomy is introduced into the harmoniously created human hypostasis.

If *Homily* 26 provides us with the perfect testimony to humanity's microcosmic character, St. Gregory's *Natural Chapters* explicitly links it to a mediatorial role in creation. While Palamas emphasizes the significance of the soul/body relationship and its microcosmic significance throughout the *Natural Chapters*, his most interesting acknowledgment of synthetic human nature comes via his discussion of the human being's triadic power. In this context, Palamas divides the parts of the human power triad into the noetic, rational, and sensory capacities, defining the various kinds of knowledge of which the human being is capable.³⁰ The intellect is ultimately involved in the attainment of all three forms of knowledge, interfacing with the senses and the sensory world through mankind's φανταστικόν, or faculty of imagination.³¹ It is evident in both the *Natural Chapters* and the passage cited from *Homily* 26 that the faculty of imagination is created as an inherent part of the human being, designed to mediate naturally between the intellect and the senses, the implications of which certainly deserve further study. Despite the frequency with which thought images are described as dangerous by ascetic literature, including by Palamas himself,³² it is evident that St. Gregory considers the imagination to have a κατὰ φύσιν function. As Palamas affirms elsewhere in the *Natural Chapters*, the thoughts formed through the φανταστικόν can be either used for the cultivation of virtue or vice, depending on the way in which they are used.³³ What is much more significant is St. Gregory's affirmation that it is the human being's somatic dimension, the possession of senses and a sensory capacity, that qualify him for "dominion of the entire earth" (κυριότητα τῆς γῆς ἁπάσης), a form of authority that is denied the angelic beings.³⁴ As Palamas states, the devil possesses no real dominion over the earth precisely because of his exclusively noetic constitution.³⁵ While the devil clearly has the capacity to influence mankind, mediatorial culpability ultimately resides with the human being and the way in which he or she uses the sensible world and its phenomena. The capacity to mediate and draw together the psychic and somatic substances into a coherent and functionally consubstantial whole is a power unique to human nature, truly establishing the human being as the crowning glory of all creation.

Our possession of a sensory dimension and a body renders us superior to angelic creatures in another way. The synthesis between the human being's rational and sensory powers enable mankind to create within the sensible world, to invent various arts and sciences, to cultivate the earth, all of which, Palamas argues, is indicative of a superior expression of creation "in the likeness of God" (κατ' εἰκόνα τοῦ Θεοῦ).³⁶ While the unfallen angels are superior in likeness – that is, καθ' ὁμοίωσιν – humanity's ability to creatively act within and upon sensible realities reflects the icon *par excellence* of the Holy Trinity's own creative power.³⁷ Arguably, there is a great deal that is implied by this passage that requires a more complete analysis. Suffice it to say for the present, this description of humanity's κατ' εἰκόνα capacity is reminiscent of a passage from Maximus's *Questions and Doubts* in which he pairs the Aristotelian δύναμις/ἐνέργεια distinction with the biblical description of humanity's creation "in the image and likeness."³⁸ As the Confessor argues, "in the image" pertains to our δύναμις, our natural power or potentiality that analogizes divinity, while "in the likeness" has to do with ἐνέργεια – that is, it is realized to the extent that we actualize our divinely bestowed power in accordance with our eschatological purpose.[39]

It could be argued that Palamas has precisely the same δύναμις/ἐνέργεια distinction in mind when he declares that the holy angels more closely resemble divinity than we do in terms of likeness, though they are lesser κατ' εἰκόνα. It is not due to the angels' exclusively spiritual constitution that they reflect in a superior fashion the divine likeness. Rather, the angels who remained faithful more closely resemble God according to their mode of actuality, while, conversely, humanity fell into corruption, violating God's image and the potential it bestows, being rendered lesser καθ' ὁμοίωσιν.[40] It is only because of humanity's post-lapsarian state that we find ourselves qualitatively lesser in relation to angelic creatures. Nevertheless, because of our unique microcosmic constitution and our superior "capacity in the image" – κατ' εἰκόνα δύναμις – all of humanity possesses *in potentia* the possibility of surpassing in honor all other created beings at the eschatological Eighth Day.

Given the views manifested in his homilies and the *Natural Chapters*, it should be no surprise that it is this microcosmic approach to the human person that defines and informs St. Gregory Palamas's defense of the practice and doctrine of hesychia. While his works on the subject, such as the *Triads* or his epistle, *To the Most Reverend Nun Xenia*, contain all of the literary nuances we would expect from a monastic informed by the Macarian and Evagrian spiritual legacies, such as Maximus himself, Palamas's discourse is consistently buttressed by a deep sense of the eschatological destiny of the entirety of human nature. As such, the spiritual achievements of the God-seeing hesychast function not as incidental miracles, but rather provide a paradigmatic foretaste of a grace-filled natural destiny intended for the totality of the human race, which shall be realized by all the faithful in Christ. Synthesizing a more Peripatetic approach to self-determination with his hesychastic doctrine, Palamas insists not only on the tripartite character of the soul but also that the participation of the incensive and appetitive elements of the soul is crucial to the attainment of the highest levels of spirituality.[41]

This is clearly expressed in St. Gregory's letter to the Nun Xenia, where he explains that the totality of the soul is wounded as a result of humanity's lapsed state. Divinely bestowed healing begins with the appetitive and incensive elements of the soul, thereby enabling the hesychastic seeker's intellectual powers to assume their proper hegemonic state and move toward the contemplation of divine truths and, ultimately, encounter divinity itself.[42] This therapeutic process would indeed include the deployment of ἐγκράτεια, the ascetic restraint of the wild movements of the passible portion of the self. Indeed, it is an inherent part of the hesychast's first steps away from his or her fallen state.[43] Nevertheless, it is evident that ἐγκράτεια fulfills a provisional purpose, only bringing about a restoration of a properly ordered internal hierarchy within the human being, but by no means constituting a proper spiritual end in itself. The proper end of what Palamas calls in *The Triads* the παθητικόν, or the passionate part of the soul, is the attainment of divinity itself, participating in concordance with the intellect in the experiences of the divine.⁴⁴ In the significantly more profound words of Palamas himself, "The soul, since it experiences divine things, doubtless possesses a passionate part, praiseworthy and divine: or rather, there is within us a single passion aspect which is capable of thus becoming praiseworthy and divine."⁴⁵

Similarly, in his letter to the Nun Xenia, St. Gregory explains that the hesychast is assimilated to the divine and heavenly archetype when the lesser powers of the soul converge on the intellect and the unified human soul becomes a coworker with God himself.⁴⁶ The noetic soul comes to function divinely when the various powers of the soul cease to behave discordantly, reflecting a unified mode of existence, or, better, a functionally consubstantial state. I would suggest this "convergence" of the soul's powers constitutes the philosophical expression of the hesychast's attempt to circumscribe his intellect within the heart – a phenomenon described and ardently defended by Palamas throughout *The Triads*. The centering of the intellect within the practitioner of noetic prayer results in the achievement of a coherent psychic self, a necessary step for the constitution of a natural microcosm, as the passible portion of the soul is called to work with the ἡγεμονικόν, moving with the intellect as it responds to the natural law of Christ and the divine dictates for human nature.⁴⁷

Perhaps the most powerful refutation of von Balthasar's interpretation of Palamas comes via St. Gregory's extended endorsement of the eschatological significance of the body and its complete participation in the highest achievements of noetic prayers. St. Gregory's insistence on corporeal participation in the experience of the uncreated light by both the Disciples of Christ on Mount Tabor as well as the practitioners of noetic prayer has been well examined and functions in itself as a refutation of the attempts to construe hesychastic prayers as a Manichean rejection of materiality.⁴⁸ Palamas is emphatic in his insistence on the complete participation of the body in the light and its reception of uncreated grace, asserting that even the physical senses themselves are elevated with the body. Explaining this process in *Homily* 34, Palamas says that the human senses pass from "flesh to spirit," thus contemplating along with the totality of the soul the ineffable glory of God.⁴⁹ This διάβασις or passage of body "to spirit" should not be construed as a process of dematerialization, but rather as change of its mode of existence and a foretaste of the Eighth Day glory of the body.

Infrequently emphasized, however, is Palamas's suggestion that the body is not only a passive observer in the process of spiritual ascent but also, like the passible portion of the soul, intended to be a co-actualizer. In fact, this is one of the ways in which St. Gregory differentiates his views from those of Barlaam the Calabrian. In his second *Triad*, Palamas notes Barlaam's objection not only to the body's participation in the spiritual life and noetic prayer but also to the cooperation of the passible aspect of the soul. He asserts, according to Palamas, "Affection for the energies common to the passionate part of the soul and to the body serves to nail the soul [that is, the higher soul] to the body and to fill the soul with darkness."⁵⁰ Perhaps, von Balthasar would have done well to attribute a "reorientalizing" tendency to Barlaam rather than Palamas, for indeed the former thinker seems to suggest that the "higher soul" is tainted by its very relationship with both the lower soul and the body – a view that is redolent of the anthropological suppositions of Origen or, perhaps, Plotinus. According to St. Gregory's counter, neither is the soul tainted by its communion with the body, nor is it restrained by their association, because they possess "common energies" (κοιναὶ ἐνέργειαι) and must therefore co-actualize and co-realize a natural human state through the co-experience of the divine, an event that is exemplified *par excellence* by the highest levels of the hesychastic life.[51] The encounter with divine grace, therefore, causes the two fundamental aspects of the human hypostasis to be elevated concordantly, as the soul transmits spiritual joy and pleasure (ἡδονή) to it,[52] which the body in turn reciprocates, ensuring a coherent and functional instance of synthetic human nature.

As a capstone to this chapter, it is important to note that the attainment of this unified mode of existence is contingent on the bestowal of divine grace, on the one hand, and the assimilation of the *natural* aspects of the human being to divinity, on the other. In short, the engagement with divine grace does not bring about the eclipse or cessation of createdness but constitutes the fulfillment of created nature itself and the ensuing consubstantial state. A seldom-quoted passage from the latter part of Palamas's first *Triad* provides the necessary proof of this symmetrical perspective. Following a passage in which he explains that the acquisition of dogmatic and, therefore, discursive theological knowledge differs in kind from the theology brought about by the experience of the uncreated light, Palamas says the following,

> But this [kind of theology] is not the perfect and comely nobility bestowed upon us from above in the beyond-radiant light and the hyper-natural union [with God], from which originates the only certain theology and which provides natural rest and brings about the movement of the powers of the soul and the body in a way that *accords with nature*. All those who reject this kind of union in turn reject every virtue and every truth.[53]

Human nature's ultimate destiny or telos is inextricably connected with the encounter and reception of uncreated grace, which brings about what Maximus the Confessor calls "ἔκβασις κατὰ φύσιν," a transcendent event that accords with the purpose and end for which human nature was created.[54]

In conclusion, the experience of Palamas's hesychast and his or her realization of an internalized consubstantiality stand as a paradigm, as an icon of the divinely ordained destiny of the totality of human nature. As such, the Palamite synthesis manifests a concrete and Aristotelian-style affirmation of human nature and its powers, providing the entirety of the human hypostasis with a share in humanity's properly realized end. Nevertheless, the authentic practitioner of hesychia is first and foremost a testimony to the deifying effects of Christ's dispensation in the flesh, which provided the avenue for created nature to assume a unified and coherent existence through its perichoretic engagement with the uncreated Trinity. Those blessed with the vision of the uncreated light reveal a foretaste of the eschatological day and the eventual stasis of all instances of human nature, bearing witness to the mode of existence that will be extended to all believers but that cannot be fully appreciated even by the most thoroughly sanctified until the second resurrection. If indeed microcosmic consubstantiality means that the soul and body exist as one unified nature, only the resurrection of the body and its reception of immortality will bring about the attainment of the creaturely eschaton.

Notes

1. Maximus, *Ambiguum* 7 (PG 91:1101B).
2. Loudovikos (2002), pp. 73–4.
3. See Thunberg (1995), p. 102.
4. Balthasar (2003), p. 55.
5. See Maximus' *Epistle* 12 (PG 91:488A-489B) and *Epistle* 15 (PG 91:552D). See Thunberg (1995), p. 102 and Sherwood (1955), pp. 51–3.
6. Maximus, *Ambiguum* 7 (PG 91:1100C). For Christian thinkers' appropriation of Porphyrian categories, see Tollefsen (2008), pp. 99–102.
7. Thunberg (1995), p. 102. Thunberg bases this assertion in part upon Maximus' *Epistle* 15 (PG 91:552D).
8. Maximus, *Opusculum* 23 (PG 91:264A). The translation is mine.
9. Törönen (2007), pp. 51–2.
10. See *Ambiguum* 7 (PG 91:1069B, 1073A). In the *Ad Thalassium* (PG 90:608D), Maximus argues that beings who reach their $τέλος/ἀρχή$ will experience the fulfilment of all desire ($πλήρωσις\ ἐφέσεως$). The inclusion of the five senses in the natural maturation of the human being is suggested in *Ambiguum* 21 (PG:1248AB).
11. See Blowers (2013). This tendency is noted, respectively, by Henri Crouzel and Panagiotis Tzamalikos. See Crouzel (1989), p. 89, and Tzamalikos (2007), pp. 45–6.
12. See Maximus, *Ambiguum* 7 (PG 91:1088C, 1092BC, and 1097D-1100A) for Maximus's defense of a holistic approach to anthropology and eschatology. As Thunberg affirms, despite his corrective of Leontius, the Confessor, nonetheless, redeploys the notion that the relationship between the soul and body analogize the union of the two natures in Christ. See Thunberg (1995), pp. 101–4.
13. Maximus, *Ambiguum* 21 (PG 91:1248AB). Maximus presents this vision in the ecclesial imagery of the *Mystagogy* (cf. PG 91:672BC).
14. See Maximus, *Ambiguum* 10 (PG 91:1137AB).
15. Maximus, *Ad Thalassium* 54 (PG 90:516B).
16. Maximus, *Ambiguum* 7 (PG91:1069B and 1073BC).
17. Maximus, *Ambiguum* 48 (PG 91:1361A).
18. Maximus, *Ambiguum* 41 (PG 91:1312BC).
19. Maximus, *Ambiguum* 41 (PG 91:1305BC).
20. Meyendorff (1974).
21. Meyendorff (1974), p. 122.
22. For example, see Romanides (1960–1). Though published decades ago, Romanides's perspective remains for many the standard critique of Meyendorff's position.
23. Meyendorff (1974), pp. 155 and 202–27.
24. Trans. Veniamin (2009), p. 206.
25. *Φύραμα* indicates a "mixture" or a "compound." For the term in context, see Χρήστου and Ζήση (eds.) (1981) vol. 9, p. 220.
26. Veniamin (2009), p. 206.
27. Veniamin (2009), pp. 206–7.
28. Χρήστου and Ζήση (eds.) (1981), vol. 10, p. 154.
29. Veniamin (2009), p. 207.

30 Gregory Palamas, *The One Hundred and Fifty Chapters* 61–3 (ed. Sinkewicz, pp. 154–6).
31 See especially Gregory Palamas, *The One Hundred and Fifty Chapters* 15–20 (ed. Sinkewicz, pp. 98–102).
32 This is implicit in *To the Most Reverend Nun Xenia*, Ware et al. (1981), vol. 4, pp. 316–17.
33 Ware et al. (1981), vol. 4, p. 353.
34 Gregory Palamas, *The One Hundred and Fifty Chapters* 62 (ed. Sinkewicz, p. 156).
35 Gregory Palamas, *The One Hundred and Fifty Chapters* 62 (ed. Sinkewicz, p. 156).
36 Gregory Palamas, *The One Hundred and Fifty Chapters* 64 (ed. Sinkewicz, p. 158).
37 Gregory Palamas, *The One Hundred and Fifty Chapters* 63 (ed. Sinkewicz, pp. 156–8).
38 Trans. Prassas (2010), pp. 156–7.
39 Trans. Prassas (2010), pp. 156–7.
40 See Gregory Palamas, *The One Hundred and Fifty Chapters* 64 (ed. Sinkewicz, p. 158).
41 *The Triads* I.ii.3 (ed. Χρήστου, vol. 1, pp. 395–6) and *To the Most Reverend Nun Xenia*, in Ware et al. (1981), vol. 4, p. 304.
42 Gregory Palamas, *To the Most Reverend Nun Xenia*, in Ware et al. (1981), vol. 4, p. 304.
43 See Gregory Palamas, *To the Most Reverend Nun Xenia*, in Ware et al. (1981), vol. 4, pp. 302–5.
44 *The Triads*, II.ii.12 (ed. Χρήστου, vol. 1, pp. 517–9).
45 Gregory Palamas, *The Triads*, II.ii.12 (trans. Gendle).
46 Gregory Palamas, *To the Most Reverend Nun Xenia*, in Ware et al. (1981), vol. 4, p. 319.
47 Gregory Palamas, *To the Most Reverend Nun Xenia*, in Ware et al. (1981), vol. 4, pp. 318–19.
48 See Meyendorff (1974), p. 155, for St. Gregory's inclusion of materiality in humanity's ultimate end.
49 Veniamin (2009), p. 207. This is a reference on the part of Palamas to Maximus' *Ambiguum* 10 (PG 91:1125D).
50 Gregory Palamas, *The Triads*, II.ii.12 (ed. Χρήστου, vol. 1, pp. 517–8). My translation.
51 Gregory Palamas, *The Triads*, II.ii.12 (ed. Χρήστου, vol. 1, p. 518).
52 Gregory Palamas, *The Triads*, II.ii.9 (ed. Χρήστου, vol. 1, pp. 514–5).
53 Gregory Palamas, *The Triads*, I.iii.15 (ed. Χρήστου, vol. 1, p. 425). My translation (and emphasis).
54 Maximus, *Ad Thalassium* (PG 90:609B).

Select bibliography

Balthasar, H. U. von (2003), *Cosmic Liturgy: The Universe According to Maximus the Confessor*, trans. Brian Daley, San Francisco CA.
Blowers, P. (2013), "Aligning and Reorienting the Passible Self: Maximus the Confessor's Virtue Ethics," *Studies in Christian Ethics* 26.3, pp. 333–50.
Crouzel, H. (1989), *Origen*, Edinburgh.
Gendle, N. (trans.) (1983), *The Triads*. Mahwah NJ.
Loudovikos, N. (2002), *Ἡ Ἀποφατικὴ Ἐκκλησιολογία τοῦ Ὁμοουσίου*, Athens.
Meyendorff, J. (1974), *A Study of Gregory Palamas*, Leighton Buzzard.
Prassas, D. (trans.) (2010), *St. Maximus the Confessor's Questions and Doubts*, Dekalb IL.
Romanides, J. (1960–1), "Notes on the Palamite Controversy and Related Topics," *Greek Orthodox Theological Review* 6.2, pp. 186–205.
Sherwood, P. (1955), *The Ascetic Life. The Four Centuries on Charity*, Westminster MD.

Thunberg, L. (1995), *Microcosm and Mediator: The Theological Anthropology of Maximus the Confessor*, 2nd ed., Peru IL.
Tollefsen, T. (2008), *The Christocentric Cosmology of St. Maximus the Confessor*, Oxford.
Törönen, M. (2007), *Union and Distinction in the Thought of St. Maximus the Confessor*, Oxford.
Tzamalikos, P. (2007), *Origen: Philosophy of History and Eschatology*, Boston and Leiden.
Veniamin, C. (trans.) (2009), *Saint Gregory Palamas: The Homilies*, South Canaan PA.
Ware, Kallistos et al. (trans.) (1981), *The Philokalia*, 4 vols., London.
Χρήστου [Chrestou], Π. Κ. and Ζήση, Θ. Ν. (eds.) *Γρηγορίου του Παλαμά. Ὁμιλίες. Ἕλληνες Πατέρες τῆς Ἐκκλησίας*, vols. 9–11, Thessaloniki, 1981.
Χρήστου [Chrestou], Π. Κ. et al. (eds.) (1962–2015), *Γρηγορίου του Παλαμά. Συγγράματα*, 6 vols., Thessaloniki.

8 Nicholas Cabasilas of Thessaloniki

The historical dimension of the person

Marie-Hélène Congourdeau

Allow me to warn you right away: this chapter will not resemble the others. It deals with the question of the person from quite a different point of view.

In contemporary historiography there exists a tendency to return to prosopography – that is, to the study of individuals or of "persons" (πρόσωπα), with the person being defined as an individual joined to a context, in relation with other persons. Being a historian, I wish to highlight this dimension of the person here. I have thus chosen to present a theologian, Nicholas Cabasilas, not taking as my point of departure his philosophical, legal, or theological work (as is usually done), but by engaging with his life story as a person issuing from a context, joined to a network of relations, and, more specifically, as a citizen of Thessaloniki in the fourteenth century. It is not irrelevant for the theological thought of Nicholas and, in particular, for his understanding of a hesychasm within reach for all baptized Christians to know that he was a politician, a diplomat, and a lawyer, and that all that made up the concrete human life of his day affected him deeply.

I thus invite you on a detour through historical territory – history being the earth in which theology grows.

In the basilica of Hagios Demetrios, on the left facing the sanctuary, one can see a large icon representing diverse saints on three horizontal levels. On the bottom level, we notice several saints of Thessaloniki: in the middle Gregory Palamas; on his right and left two other Metropolitan Saints, Methodius and Symeon; beside them, on each side, two monks, Cyril (brother of Methodius) and David of Thessaloniki; and beside these monks, still on one side and the other, two laymen: to the left of David, St. Demetrios, and to the right of Cyril, Nicholas Cabasilas. Four women, including Theodora of Thessaloniki, complete the theoretical framework on each side.

On the other hand, a contemporary icon, spotted on the Internet without an indication of the source, shows Nicholas Cabasilas front and center, writing, and in the background the city of Thessaloniki of his day: one can distinguish the ramparts of land and sea, the acropolis and fortress, Hagios Demetrios, the *Rotunda*.

Nicholas Cabasilas, theologian of the sacraments and of the liturgy, canonized in 1983 by the Patriarchate of Constantinople, is thus essentially perceived to be a saint of Thessaloniki. He, incidentally, always considered himself to be a son of

Thessaloniki, even if he spent part of his life at Constantinople. It is this son of Thessaloniki that I would like to present today.

Part one: an enthusiastic Thessalonian

His family

Nicholas was born and raised in Thessaloniki, yet his ancestry is shrouded in mystery. We know him by the name of Nicholas Cabasilas. And in fact, he descends from one of the great Thessalonian families of the beginning of the fourteenth century: the Cabasilas family. The *Prosopographisches Lexikon für Palaiologenzeit* (PLP),[1] which takes an inventory of all the personalities whose names appear in Byzantine sources of the last three centuries of Byzantium, enumerates no less than 14 Cabasilas's originating from Thessaloniki.[2] We can connect Nicholas to two of these Thessalonian Cabasilas'. The first is his mother, whom the chronicler Sphrantzes describes in the following century as "the sister of three brothers, all bishops, surnamed Cabasilas and mother of the most wise Nicholas Cabasilas"; he teaches us also that from Constantinople she reached "Thessaloniki, where her brother Nil Cabasilas was bishop." He tells us that she raised Thomaïs, an orphan girl, lived with her at the monastery of St. Theodora of Thessaloniki and bequeathed her all her wealth.[3] Of her relationship with Nicholas, we know only that she was his mother, and that despite this, she bequeathed all her wealth to someone else. In all the writings of Nicholas, we incidentally find not the least mention of this unusual mother.

Her brother Nil, archbishop of Thessaloniki from 1358 to 1362, tells us no more regarding his sister. By contrast, we know that, likely acting as Nicholas's first professor of rhetoric, his relationship with his nephew was extremely amicable. In his first letter addressed to his father, Nicholas mentions his "admirable uncle."[4] We elsewhere have a most affectionate letter from Nil, sent to Nicholas regarding a eulogy to St. Demetrios in which his promising nephew showed himself a little too enthusiastic, placing Demetrios above St. John the Forerunner, something that upset certain punctilious souls.[5] The epitaph written by Nicholas at the death of his uncle bears the utmost warmth: "Why do you shed so many tears?" he asks the city. And the city responds: "I have lost the one whom I bore, who nourished those in my loins."[6] We also know that Nicholas gathered the scattered papers of his uncle and published his substantial work on the Holy Spirit, accompanying it with a laudatory preface, which allows us today to reconstruct Nil's theological scholarship.[7] Let us recall that this treatise by Nil edited by Nicholas served as a basis for the thought of the Byzantine theologians at the Council of Florence.[8]

If we know Nicholas by the name of Cabasilas, the manuscripts in closest chronological proximity to him present him as "Nicholas Chamaetos and Cabasilas."[9] Since his mother is a Cabasilas, his father is thus a Chamaetos. The most we can say is that Chamaetos is not an illustrious name. The PLP knows of only two personalities by this name: our Nicholas and a John Chamaetos, who was a public official and *kastrophylax* of Thessaloniki under the government of Anna Palaiologina, the widow of Andronicus III: such is what is revealed by an inscription still legible on a door of the ramparts of the acropolis.[10] It is hardly a prestigious title next to the eminent titles of the aristocratic Cabasilas family. Was this a misalliance? The name Chamaetos is of popular origin, perhaps foreign (Epirote?).[11] Whatever it may be, Nicholas stayed very close to his father, to whom he addressed 6 of his 18 extant letters. During the civil war of 1341–1347, his father was a supporter of Anna Palaiologina (an attitude that may well have ruffled the Cabasilas family, being resolute Cantacuzenists). His death in 1363 plunged his son Nicholas into the greatest dejection, as is witnessed by an exchange of letters with Demetrios Kydones.[12]

His teachers

Nicholas undertook the first part of his studies at Thessaloniki (which corresponds to the Western *trivium*). He mentions this first training in his letters sent from Constantinople to his old friend and fellow-student Synadenos (another great name of Thessaloniki).

> I laughed when I read your letter, for it reminded me of our discussions in which, during debates, something was included to laugh about. But being here (in Constantinople), I was like Ulysses who placed the warmth of the hearth above exploits in foreign lands. For reading in my friend's letter how things used to be, I was with you in memory and my spirit drew up for itself the city as if it were a painting.[13]

At Thessaloniki, then, Nicholas was part of a circle of students who took part in intellectual debates "for fun." Demetrios Kydones belonged to this circle, as witnessed by the affectionate and mischievous tone of most of the letters they exchanged. We know, moreover, that Demetrios had had Nil as teacher of rhetoric. He indeed says in his *Apologia to the Greek Orthodox*,

> This was the man (Nil) who trained me, when I was still very young, in the study of rhetoric, who gave me exercises in disputation and pushed me to speak as I grew older: I trained with him and everything that had to do with rhetoric was common to us.[14]

This acknowledgment throws some light on the training that Demetrios, Nicholas, Synadenos, and their other fellow students shared at Thessaloniki.

But Nicholas had other teachers at Thessaloniki who help clarify other aspects of his personality and foreshadow his theological work. One of these was Dorotheos Vlatis, one of the future founders of the Vlatadon monastery. In a letter to his father, complaining that his old friends had forgotten him during his Constantinopolitan exile (that is to say, during his studies in the capital), Nicholas adds, "From this account I exclude my father the most holy Vlatis: for through his giving even a simple gesture I am ready to concede all to him."[15] He thus considered the "most holy Vlatis" as his father – that is, his spiritual father. Dorotheus would become, from 1341, the companion in troubles and confidant of Gregory Palamas. We can thus consider that Nicholas received, on a spiritual level, an education close to hesychast spirituality. It is even possible that he took part in the spiritual gatherings organized by Isidore Boucheiras, another future companion of Palamas and future patriarch of Constantinople. Indeed, we know that Demetrios Kydones and his family were very close to Isidore.[16] Nicholas's promotion of a kind of "lay hesychasm" at the end of his life could be considered a fruit of the spiritual teaching of Isidore and of his spiritual gatherings for families.

His eulogy of St. Demetrios

A witness to Nicholas's enthusiasm for his native city can be found in his first work of rhetoric, which served as a kind of final year assignment delivered before the Hypatos of the Philosophers: a eulogy to St. Demetrios, patron saint of Thessaloniki.

This eulogy is known mostly for its (theological) misconduct, which was responsible for the charming letter from Uncle Nil to his audacious nephew:

> Know this, that the rumour regarding the meaning of your works, against which certain bring accusation, has reached even me. I asked for the cause of their grievance, and they replied that it was the comparison that troubled them, since according to the address, the superiority of the Myrrhstreamer over the Forerunner is proven. Since he who maintained this was among the learned, I answered: "Well then, if it has been proven, one must certainly yield to the proof. Nevertheless, did he prove the superiority of the martyr over the Forerunner in an absolute sense, or from a particular point of view?" Since he replied that he had not thought about this but that whichever way it was made no difference, I grew greatly irritated and I said that it was not proofs that these people needed, but beatings.[17]

What will occupy us here is not Nicholas's enthusiasm, quite common in rhetorical eulogies, especially in the eulogies of Demetrios. At roughly the same time, a certain Chionios complained to the chartophylax of the Metropolis of Thessaloniki that some foreign residents were gathering in the church of St. Demetrios, passing by the church of the savior. The chartophylax replied that the Thessalonians "venerate the martyr more than Christ" (πλέον τιμῶσι οἱ Θεσσαλονικεῖς τοῦ Χριστοῦ).[18] Nicholas is thus not alone in allowing himself to be carried away by his love for the saint of the city.

More interesting for us is the description that he gives, in this eulogy, of Thessaloniki. Here are some passages:

> There are many worthy reasons for admiring the city: how could it not jump out at the listener that it is not my own patrimony that I praise, but that of

the most beautiful and best of men? For we cannot say that Demetrios is a source of praise for Thessaloniki, but that Thessaloniki is not one for him. On the contrary, she who was founded from the first to govern many other cities is magnified by all her members, but (on her part) all who come from her contribute to placing them among the blessed, and she proves higher than the most excellent cities.[19]

Demetrios and Thessaloniki are thus, one for the other, sources of glory. Nicholas praises the quality of the air, the location, the beauty, the grandeur, all the blessings associated with the sea. But it is the education received there that constitutes the superiority of Thessaloniki over other cities.

> She boasts many benefits that make her beautiful, but the greatest, which makes her worthy of the highest praise, is her capacity for rhetoric, so high that she is admired for it more than any other city. She has such a special relationship with the Hellenic art of rhetoric [. . .] that this quality alone suffices for her own happiness, and she can besides bring this happiness to other cities, establishing rhetoric like colonies, using the example of the ancient city of Athens. So much so that there is no one, I think, among the Greeks who live today anywhere in our land who would rank Thessaloniki on a par with his homeland, and who would not consider her the mother of his homeland's muse, considering that it is on account of being of the race of the Thessalonians that he is deemed worthy of respect. [. . .] What city, among all others, continually bears such excellent orators thus, companions of Plato and Aristotle? [. . .] The music of Orpheus, his harmony, his art of seduction, of charming and all these things, no other city can present them to us.
>
> Such is my sentiment towards this city, and it is in this manner that she has safeguarded the laws of the Greeks, but not by simply fastening on the letter of the law. I indeed leave aside sacred philosophy and those who devote themselves to it (the monks), almost as numerous as in all the rest of Greece, and who are such excellent craftsmen of virtues that not only do they themselves enjoy their art, but they can come to the aid of numerous others and stand surety before God [. . .] And certainly, guaranteeing the equality of public life and justice, living a life according to God piously, preferring what pleases Him to her own life, hastening above all towards all that is excellent, and safeguarding reality in accordance with laws and justice, [. . .] does not this city live all this more than any other? Thus, in all things she leads to happiness, and a wealth of good fortune falls to her, to the extent that she lacks nothing, whether with regard to the nature of the earth or the virtue of her people, for these two benefits are shared within her, and compete with one another.[20]

Part two: a lawyer of Thessaloniki

Nicholas Cabasilas is not only a patriot. He is also a pure product of fourteenth-century Thessaloniki, which was not only a city of arts and rhetoric but also home of lawyers.

The period of the Zealots

A period of his youth shows how he put into practice all that his Thessalonian education taught him – namely, his role in the Zealot Crisis.[21]

By 1346, the city had been governed by the Zealots for four years. We are in the midst of a civil war between John Cantacuzenos and John Palaeologos for the succession following the death of Andronicus III. In 1342, when the governor of Thessaloniki prepared to give the city to Cantacuzenos, the Zealots, who were partisans of John Palaeologos, but above all enemies of Cantacuzenos, took power. They aligned themselves with the Empress Anna Palaeologina, the widow of Andronicus III, and Andronicus' son John Palaeologos. The Zealot government was accompanied by abuses, pillaging, and murders, and constituted a kind of "revolution," an overthrow where the poor were to take the place of the rich. It was in this context that Cabasilas, his studies now complete, returned to his hometown and made his first public intervention.

For now, the governor of Thessaloniki, John Apokaukos, having reduced the Zealots to silence, decided to place the city in the Cantacuzenos camp. In order to do this, he sent a diplomatic mission to Manuel, the son of Cantacuzenos, who was then in Veria. One of the two ambassadors chosen for this delicate task was, in fact, Nicholas Cabasilas. He would carry out the task with great skill, ensuring that Thessaloniki kept its privileges and that its inhabitants received important advantages. We thus have here not simply a rhetorician (something we knew already) but a lawyer, fully up-to-date with the legal prerogatives of his city, and a diplomat (John Cantancuzenos knew well how to make use of these abilities). This fact sheds particular light on his insistence, beginning with the *Eulogy of St. Demetrios*, on the legal tradition of Thessaloniki.

Admittedly, the success of his diplomatic mission would be short lived, for the Zealots would rise up, led by Andrew Palaeologos, and massacre the Senate of the city, guilty of having wanted to ally with Cantancuzenos. The massacre extended from the acropolis to the city and numerous murders and ransackings ruined the negotiators' efforts. Thessaloniki would remain in rebellion against Cantancuzenos until 1350.[22]

But this episode reveals a Cabasilas much less naïve than we might have supposed if we had only the rhetorical works of his youth. Thus, as much as rhetoric, the science of law is during this period the privilege of Thessaloniki, and in this also, Nicholas reveals himself to be a son of this city. If we compare his legal works, all stemming from his youth, with the letters of the young student at Constantinople, we observe that it is only after his return to Thessaloniki that he threw himself wholeheartedly into legal studies.

Thessaloniki, the city of justice

Thessaloniki appears at this time to be the city of justice *par excellence*. Cabasilas himself mentions it in his eulogy to St. Demetrios.[23]

It is to the Senate of Thessaloniki that Nikephorus Choumnos (who was governor of the city for two years) addressed his discourse *On Justice*, in the context of the judicial reform of Andronicus II. After having paid his due to the laws of the genre by delivering a eulogy of the city and its inhabitants, he outlines some general considerations on justice, which deal with public safety, the security of possessions, confidence in the impartiality of judges, the redistribution of goods, and the reduction of inequalities (we see here the corrective justice of Aristotle's *Nichomachean Ethics*). This is followed by more particular considerations on the exercise of justice: he rails against the corruption of the lawyers "who have no interest in the law [. . .] and sacrifice their souls to gain a little gold" and denounces the judges who accept bribes to bolster one of the parties involved. He concludes with a portrait of a Thessaloniki returned to justice "such that we might say: the city of the Thessalonians [. . .] has more than other cities made justice her adornment."[24]

But if there is one who represents in an exemplary way the particular connection that Thessaloniki, during this period, has with reflection on justice and law, it is certainly Thomas Magistros (ca. 1275–post-1347). In his discourse Περὶ Βασιλείας, he expresses the idea that justice is to kingship what ramparts are to a city. A state's best protection is, as much as her military strength, the fact that the emperor "endeavors in the first place never to do anything contrary to the laws" and thus to be "an example of justice." For justice and the respect of the laws are inseparable. Further, in his Περὶ πολιτείας, he describes the harmonious city: a city that Aristotle would not have disavowed, where solidarity between rich and poor is practiced, and where respect for the law and justice protects the weak from the abuses of the strong.[25]

Justice, founded on laws, is also given pride of place by the two great jurists of Thessaloniki during this period: Matthew Vlastaris and Constantine Harmenopoulos. Vlastaris, under letter *Delta* in his *Canonical Collection*, defines justice (Δικαιοσύνη) as "a firm and continuous will to render to each the right that is his due."[26] We are still in a context that is strongly influenced by Aristotle, principally by Book V of the *Nichomachean Ethics*. Constantine Harmenopoulos, who is an exact contemporary of Cabasilas (they are roughly the same age), opens his *Hexabiblos* with a Περὶ διακαιοσύνης ("on justice"). He addresses those who wish to serve as judges, basing his argument on a series of quotations from the Bible, the Fathers (Basil, John Chrysostom, Gregory of Nyssa), and from Plato and Demosthenes (curiously, he does not cite Aristotle). The judge must love justice, fear the last judgment, and be well versed in the law: "That he always meditate upon the laws, endeavoring to know their meaning and not simply the bare letter."[27] I cannot help but relate this point to a phrase in Nicholas's eulogy to St. Demetrios: "Thessaloniki [. . .] has safeguarded the laws of the Greeks, but not by simply fastening on the letter of the law."[28]

The main features of this Thessalonian school of reflection on law and justice, in the first half of the fourteenth century, are thus concern for social justice (based on the thought of the fourth-century Fathers) and respect for the laws (Roman law, which guarantees justice, according to the definition that opens Justinian's *Digest*: "The law is the art of the good and of equality"),[29] an insistence on the impartiality of judges, and the fight against the corruption and greed of the magistrates. All these traits, then, can be found in Nicholas Cabasilas.

Nicholas Cabasilas and the law

In the years 1345–1354, Nicholas composed a series of treatises on legal matters, some of which he would later improve through redaction, but whose main substance dates from the years of his youth.

The first is his discourse on usury (*Περὶ τόκων*).[30] Contrary to the superficial readings that have been made of this text (Nicholas defending a naïve position based on the prohibition of lending at interest in the Bible and the Fathers, without any reference to the economic reality of his day), he develops a reflection that takes into account both the excesses of consumer loans, which bring about a transfer of riches from the poor to the rich by means of interest (thus showing himself to be an heir of the Cappadocian Fathers), but also the existence of Byzantine laws that authorize loaning at interest. This treatise provides an original contribution on the role of law in economic and social matters: the laws authorize the levying of interest, not in order to liberalize the practice, but to frame and limit its perverse effects. The concrete and quantified examples he develops show his firm grasp of the Byzantine laws such as they are discussed in Harmenopoulos's *Hexabiblos* published in 1345. Nicholas demonstrates his concern to reconcile the exigencies of social justice with those of the law that frames the economy, without bridling the latter.

His *Supplication to the Empress Regarding Interest*,[31] where he asks the empress, who is then governing Thessaloniki, to put a moratorium into effect on the interests decided previously by Andronicus III, is an illustration of this intellectual attitude, since Nicholas shows himself to be fully up-to-date with the different laws and mechanisms for lending at interest. For example, he mentions the interest of maritime loans "at high risk," which integrates the risks taken by the lender.

His discourse *Against Abuses by the Authorities*[32] presents itself as an indictment of the corruption of the *archontes* (rulers), with the presentation and then refutation of the arguments of the defense. He here insists on respect for legality and proves his firm grasp of both civil and ecclesiastical law. Here again, he deploys a subtle legal argument in the service of a judicial eloquence quite familiar with the workings of legal proceedings.

A rough draft of a discourse, found by I. Ševčenko in a manuscript, gives us a very concrete example of Nicholas Cabasilas's dependence with regard to this legal tradition. He mentions the existence of forced contracts: "When we drag the weakest by force towards a purchase or a sale that they do not want." He castigates in this regard "those who wish to enrich themselves without regard for the Law or the laws."[33] He hereby echoes a Byzantine tradition, safeguarded in the legal libraries of Thessaloniki and in the thought of its scholars, according to which the state can intervene in economic life for the defense of the weak by imposing limits on the freedom of contracts: when one of the two parties is forced by reason of necessity, a contract, even one agreed to "freely" on a formal level, is invalid. The role of the law is thus to restore balance to such power struggles and reestablish justice.[34] We here find both the theory developed in the *Nichomachean*

Ethics as well as the Byzantine judicial practice, which invalidates a sale when the price is less than half the value of what is being sold.

Nicholas's legal education finds its way even into his mature theological works. His reflection on the law helped him understand the Western theology of redemption (or atonement), which he may have learned through the translations of Thomas Aquinas made by his friend Kydones. He discusses this theology of redemption in Book I of his *Life in Christ* when he mentions the motive for the Incarnation of the Word:

> Since he that was due to settle this debt (towards God) [. . .] was reduced to slavery by those very ones whom he ought to vanquish (the demons), and since God who was able had no debt, [. . .] for this reason, it was necessary that one and the other should unite, that the two natures might be one and the same being, both he who **ought** to fight the battle, and he who **could** win.[35]

But he replaces this scheme in his own vision of redemption, which is resolutely Orthodox:

> It was necessary, in any case, that human nature, according with the work for which it was made in the beginning, would some day offer itself and present a human being capable of working in a manner appropriate to the Creator's design. For God did not create human nature with any other goal, and He knew that it was to this end that later it would serve. The tools destined for certain crafts, we force to adapt to other crafts, so much so that it is not at all necessary that they absolutely accord with their purpose. But God, in creating humanity, sought this: to receive from it the mother he needed for his birth, and from the beginning he established this need as a sort of rule to follow in the creation of man.[36]

He thus integrates the juridical idea of the debt (a subject he is readily familiar with on a strictly secular level) within a frame of the great patristic tradition that makes of the Incarnation of God and the deification of man the goal itself of creation. For him, the Incarnation was planned from the beginning: the sacrificial character of the atonement (the cross) is due to the additional obstacles placed between man and God by sin.

In the context of this original wound, God brought about the salvation of man "by judgment and justice" (κρίσει τινὶ καὶ δικαιοσύνῃ):[37]

> He did not capture those who were prisoners, but he paid the ransom. He bound the strong one not because he was more powerful than he, but because he had been condemned by a just sentence. [. . .] He destroyed the tyranny in the souls of men, not because he had the power to destroy it, but because it was just that it should be destroyed (ὅτι λυθῆναι δίκαιον ἦν).[38]

We have here the reasoning of a man profoundly attentive to the concept of justice, to the extent of having what we might call a respect for "due process."

Thus, even in his theological synthesis, Nicholas Cabasilas comes across as an exemplary representative of the Thessalonian legal school of his day, which exalts the law and puts it at the service of justice.

Part three: a Christian of Thessaloniki

A last aspect of the Thessalonian patriotism of Nicholas Cabasilas is his attachment to the Church of Thessaloniki.

The officials of the metropolis

Nicholas Cabasilas collected 18 of his own letters for the publication of his personal correspondence. Of these 18 letters, 6 are addressed to his father, 2 to his childhood friend Demetrios Kydones, and 2 to reigning emperors. The other eight are addressed to six old fellow students from his first years of study at Thessaloniki.

Who are these Thessalonian friends for whom Nicholas feels such a loyal affection that he insisted on preserving, for posterity, the letters he addressed to them?

Three of them are officials of the Metropolis of Thessaloniki: Synadenos, *ostiarios* (doorkeeper) of the Metropolis; Pasidonis, great *sakellarios* of the Metropolis; and the anonymous *hypomnimatographer* of the Metropolis. A fourth, Tarchaneiotis, is a rhetorician, but he is the son of a great chartophylax of the Metropolis of Thessaloniki. In addition, we have Dositheus Karantinos, who is not a member of the Metropolis clergy, but priest of a church in Thessaloniki and then monk at the monastery founded by Dorotheus and Mark Vlatis (the monastery τῶν Βλατάδων). Finally, a last correspondent, Doukopoulos Manikaïtis, is a judge in Thessaloniki.

Of all the correspondents who had the privilege of receiving a letter from the pen of Cabasilas, only the two emperors (John VI Cantacuzenos and Manuel II) are not Thessalonians, and even this is only half-true in the case of Manuel II, who governed the city several times and defended it against Turkish incursions.[39] Nicholas Cabasilas thus maintains relationships, throughout his life, with his native city, but especially with its clergy and Metropolis.

"The admirable one of Thessaloniki"

I will end with a theme that continues to divide historians – namely, the relationship between Nicholas Cabasilas and Gregory Palamas. I leave to one side the Palamite controversy in its theological aspect to concentrate on the relationship between Nicholas, citizen of Thessaloniki, and he who would become archbishop of the city from 1347 (even if he could not enter the city until 1350) until his death in 1359.

In 1355, returning from a forced exile in Anatolia, where he was held hostage by the Ottomans, Gregory had to take part, in the presence of the emperor John V and the papal legate, in a debate with the philosopher Nicephorus Gregoras with regard to his theology that distinguishes essence and energies in God. The next day, Gregoras gave a heavily biased summary in which he ridicules Palamas.[40]

Copies of this summary circulated in Thessaloniki, and Nicholas Cabasilas takes up his pen to refute the "babblings (λαρήματα) of Gregoras."[41]

Let us pass over the sarcasm that Nicholas deploys on meeting Gregoras, who represented for him an intellectual full of himself and a radical Platonist whose doctrines troubled the good Aristotelian Cabasilas. What interests us here is that, while the debate between Palamas and Gregoras had to do with the heart of Palamite theology – namely, the distinction between the essence and energies of God – Nicholas does not even make the faintest allusion to it. He simply defends Palamas, whom he deems unjustly slandered. Even better, it is neither the theologian or even the person of Gregory Palamas that Nicholas defends, but the archbishop of Thessaloniki, his archbishop. One only needs to pick up on the expressions he uses to speak about Palamas: he calls him "the shepherd (of the Thessalonians)," "the admirable one (θαυμαστός) of Thessaloniki," "the most divine bishop of Thessaloniki," "the most divine Gregory," "the most divine of Thessaloniki." The insistence on this "most divine" (θειότατος) is significant: it is in fact an adjective that, in the patriarchal and metropolitan chancellery of this period, was used to designate a metropolitan or an archbishop; the term "admirable" (θαυμαστός) was likewise used to designate a bishop.[42] It is thus as the archbishop of Thessaloniki, his archbishop, that Nicholas defends Palamas.

Furthermore, what provoked Cabasilas's anger were the letters Gregoras sent to Thessaloniki in which he "asks for the praises of the Thessalonians for the very outrages which he pronounces against their pastor, whom they honor to the point of entrusting to him their own souls." It is as a Christian of Thessaloniki, a spokesperson for those Thessalonians who honor their pastor, that Cabasilas defends this pastor who is also his own. We have here an echo of the attachment that the Thessalonians could have for their archbishop, irrespective even of the theological controversy of which he was the center and to which he himself rarely alluded in his homilies to the people of Thessaloniki.

***

Considering Nicholas Cabasilas not only as an author and a theologian but also as a person whose thought is developed in a definite *milieu* – Thessaloniki in the fourteenth century – can no doubt help us better understand his writings. Indeed, his thought – whether legal or theological – grew out of his education, the controversies that troubled his time, his experience, and his personal reflection.

This purely historical detour through the relationship of Cabasilas with his native town casts a light on his personal contribution to Byzantine spirituality. Nicholas is not a man of the desert nor a theoretician of ascetic studies. He is a man of the city, the man of one city, Thessaloniki, and loyal son of its archbishop: not the theologian of a hesychasm for the monks and ascetics, but of a hesychasm for all baptized Christians, more specifically the urban baptized, those who live in the city and who participate in the sacraments in the basilicas as well as the small monastic sanctuaries of the city. Thessaloniki was in his day full of these, as we can still see today: most of the architectural and artistic treasures of Thessaloniki date from the fourteenth century.

This detour via the history of a person, the theologian Nicholas Cabasilas, taking into account the context in which his thought developed, allows us to measure the concrete, and not only conceptual, richness of the concept of the human person, quite distinct from that of a single individual.

Notes

1. Trapp et al.. (1976–1991).
2. PLP, fasc. 5, 1981.
3. Sphrantzes, *Cronaca*, c. 18, 1–3, ed. R. Maisano, Palerme, 2008, pp. 86–8.
4. Nicholas Cabasilas, *Ep.*. 1, Enepekides (ed.) (1953), p. 29. French translation in Congourdeau (trans.) (2010), p. 2.
5. Nil Cabasilas, *Letter to His Nephew Nicholas*, Lampros (ed.) (1905), here pp. 305–6. French translation in Congourdeau (trans.) (2010), pp. 24–7.
6. Nicholas Cabasilas, *Epigram on the Death of His Uncle Nil*, in Garzya (ed.) (1956), pp. 53–9.
7. Cf. Nicholas Cabasilas, *Protheoria* (PG 149:677–80).
8. Cf. Laurent (1971).
9. Τοῦ [. . .] κυροῦ Νικολάου Καβάσιλα τοῦ καὶ Χαμαέτου. See, for example, the MS Paris. gr. 1213: cf. Nicholas Cabasilas, *The Life in Christ* vol. 1 (SC 355 :76).
10. Cf. Spieser (1973), pp. 175–6 (inscription 28).
11. Cf. Angelopoulos (1977), pp. 367–9.
12. On the admiration of Chamaetos for Anna Palaiologina, cf. Nicholas Cabasilas, *Eulogy of the most pious Augusta*, ed. Jugie (1911). On Nicholas' grief at the death of his father, cf. Nicholas Cabasilas, *Ep.* 14, Enepekides (ed.) (1953), pp. 41–2. French translation in Congourdeau (2010), pp. 82–5.
13. Nicholas Cabasilas, *Ep.* 7, Enepekides (ed.) (1953), pp. 34–5. French translation in Congourdeau (2010), pp. 52–5.
14. Demetrios Kydones, *Apologie aux Grecs*, edited by G. Mercati, *Notizie di Procoro e Demetrio Cidone, Manuele Caleca e Teodoro Meliteniota ed altri appunti per la storia della teologia e della letteratura bizantina del secolo XIV*, Studi e Testi 56, Vatican, 1931, p. 359–403; here at p. 391.
15. Nicholas Cabasilas, *Ep.* 5: Enepekides (ed.) (1953), pp. 32–3. French translation in Congourdeau (2010), pp. 30–3.
16. Cf. Saint-Guillain (2001).
17. Nil Cabasilas, *Letter to His Nephew Nicholas*: Sp. Lampros (ed.) (1905), pp. 34–5. French translation in Congourdeau (2010), p. 26.
18. Cf. Hunger et al.. (eds.) (1995), n° 111, pp. 104–17.
19. Nicholas Cabasilas, *Eulogy of Saint Demetrios*, § 3, in Ioannou (ed.) (1884), pp. 67–114 here, p. 69; my translation.
20. *Ibidem*, § 4, p. 70.
21. On the causes, progression, and sources of this crisis, see Congourdeau (dir.) (2013a).
22. On the diplomatic mission of Cabasilas to Veroia, see Congourdeau (dir.) (2013a), p. 64–74, a French translation of John Cantacuzenos, *Histories* III, 93–4 in L. Schopen (ed.), *Corpus Scriptorum Historiae Buzantinae* 21, Bonn, 1832, pp. 568–82. On the end of zealot dissidence, cf. Estangüi Gómez (2014).
23. Nicholas Cabasilas, *Eulogy of Saint Demetrios*, § 5 in Ioannou (ed.) (1884), pp. 70–1.
24. Nicephorus Choumnos, Θεσσαλονικεῦσι συμβουλευτικός, περὶ δικαιοσύνης, ed. Boissonnade, *Anecdota Graeca*, II, Paris, 1830, pp. 137–87. Translation mine.
25. Cf. Triantare-Mara (2009). Translation mine.
26. Δικαιοσύνη ἐστὶ σταθηρὰ καὶ διηνεκὴς βούλησις ἑκάστῳ τὸ ἴδιον ἀπονέμουσα δίκαιον (Matthieu Blastarès, Σύνταγμα τῶν κανόνων, Δ, ch. 6: περὶ δικαιοσύνης in G. A. Rhalles et M. Potles (eds.), Σύνταγμα τῶν θείων καὶ ἱερῶν κανόνων, VI, Athens, 1859, p. 213. This principle goes back to Justinian's code.

27 τούς τε νόμους ἀεὶ μελετάτω, τὴν διάνοιαν τούτων, μὴ τὰ ῥήματα μόνον, εἰδέναι σπουδάζων: Constantin Harménopoulos, Ἑξάβιβλος, I, 1, ed. C. G. Pitsakis, Athens, 1971, p. 5.
28 Nicholas Cabasilas, *Eulogy of Saint Demetrios*, § 5 in Ioannou (ed.) (1884), p. 70.
29 *Ius est ars boni et aequi* (Justinian, *Digest*, I, 1, 1, *proemium*).
30 Nicholas Cabasilas, *On usury* (PG 150:728–50). Cf. Congourdeau (2013b), pp. 73–88.
31 Edition, translation, and commentary in Congourdeau and Delouis (eds. and trans.) (2010).
32 Edited by I. Ševčenko: Ševčenko (ed.) (1957).
33 Cf. Ševčenko (1960).
34 Cf. Laiou (1999).
35 Nicholas Cabasilas, *Life in Christ*, I, 42 (SC 355:118–19). Emphasis mine.
36 Nicholas Cabasilas, *Homily on the Annunciation*, ch. 8, ed. M. Jugie, *Homélies mariales byzantines II*, *Patrologia Orientalis* 19, fasc. 3. Paris, 1925–1926, p. 492–3. French translation in Ricard (2013).
37 Nicholas Cabasilas, *Life in Christ* I, 30 (SC 355:104–5).
38 Nicholas Cabasilas, *Life in Christ* I, 30 (SC 355:104–5).
39 Manuel II, *Ep.* 6 in Dennis (ed.) (1977); French translation in Congourdeau (2010), pp. 136–41.
40 Cf. Nicephorus Gregoras, *Histoire Romaine*, c. XXX, ed. L. Schopen, *Nicephori Gregorae Byzantina historia Graece et Latine*, vol. II (Corpus Scriptorum Historiae Byzantinae 32), Bonn, 1830, pp. 266–348.
41 Nicholas Cabasilas, *Against the babblings of Gregoras* in Garzya (ed.) (1954). The edition is complemented by Garzya (1957).
42 Cf. Darrouzès (1969).

Select bibliography

Angelopoulos, A. A. (1977), "Τὸ γενεαλογικὸν δένδρον τῆς οἰκογενείας τῶν Καβασιλῶν," *Makedonika* 17, pp. 367–95.
Congourdeau, M.-H. (trans.) (2010), *Correspondance de Nicolas Cabasilas*, Paris.
Congourdeau, M.-H. (dir.) (2013a), *Les Zélotes. Une révolte urbaine à Thessalonique au 14e siècle. Le dossier des sources*, Paris.
Congourdeau, M.-H. (2013b), "Nicolas Cabasilas et son discours sur les intérêts," in C. Gastgeber et al. (eds.), *Pour l'amour de Byzance. Hommage à Paolo Odorico*, Eastern and Central European Studies III, Frankfurt am Main, pp. 73–88.
Congourdeau, M.-H. and Delouis, O. (eds. and trans.) (2010), "La Supplique à la très pieuse augusta sur l'intérêt de Nicolas Cabasilas," *Mélanges Cécile Morrisson*, *Travaux et Mémoires* 16, pp. 205–36.
Darrouzès, J. (1969), "*Ekthésis néa*, Manuel des pittakia du XIVe s.," *Revue des Études Byzantines* 27, pp. 5–127.
Dennis, G. T. (ed.) (1977), *The Letters of Manuel Palaeologus* (Corpus Fontium Historiae Byzantinae 8), Washington DC.
Enepekides, P. (ed.) (1953), "Der Briefwechsel des Mystikers Nikolaos Kabasilas. Kommentierte Textausgabe," *Byzantinische Zeitschrift* 46, pp. 18–46.
Estangüi Gómez, R. (2014), "Le séjour de Jean VI Kantakouzènos à Thessalonique et la fin du régime des Zélotes (septembre 1349–décembre 1350)," in M.-H. Congourdeau (ed.), *Thessalonique au temps des Zélotes*, Actes de la table ronde organisée dans le cadre du 22ᵉ Congrès international des études byzantines à Sofia, le 25 août 2011, Paris, pp. 55–88.
Garzya, A. (ed.) (1954), "Un opuscule inédit de Nicolas Cabasilas," *Byzantion* 24, 1954, pp. 521–32.

Garzya, A. (ed.) (1956), "Versi inediti di Nicola Cabasila," *Bollettino della Badia Greca di Grottaferrata* 10, pp. 52–9.
Garzya, A. (1957), "Due note. II. Postilla cabasiliana," *Giornale italiano di filologia* 10, pp. 156–71.
Hunger, H. et al. (eds.) (1995), *Das Register des Patriarchats von Konstantinopel. II, Edition und Übersetzung der Urkunden aus den Jahren 1337–1350*, Vienna.
Ioannou, Th. (ed.) (1884), *Μνημεία ἁγιολογικά νυν πρώτον εκδιδόμενα*, Venice.
Jugie, M. (ed.) (1911), "Nicolas Cabasilas. Panégyriques inédits de Mathieu Cantacuzène et d'Anne Paléologine," *IRAIK* 15, pp. 112–21.
Laiou, A. (1999), *"Nummus parit nummos*: L'usurier, le juriste et le philosophe à Byzance," *Comptes-Rendus des séances de l'Académie des Inscriptions et Belles-Lettres* 143/2, pp. 583–604.
Lampros, S. (ed.) (1905), "Ἀναγραφὴ ἔργων Νικολάου Καβασίλα καὶ Δημητρίου Κυδώνη ἐν τῷ Παρισιακῷ κώδικι 1213," *Neos Hellenomnemon* 2, pp. 299–323.
Laurent, V. (1971), *Les Mémoires du Grand Ecclésiarque de l'Eglise de Constantinople, Sylvestre Syropoulos sur le concile de Florence 1438–1439*, Paris.
Ricard, M. (2013), "Nicolas Cabasilas, Homélie sur l'Annonciation à notre très sainte Souveraine Mère de Dieu et toujours Vierge Marie," *Collectanea Cisterciensia* 75.4, pp. 385–410.
Saint-Guillain, G. (2001), "Manouèl Kydonès (vers 1300–1341), diplomate byzantin, père de Dèmètrios Kydonès," *Revue des Études Byzantines* 64–5, pp. 341–57.
Ševčenko, I. (1957), "Nicholas Cabasilas' Anti-zealot Discourse: a Reinterpretation," *Dumbarton Oaks Papers* 11, pp. 81–125.
Ševčenko, I. (1960), "The Author's Draft of Nicolas Cabasilas' Anti-Zealot Discourse in Paris gr. 1276," *Dumbarton Oaks Papers* 14, pp. 179–201.
Spieser, J. M. (1973), "Les inscriptions de Thessalonique," *Travaux et Mémoires* 5, pp. 145–80.
Trapp, E. et al. (1976–1991), *Prosopographisches Lexikon für Palaiologenzeit*, fasc. 1–12, Vienna.
Triantare-Mara, S. (2009), *Πολιτική ρητορική και επικοινωνία τον 14ο και τον 21ο αιώνα: Θωμά Μαγίστρου, Λόγος περί βασιλείας και πολιτείας*, Thessaloniki.

9 Freedom, necessity, and the laws of nature in the thought of Gennadios Scholarios

Matthew C. Briel

In March of 1672, Dositheos's synod of Jerusalem met and produced a *Confession* that rejected Cyril Lucaris's *Confession* and outlined the ways in which Orthodox dogma differs from Calvinism. The third decree of that Jerusalem *Confession* has a powerful and distinctive account of divine providence that is presented as the Orthodox alternative to John Calvin and Cyril Lucaris's predestination.[1] It is noteworthy, however, that the terms and ideas, especially of the technical usage of grace, God's foreknowledge, and human cooperation, were not developed as a theological account in response to the challenge of Calvinism in the seventeenth century, nor are they simply passive translations of Latin Scholastic concepts. Rather, they were developed 200 years earlier by erstwhile Patriarch Gennadios Scholarios in response to a different kind of challenge. In this chapter, I examine the contribution that Scholarios makes to the Orthodox account of God's providence in three stages. First, I discuss the ides that drove Scholarios to write his theology of providence. Second, I discuss his account itself, and third, I illustrate this by the remarkably similar account of providence in an English mystery writer of the mid-twentieth century.

Perhaps the greatest theological challenge in fifteenth-century Greek theology came not from the Latin West or even from Islam but from within the Byzantine Empire itself. Gemistos Pletho, who lived nearly a century before he died in 1454, was considered by his contemporaries to be the greatest intellect of his generation.[2] Pletho was a fascinating figure who was asked to leave Constantinople around 1410 because, it seems, he had developed his own philosophical system that included polytheism. Pletho certainly would have kept this teaching private, but some rumors of his unorthodoxy circulated, and the emperor Manuel II Palaiologos suggested that Pletho move to Mistras in the Peloponnese, which he promptly did. Now, this exile was not like Ovid's sojourn among the Scythians. Mistras was a new regional capital farther away from the threatening Turks than Constantinople and the home of a rich intellectual life. Pletho soon became the center of that intellectual life, attracting students away from Constantinople, Thessaloniki, and even Italy.

Pletho was a polymath who considered himself the intellectual heir to Plato. He slowly developed a polytheistic theology that was deeply indebted to Proklos and Plotinos. All of reality is in some sense related to and drawn back to the One.

For Pletho, there is no fundamental distinction between the One and the many in terms of being. Put simply, Pletho's account of being is univocal. Even more radically, for Pletho, the ontological gap between creator and creature revealed in the Old Testament simply does not exist. In classical Christian theology, God is considered to have a kind of existence that is necessary, while creatures have a qualitatively different kind of existence that is not necessary. For Pletho, however, the difference of being between the creator and the creature is only one of degree.

Indeed, in Pletho's account of the world and the divinity, there is only one account of being. As in Proklos's system, the difference between God's existence and creaturely existence is a matter of degree, and Pletho can say that the soul is a piece of the divinity in his letter to Bessarion.[3] There is no essential difference. For mainstream Christian theological accounts, there is a chasm envisioned between the being of God and that of creatures. God is normally considered to have a kind of existence that is necessary, while creatures have a qualitatively different kind of existence that is not necessary.

This, it seems to me, is the metaphysical foundation for all of his thought that he developed as he took on pupils, some of whom were privy to this secret teaching and others were not. In those decades in Mystras, Pletho secretly worked on his *magnum opus*, the *Nomoi* or *Laws*, which is a sort of neo-pagan version of Plato's *Republic*.[4] Only fragments of the text survive because when Pletho's codex was found and read after his death, the rulers of the Peloponnese were shocked by its contents and asked Scholarios whether they ought to burn it, and he encouraged them to do just that. One section does, however, survive today because Pletho circulated it well before he died.

In 1438 Pletho, Scholarios and the philosopher George Amiroutzes were brought as lay advisors to the Orthodox delegation at the Council of Ferrara. At the end of that year, the council moved to Florence, where the seeds of the Renaissance had already been planted. By January of 1439, Pletho had grown bored with the ecclesiastical wranglings of the official meetings and began spending his time with hospitable Florentine humanists. Pletho was a celebrity in this city of Cosimo de Medici, and by the spring, he was giving something like a modern academic paper on the differences between Aristotle and Plato.

It was in this setting that he circulated his tract on fate, the only complete surviving tract from Pletho's *Laws*. It was immediately popular. At least 17 manuscripts, most of them from the fifteenth century, survive today.[5] In *De fato*, Pletho argues that everything in the world is determined because God is all-powerful and directly involved in the running of the world. Any arbitrariness in the world would be a sign of God's mismanagement. How, Pletho asks, could cause A produce the result B one day and the result C the next day? It seems that God decides to bring about a worse case in one of the two results: therefore, in an undetermined world, Pletho argues, God is not perfect. Rather, everything must be determined.

Readers and listeners were fascinated if troubled by Pletho's account of a fated universe. Christians such as Scholarios, desiring a coherent theological account of man and the world, were not satisfied with Pletho's description of a world in which everything, including human actions, is determined. The only freedom that

Pletho offers is that of the Stoics, pithily put by Seneca: *ducunt volentem fata nolentem trahunt* – the fates lead the willing but drag the unwilling.[6] The only free action for Pletho is resignation to the inevitable.

Clearly, an alternative account for human freedom and God's action in the world was necessary. But the traditional philosophical support for an Orthodox theology of providence, dependent on Aristotelian terminology *via* John Damascene, was yanked out from under the theologians by Pletho at the same time that he circulated his tract on fate. In his lectures, which he would circulate under the title *On the Differences Between Aristotle and Plato*, Pletho criticizes Aristotle precisely on the action of God in the world.[7] The metaphysical foundation for their theologies of providence now gone, fifteenth-century theologians, including Scholarios, had a case of vertigo.

Pletho, stripping Aristotle of his thick commentary tradition, demonstrates Aristotle's inconsistency in his doctrine of causality. Aristotle is very clear that 1) every cause must necessarily and determinately produce its effect and 2) that every occurrence must have a cause. But in order to explain human freedom in this tightly bound system of cause and effect, Aristotle introduces the concept of τύχη, or a result without a definite cause. Pletho relished in Aristotle's inconsistency.

Scholarios could not simply repeat the earlier Greek theological tradition on the question of providence, because there had been no theological account of how God can act in this world and humans be free without a limitation on one of the two. Now, there were two main theological trajectories on the question of providence. One, the earlier, was initiated by Origen, took on a mature form in John Chrysostom, and was codified in John Damascene's *Precise Exposition of the Orthodox Faith* in the form that God foreknows everything that will happen, but he does not predetermine everything. God only predetermines the effects of necessary causes – that is, not those things that depend on us (τὰ οὐκ ἐφ ἡμῖν) or come of our own volition.[8] But this would not satisfy Pletho's critique; it is too much like Aristotle's account of τύχη, and it limits God's power. Furthermore, the philosopher would ask, how can anything be known if it is not defined – that is, determined?

A later and more focused theological trajectory develops from this initial baseline of John Damascene and asks the question, is the hour of death determined by God?[9] Wrapped around that specific question is a host of other problems about divine providence and human freedom. By saying that God determined the hour of death, a consistent thinker had to argue that the other events and actions of a man's life were also determined. By Middle and Late Byzantium, a certain strand of metaphysically rigorous and consistent thinkers such as Nicholas of Methone and Theodore Metochites tended to argue that the hour of death was predetermined. But Orthodox theologians were rightly anxious to preserve a strong sense of human freedom, and so authors such as Mark Eugenikos attempted to make compromises such as God does not predetermine the lives of sinners, only of saints. Sinners, after all, are not acting according to God's plan: how could God positively predetermine sin?

Scholarios wrote several hundreds pages from 1440 to 1458 of faltering attempts to account for how God can know and determine everything that happens while retaining human liberty. But it was not until he retired to the monastery of St. John the Forerunner in Serres, 50 miles northeast of Thessaloniki, that Scholarios presented a coherent account of God's providence, which, while retaining the mystery of divine grace and human action, greatly diminishes the compromises that earlier Greek theologians had made. He does this in his five tracts on providence, which he wrote between 1458 and 1468.[10]

Let me now sketch the outlines of Scholarios's account. First, since God, whose existence is qualitatively different from ours, exists outside of time, there is no such thing as foreknowledge properly speaking in God. Rather, God knows everything that exists as present tense. Second, the problem of his knowledge of sin is explained as known negatively.[11] So, for instance, if I freely choose to sin tomorrow, God can know that I will sin tomorrow. He knows it with certainty but does not compel me to sin; that is, my action remains free because God knows sin not in itself but only negatively. Everything that exists is good, and sin is a lack of existence, so it cannot properly be known.[12] Imagine wormholes in a wormy apple. Everything around those empty spaces – that is, the flesh of the apple – is good and known. The lack or privation of apple flesh exists within the apple. The hole itself is not known because it is empty space. But the very shape of that hole, its contours and deviations, can be known. In fact, everything about the hole can be known through knowing the flesh of the apple. Now, since evil is a privation of being, the being that is (and will be) left with holes or gaps is fully known, determined, and predetermined by God. In this knowledge and predetermination of the good, God also knows evil, albeit negatively.

Now, beyond the question of God's knowledge, Scholarios also has a distinctive way of describing God's being and intervention in the world. Against Pletho's univocity of being, Scholarios argues that only God properly exists: creaturely existence is utterly dependent upon, and different from, God's existence. Since God is the ground of all existence, his activity in creation is explained as συντρέχειν, a running alongside or concurrence – a word used at the council of Chalcedon to explain how the two natures of Christ coexist.[13] And it is this Christological analogy of the simultaneous operation of the human and the divine that is central to understanding Scholarios. Scholarios extends John Damascene's account of the human nature of Christ in which the creaturely nature is conceived as an instrument of the divine to the realm of human actions in general. All causes other than God are, acccording to Scholarios, instrumental causes. In addition to being the final cause for intelligent creation – that is, angels and men who find their purpose in participation in God, God is also the efficient cause of everything that happens. So we can see that God's providence is not limited, but what about human freedom?

Freedom seems to be extended to human beings, because God also shares his efficient causality with the beings who are endowed with intelligence. But this creates a problem. Who, then, is really responsible for any action? An evil act is easily enough "up to" human beings. But who is responsible for a good action? If God is the efficient cause – that is, the agent who is responsible for everything in the world – how can human beings be responsible for anything but sin? If God is the efficient cause by grace, would not that grace compel a good action? Here is where Scholarios's Christological language becomes essential. Grace and God's efficient causality is the cause of any good action, but that is not necessarily prior to, or compelling of, a good action. Any good human action has its initiative in the human will concurrent with divine action. That is, any good act is due to the cooperation of God and man, and Scholarios refuses to dissect this mysterious συνεργισμός in the way that, perhaps, the later Augustinian tradition did. Instead, in Scholarios's Christological account, any good human action is due to the human will agreeing with but not forced by the divine will.

Thus in Scholarios's account of providence, the mystery of the initiative of a good human action is retained. He provides a theological account of divine providence that preserves divine omnipotence and omniscience with full human liberty.

Let me conclude with a borrowed analogy. Scholarios gives a philosophical-theological account for a reality that has been expressed most fully but less precisely by artists such as Dorothy Sayers. In her theological essay, *The Mind of the Maker*, she compares the freedom of the characters of a novel-in-progress in the mind of an author to the freedom of human beings in God's universe. She writes,

> The process which I shall now try to explain is something for which the reader must take my word. I cannot easily point to any successful examples in literature, because it is the whole essence of such a process that, if it is successful, nothing in the finished work will betray it. I can only state, as matter of experience, that if the characters and the situation are rightly conceived together, as integral parts of the same unity, then there will be no need to force them to the right solution of that situation. If each is allowed to develop in conformity with its proper nature, they will arrive of their own accord at a point of unity, which will be the same unity that preexisted in the original idea. In language to which we are accustomed in other connections, neither predestination nor free will is everything, but, if the will acts freely in accordance with its true nature, it achieves by grace and not by judgment the eternal will of its maker, though possibly by a process unlike, and longer than, that which might have been imposed upon it by force.[14]

Notes

1 Decree III of Dositheois's *Confession of Faith* was written against Cyril Lukaris and borrows from Thomas directly or indirectly. It seems to betray some knowledge of Scholarios's theology of providence, especially his understanding of God foreseeing human merits. *Confession of Faith* and *Acts of the Council* found in Michaelescu (1904), pp. 123–82. Michaelescu (1904), pp. 174–5 argues for Dositheos's dependence on the scholastics. Traditionally seen as finding the truth between Catholicism and Calvinism, it has been generally accepted by scholars since the mid-nineteenth

century that some similarities exist between Dositheos and scholasticism; in addition to Michaelescu, see also Papadopoulos (1907), pp. 104–8.
2 See, among many others, Hladky (2014).
3 See Pletho's two letters to Cardinal Bessarion. Letters 19 and 21 in ed. Mohler III. Compare *Procli In Parmenides* 829.
4 For a study, see Siniossoglou (2011).
5 According to a search on the Greek manuscript database, Pinakes (pinakes.irht.cnrs.fr).
6 Seneca, *Ep.* 107.11: *ducunt volentem fata nolentem trahunt*.
7 Lagarde (ed.) (1973).
8 See John Damascene, *Exact exposition*, ch. 43: ed. Ledrux (SC 535).
9 For helpful surveys of primary literature see Beck (1937) and the introduction by W. Lackner to Blemmydes (1985), pp. i – xciv.
10 Gennadius Scholarius, *On Providence in Five Tracts*: Petit, Siderides and Jugie (eds.) (1928–36), vol. 1: Tract One, pp. 390–412; Tract Two, pp. 412–26; Tract Three, pp. 427–39; Tract Four, pp. 440–53; Tract Five, pp. 453–60. I intend to publish a translation and commentary on these texts in the near future.
11 See especially paragraph 13 of Tract 1.
12 Although Scholarios almost certainly is influenced by Thomas Aquinas at this point, his train of thought is in line with the deepest traditions of Greek theology. Cf., for instance, Photios's claim in Question 18 of the Amphilochia that the one who lacks virtue and piety is not seen by God (lines 12–20) in Westerink (ed.) (1986), p. 62. For the influence of Thomas Aquinas, consider Scholarios's notes on Thomas's *summa contra gentiles* book 1, chapters 67–71, in Petit, Siderides and Jugie (eds.) (1928–36), vol. 5, pp. 43–6. Finally, Thomas addresses this point in detail in paragraphs 2614–2615 of his commentary on Aristotle's *Metaphysics* – a text that Scholarios certainly knew and may well have translated (the manuscript of this Greek translation of Thomas' commentary on the *Metaphysics* was destroyed in the seventeenth century fire at the Library of El Escorial).
13 See Tract 1, paragraph 16.
14 Sayers (1987), p. 75. Compare this to the remarkably similar insight of J. R. R. Tolkein in letter 163 to W H Auden on writing *The Lord of the Rings*. Carpenter and Tolkien (eds.) (1981), pp. 211–17, especially the end.

Select bibliography

Beck, P. Hildebrand (= Hans-Georg Beck) (1937), *Vorsehung und Vorherbestimmung in der theologischen Literatur der Byzantiner*, Orientalia Christiana Analecta 114, Vatican City.
Blemmydes, N. (1985), *Gegen die Vorherbestimmung der Todesstunde*, ed., trans. and comm. W. Lackner, Corpus Philosophorum Medii Aevii, Philosophi Byzantini 2, Leiden.
Carpenter, H. and Tolkien, C. (eds.) (1981), *The Letters of J. R. R. Tolkien*, Boston MA.
Hladky, V. (2014), *The Philosophy of Gemistos Plethon. Platonism in Late Byzantium, between Hellenism and Orthodoxy*, Farnham.
Lagarde, B. (ed.) (1973), "Le '*de differentiis*' de Pléthon d'après l'autographe de la Marcienne," *Byzantion* 43 (1973), pp. 312–43.
Michaelescu, J. (1904), Θησαυρὸς τῆς Ὀρθοδοξίας, Leipzig.
Papadopoulos, C. (1907), "Δοσίθεος Πατριάρχης Ἱεροσολύμων," Νέα Σιών 5, pp. 97–168.
Petit, L. et al. (eds.) (1928–36), *Oeuvres complètes de Georges Scholarios*, 8 vols., Paris.
Sayers, D. L. (1987), *The Mind of the Maker*, New York.
Siniossoglou, N. (2011), *Radical Platonism in Byzantium*, Cambridge.
Westerink, L. G. (ed.) (1986), *Photius: Epistulae et Amphilochia*, vol. 4, Leipzig.

Section IV
Modern

10 Flesh and Spirit
Divergent Orthodox readings of the iconic body in Byzantium and the twentieth century

Evan Freeman

If a common thread runs through the entire history of Orthodox icons, it is neither the ubiquity of gold leaf nor the hieratic frontality of the figure, but the figure itself: the human body. The body's prominence in icons reflects the central role that the human body plays in Christian salvation history and the spiritual life of the believer. According to the Christian reading of Genesis, God creates the human person in his divine image as an integrated spiritual and material being.[1] Traditional Christian theology understands the body as an integral part of the human person and inherently good, and thus rejects the kind of dualism associated with Platonism and Gnosticism that exalts the spirit and denigrates the flesh.[2] Although the human body becomes a locus of sin and death after Adam and Eve eat the fruit in Genesis, nevertheless, through the Incarnation, death, and bodily resurrection and ascension of Christ, the body ultimately becomes a locus of rapprochement between creation and Creator.[3] The body remains a contested site in the ongoing life of the Christian believer: on the one hand, it is prone to misuse through the passions; on the other, it is a means for glorifying God.[4] In icons, this inherent and potential goodness of the body is reflected in the bodies of Christ and the saints, which dominate both portrait and narrative compositions.[5] Icons may include plants, animals, buildings, or landscapes, but these are rarely more than supporting characters or attributes for human subjects.[6] The human body, the outward manifestation of the human person created in the image of God, is without question the primary subject of Orthodox icons.

But while the body remains the central subject of Orthodox iconography to the present day, Orthodox interpretations of the iconic body from Byzantium to the twentieth century are surprisingly dissonant. Byzantine writers across the centuries repeatedly emphasized the incarnational basis and lifelike appearance of icons. Byzantine viewers frequently responded to these embodied images with similarly embodied responses such as tears and groans. In contrast, influential twentieth-century Orthodox writers Evgeny Trubetskoy, Pavel Florensky, and Leonid Ouspensky – three pivotal figures in the modern Orthodox "rediscovery" of the icon – departed from the incarnational basis of Byzantine icon theory. These writers applied a uniquely modern understanding of abstraction as a symbolic representation of spirituality to define icons not as images of the incarnate Christ and his saints in the world, but as disembodied figures in the heavenly realm. For them, the viewer's response should be likewise dispassionate and spiritual. Where the Byzantines emphasized the incarnational basis and lifelike appearance of the holy figures in icons, modern Orthodox theology viewed icons as non-naturalistic, symbolic representations of the spiritualized bodies of Christ and the saints in the heavenly realm – a modern reinterpretation.

Embodied holiness in Byzantium

Christian images and the bodies of the saints were closely connected from the beginning. The Christian cult of images emerged in tandem with the veneration of the bodily relics of the martyrs and saints.[7] In the pre-Iconoclast period, reliquaries, ampullae, and other pilgrim souvenirs often contained relics, while at the same time depicting associated holy figures or events.[8] Such objects employ a dual strategy for making holy bodies physically and visually present to Christian pilgrims. After the official triumph of images over Iconoclasm in the ninth century, a spike in textual accounts of healing miracles associated with saints' relics suggests an ongoing connection between the veneration of icons and the bodily remains of the saints through the Middle Byzantine period.[9] Moreover, according to Byzantine tradition, many of the earliest icons were themselves contact relics. *Acheiropoieta* icons, images "not made by [human] hands," were believed to result from the imprinting of a holy body onto a material surface through direct physical contact.[10] St. John of Damascus recounts such a legend:

> A story has come down to us by tradition: Abgar, the prince of Edessa, ardently burning with divine love at the fame of the Lord, sent ambassadors to beg for a visitation. If he declined to come, he commanded that a likeness be fashioned of him by an artist. When he who knows everything and can do everything learnt this, he took a strip of cloth and lifted it to his face, marking it with his own form. The cloth survives to this day.[11]

According to such traditional accounts, many of the earliest and most revered icons were not artistic representations of Christ or the saints, but direct imprints of their physical bodies onto material surfaces. The Byzantines prized such icon relics for their direct connection to Christ's physical body.[12] The evidence is clear that the emergence and ongoing creation and veneration of Christian images of holy bodies was inextricably, and often even physically, linked with the saints' bodies themselves.

During the Iconoclast controversy of the eighth and ninth centuries, iconodules such as John of Damascus recounted the *acheiropoieta* legends because they reinforced the incarnational argument in favor of icons. According to John, images of the invisible God were rightly forbidden in the Old Testament. It was only when God manifested himself as a human being that depicting the outward appearance of the incarnate God became possible:

> I am emboldened to depict the invisible God, not as invisible, but as he became visible for our sake, by participation in flesh and blood. I do not

depict the invisible divinity, but I depict God made visible in the flesh. For if it is impossible to depict the soul, how much more God, who gives the soul its immateriality?[13]

For John of Damascus, the invisible God is as impossible to depict as the human soul, but when God becomes flesh and blood in Christ, his outward physical appearance can be represented.[14]

Later, Patriarch Nikephoros I of Constantinople nuanced the iconodule position, arguing that icons were distinct in *essence* (οὐσίᾳ), but similar in *likeness* (ὁμοίωμα), to the holy persons they depicted.[15] In other words, an icon of Christ, fashioned by human hands from materials such as paint and wood, was not Christ. Icon and archetype could not be collapsed. Charles Barber explains, "It is possible to describe the icon as a directed absence. Because the image cannot make the one represented present, it becomes the point of departure for the contemplation of that person."[16] Nevertheless, inasmuch as an image accurately represented Christ's visible, bodily form, the icon shared a "formal" relationship with Christ.[17] The implications of this iconodule position challenge both the modern perception of icons as unrealistic, as well as the widespread argument in contemporary Orthodox theological writings that icons employ abstraction to convey spiritual themes. According to Barber,

> This person, a historical entity, can give himself to visualization only in his manifest form. This does not imply an abstraction of the human body into a conceptual style. Rather, the implication is the opposite, in that what is visualizable is a corporeal human being. It is the icon's function to render this person in an accurate and credible manner. Indeed, it suggests a desire for naturalism in the specific rendering of the individual.[18]

For the Byzantine iconodules, the theological permissibility of icons hinged on God's manifestation in a human body and the ability of icons to represent this body with accuracy.

It should not be surprising, then, that Byzantine texts are full of legends, miracles, and eyewitness accounts vouching for icons' accurate representation of their prototypes.[19] In addition to the *acheiropoieta* legends already mentioned, various traditions held that the earliest icons of the Virgin and Child were painted by eyewitnesses such as St. Luke the Evangelist while the Virgin and Child sat as models.[20] Hans Belting describes the surprising demand for verisimilitude that such legends imply:

> Only if one was sure that the painter had recorded the actual living model with the accuracy we today tend to attribute to a photograph, as in the case of St. Luke or the painter whom the Three Kings brought with them to Bethlehem to portray the Mother and Child, could one verify the authenticity of the results.[21]

So, contrary to modern characterizations of icons as schematic or abstract, such Byzantine traditions envision icons as accurate portraits created from living models.[22]

As Henry Maguire and Alexander Kazhdan have shown, Byzantine hagiographies repeatedly testify to the accurate rendering of the saint's physical appearance in his or her icon.[23] Often, eyewitnesses who knew the saint in life offered confirmation that the icon looked as the saint once did: "In the Vita of Athanasios of Athos: Kosmas, the one-time sacristan of the Lavra of Athanasios, saw the portrait of his former hegoumenos and immediately acknowledged its great degree of likeness (πρὸς τὸ ὁμοιότατον ἀκριβῶς ἐξειργασμένον) with the original."[24] In another common hagiographical trope, saints appeared in visions or dreams and were recognizable because they looked exactly as they did in their icons.[25] When an iconographer found himself frustrated in his efforts to represent a saint whom he had never seen, many an accommodating saint miraculously appeared to sit and model for his or her portrait, much like the Theotokos in the accounts of St. Luke's iconpainting.[26] So according to Byzantine hagiographies, there was no difference between how a saint appeared in life, in a dream or vision, and in an icon.

In addition to viewing the icon as an accurate "likeness" of the holy person depicted, Byzantine viewers repeatedly describe the holy figures in icons as remarkably *lifelike* – a fact that has often vexed modern viewers for whom Byzantine icons appear anything but true to life.[27] In the Greek Life of Saint Pankratios of Taormina, probably dating as late as the eighth or ninth century, the saint's disciple, Evagrius, depicts his master exactly as he knew him in life:

> I also depicted the appearance of my lord Pankratios in an image, precisely as he once was. And when I see his reverend appearance in the image, it seems to me then that I meet with him in the flesh and look upon him.[28]

Evagrius's icon is not only an *accurate* likeness of the saint, but it is also so *lifelike* that when Evagrius stands in front of the image, he feels as if he is meeting his old master face-to-face once again. This "lifelike" appearance of the saints in icons is a common rhetorical *topos* borrowed from antiquity that also appears repeatedly in Byzantine descriptions of works of art, a genre called *ekphrasis*.[29] According to such texts, depictions of Christ and the saints in icons appear to be made of real flesh, seem to exhibit emotions, look as though they are about to speak, and even seem to lean out of the image frame into the physical space of the viewer.[30] Among the most famous examples from this genre is Patriarch Photios the Great's description of the mosaic image of the Virgin in the apse of Hagia Sophia in Constantinople:

> Such exactitude has the art of painting, which is a reflection of inspiration from above, set up a lifelike imitation [ἀκριβῶς εἰς φύσιν τὴν μίμησιν] [. . .] You might think [the Virgin] not incapable of speaking [. . .] to such an extent have the lips been made flesh by the colors [Οὕτω διεσαρκώθη τὰ χείλη τοῖς χρώμασιν].[31]

In his description of the church built by Stylianus Zaoutzas, Emperor Leo VI the Wise describes figures in an icon of the ascension as appearing to exhibit emotions like living people: "His Mother, who has transformed motherhood, and His disciples are standing there, fashioned with such lifelike character by the painter, that they seem indeed to be seized by the various emotions of living persons."[32] And in his famous description of the Church of the Holy Apostles in Constantinople, Nicholas Mesarites describes the mosaic image of Christ in the central dome as appearing to lean out into the space of the viewer:

> This dome shows in pictured form the God-Man Christ, leaning and gazing out as though from the rim of heaven, at the point where the dome begins, toward the floor of the Church and everything in it [. . .] Wherefore one can see Him, to use the words of the Song, looking forth at the windows, leaning out as far as His navel through the lattice at the summit of the dome like an earnest and vehement lover.[33]

Byzantine rhetoricians repeatedly describe the holy figures in icons as embodied, appearing to exhibit emotion, and giving the impression of occupying the same space as the viewer.

These emotional, embodied qualities that Byzantine viewers perceived in their icons elicited mutually emotional and embodied responses. Liz James has argued for the importance of touch in Byzantium, particularly for interacting with icons. "Written sources contain many stories about people holding, kissing, hugging, biting, consuming works of art."[34] *Ekphrastic* texts describe viewers moved to tears and even beating their breasts in responses to icons. In the fourth century, a Bishop Asterios described his emotional response to a compelling depiction of the martyrdom of St. Euphemia.

> But now tears come to my eyes and sadness interrupts my speech; for the artist has so clearly painted the drops of blood that you might think them to be trickling down in very truth from her lips, and so you might depart weeping.[35]

In his description of a martyrdom cycle in the *Life of Tarasios*, written between 843 and 847, Ignatios the Deacon similarly describes an intense emotional, oral, and even physical response to images of martyrdom.

> For who would see a man represented in colors and struggling for truth, disdaining fire [. . .] and would not be drenched in warm tears and groan in compunction? Who, seeing a man [. . .] finally tortured to death, would not leave the scene beating his breast in the affliction of his heart?[36]

In such texts, which may seem exaggerated to the modern reader, Byzantine writers rely on standard rhetorical *topoi* to describe these works of art.[37] Nevertheless, the consistency with which the Byzantines describe such emotional and physical reactions to what appeared to them to be very lifelike images of Christ and his saints cannot be dismissed or ignored.[38] Brubaker notes that even if the modern reader is skeptical that these texts accurately describe how the Byzantines saw icons, it remains the case that these texts reveal how the Byzantines believed they *ought* to see and respond to icons, and it would have been unavoidable for such ubiquitous rhetorical themes not to have influenced the expectations with which Byzantine viewers approached icons.[39] According to James and Webb, eliciting such embodied, emotional responses to works of art and their subject matter was indeed the very purpose of *ekphrastic* texts.[40]

Holiness disembodied

For the Byzantines, icons were accurate, embodied images of Christ and the saints, and they prompted emotional and physical responses from their equally embodied viewers. But in the twentieth century, Orthodox thinkers reinterpreted the icon through a lens of modernist aesthetics, challenging the incarnational basis of Byzantine icon theory. Although icons never fell out of use in the Orthodox Church, and indeed continued to be displayed and venerated in churches and private devotional spaces, a new modern curiosity about Byzantine and early Russian icons emerged in Russia in the nineteenth and early twentieth century, leading to their reinterpretation. This new modern interest in medieval icons has come to be known as the "discovery" or "rediscovery" of the icon.[41] This "rediscovery" followed a period in Russian history marked by an emulation of Western European culture during the seventeenth and eighteenth centuries. During this period, Orthodox icons often imitated Western sacred art in terms of subject matter, composition, and style. But in the nineteenth century, particularly after the French invasion of 1812, nationalism and Romantic antiquarianism prompted a new curiosity in Russia's cultural heritage, a trend exemplified by the pro-Russian, anti-Western Slavophile movement.[42] Byzantine-style icons, which had long been associated with Old Believer and peasant piety, now became emblematic of Russia's unique cultural character.[43] By the end of the nineteenth and beginning of the twentieth century, new art restoration techniques enabled conservators to strip away layers of soot, darkened varnish, and overpainting to reveal the original layers of paint on many of Russia's oldest surviving icons.[44] The newly restored icons were exhibited in Russia and abroad and were celebrated for their apparent similarities to modern art. Modern scholars, critics, and avant-garde artists viewed icons as proto-modern, since they seemed to flatten and stylize forms and employ vibrant, expressive colors much as modern art often did.[45] As late as 1958, in his article "Byzantine Parallels," the American art critic Clement Greenberg stated,

> The tendency of modernist painting has been to turn the conventions of sculptural naturalism inside out [. . .] In Late Roman and in Byzantine art, the naturalistic devices of Greco-Roman painting were turned inside out to reaffirm the flatness of the pictorial space [. . .] Byzantine painting and mosaic moved from the beginning toward a vision of full color in which the role of light-and-dark contrast was radically diminished. In Gauguin and in Late Impressionism, something similar had already begun to happen.[46]

Viewed through this modernist lens, icons were rarely encountered on their own terms and studied within the context of their original cultural meanings and functions. Robert Nelson has shown that in their reception of Byzantine art, modern artists and critics emphasized precisely those stylistic qualities like flatness and expressive color that seemed to anticipate and justify modern art itself.[47]

Surprisingly, it was this modern, aesthetic appraisal of the icon's style as abstract, rather than historical Byzantine icon theory or liturgical functions, that formed the foundation of the modern Orthodox interpretation of the icon in the twentieth century.[48] A new "traditionalist" movement represented by theologians such as Evgeny Trubetskoy and Pavel Florensky, and painters influenced by this theology such as Leonid Ouspensky, the monk Gregory Krug, and Photios Kontoglou, advocated a rejection of seventeenth- and eighteenth-century icon styles that reflected European influence in favor of a revivalist style that imitated Byzantine or medieval Russian icons. Seventeenth- and eighteenth-century icons were condemned for being too naturalistic and therefore only representing the visible, material world, while the icons of Byzantium and medieval Russia were hailed for their abstraction, which was interpreted as symbolizing the spiritual realm.[49] Paradoxically, it was by echoing the modernist rejection of naturalism and appealing to the modernist appraisal of the icon as abstract, rather than to historical Byzantine icon theory, that writers such as Trubetskoy, Florensky, and Ouspensky justified the new iconographic traditionalism. So while contemporary iconographers such as Ouspensky, Krug, and Kontoglou began emulating Byzantine and early Russian icons, modern Orthodox icon theology increasingly deviated from the historical Byzantine understanding of the icon. Where the Byzantines had emphasized the incarnational basis and lifelike appearance of the icon, twentieth-century writers now emphasized the mystical origin and spiritualized appearance of the iconic body: historical icon theology was being inverted.

Among the earliest of such modern Orthodox interpretations of the icon were three short essays by Prince Evgeny Trubetskoy (1863–1920), a philosopher of the Russian Religious Renaissance whose writings were strongly influenced by the philosophy of Vladimir Solovyov.[50] Trubetskoy's impressionistic reflections on Russian icons focus on many of the same formal qualities emphasized by modern artists and critics, and attempt to connect them with the eschatological theology of Solovyov.[51] Trubetskoy published his essays in 1915, 1916, and 1917, and contrasted what he perceived to be the eschatological vision presented in Russian icons with the sin and suffering of the modern world, represented by the unfolding atrocities of the First World War.[52] Drawing on Solovyov's concept of "all-unity" (*vseedinstvo*), and focusing on stylistic aspects of the icon such as color and the elongation of the figure, Trubetskoy argues that icons offer a vision of the future cosmos as church in a state of total unity and peace.[53] The figures in icons represent "the future man-within-the-church,"[54] and Trubetskoy contrasts the "ascetic," "attenuated,"[55] and often elongated[56] bodies and "gaunt faces"[57] in icons with what he views as the source of the world's present suffering:

> The "biologism" that makes the body's gratification an absolute law justifying not only man's grossly utilitarian and cruel view of the lower creatures but also the right of any nation to wage bloody war on other nations as if they happen to prevent it from getting its fill.[58]

For Trubetskoy, Solovyov's eschatological theology offered an answer to the suffering of the First World War, and the holy figures in icons illustrated Solovyov's eschatological vision.

Trubetskoy argues that it is not so much the individual panel icon but church architecture and monumental iconography as a whole that offer this eschatological vision of the entire cosmos in harmony.[59]

> The whole universe must become a temple of God. All creatures – man, angels, animals – must come into its fold. In this idea of a world-embracing church rests the religious hope for peace among all creation, against universal war, universal bloodshed and trouble.[60]

The subordination of individual bodies to the unified architectural and iconographic program exemplify the future unity of the cosmos:

> The icon is subordinated to the *architectural design* of the church [. . .] The architectural aspect more than any other deepens the chasm between ancient icon painting and realistic painting. We see human figures shaped to conform to the lines of a church, now too rectilinear, now unnaturally curved, to harmonize with the curve of a vault. The heavenward thrust of a narrow, tall iconostasis may call for extremely elongated figures; the heads then look disproportionately small for the bodies; the shoulders are unnaturally narrow, which emphasizes the ascetic emaciation of the whole image.[61]

By subordinating individual figures to the architectural whole, the church program presents an eschatological image of Solovyov's "all-unity."

Trubetskoy also argues that icons depict the body in a way that is meant to differentiate the holy figure from the viewer.

> The position of the saint's body, and that of his crossed arms in relation to each other, and the way his fingers are folded in benediction; the extremely restricted movement; the exclusion of anything that would make the Saviour and the saints look "like unto our selves."[62]

Even animals are stylized in such a way as to look unlike "the animals we know" in order to "prefigure the new creatures, already aware of having come under a new, not the biological, law."[63] Emphasizing the eschatological vision of icons, Trubetskoy argues, "It was the artist's task to depict a new way of life, still unknown to us, and of course he could do this only symbolically, not by copying *our* reality."[64] By highlighting the modern aesthetic reading of medieval icons as non-naturalistic and interpreting the iconic body as otherworldly in this way, Trubetskoy set the stage for the later writings of Florensky and Ouspensky.[65]

Trubetskoy's impressionistic interpretation of icons as images of another world was advanced with greater sophistication by another prominent figure of the Russian Religious Renaissance, the polymath and priest, Pavel Florensky

(1882–1937).⁶⁶ Florensky worked to defend ecclesiastical treasures from the anti-religion policies of the Soviets as a member of the Commission for the Preservation of Monuments and Antiquities of the Lavra of the Trinity and St. Sergius in Sergiev Posad.⁶⁷ Florensky was also an active figure in the Russian Symbolist movement, which strongly influenced his understanding of icons.⁶⁸ Where Trubetskoy's reading of the icon focused on asceticism and Solovyov's eschatological vision of all-unity, Florensky attempted to interpret the icon in terms of a deeply Platonic cosmology and Symbolist aesthetics.⁶⁹

Florensky's icon theory begins with a view of a Platonic cosmos divided into two realms: the material world and a spiritual world of ideas.⁷⁰ Icons, like dreams, represent a boundary between these two worlds.⁷¹ Florensky's definition of art as a revelation of the ideal realm is overtly Neoplatonic:

> In creating the work of art, the psyche or soul of the artist ascends from the earthly realm into the heavenly; there, free of all images, the soul is fed in contemplation by the essences of the highest realm, knowing the permanent *noumena* of things; then, satiated with this knowing, it descends again to the earthly realm. And precisely at the boundary between the two worlds, the soul's spiritual knowledge assumes the shapes of symbolic imagery: and it is these images that make permanent the work of art. Art is thus materialized dream, separated from the ordinary consciousness of waking life.⁷²

From this perspective, the iconographer is, above all, a mystic, and icons are "doors" or "windows" to the spiritual realm of ideas.

In contrast with Byzantine traditions that attributed the origins of the icon to imprints of holy bodies (*acheiropoieta* icons) and paintings made from life models (e.g., St. Luke's icons of the Virgin), Florensky argues that new icons originate with visions of the spiritual realm: "Ones wherein the iconpainter records his own spiritual experience arising from either direct vision or from mystical dream."⁷³ Art created by observation of living models is incapable of revealing the spiritual realm:

> When contemporary artists look about for human models in order to paint sacred images, then they are already proving that they do not clearly see the sacred person their imagery depicts; for if they did, then every alien image from the earthly world would be for them a hindrance and not a help to spiritual contemplation.⁷⁴

In striking contrast with Byzantine accounts, Florensky explains that even if a saint is alive, the inspiration for the saint's icon must still come from a mystical vision and not from direct observation of the saint's outward form:

> Even when the icon is a portrait icon, it is clear that in order for it to be an icon, it must in the iconpainter be based in a vision (for example, a vision of spiritual light in the person – even though that person is still living on earth).⁷⁵

Florensky, therefore, actively disassociates the origin of the icon from the material body, connecting it instead with the iconographer's vision of the spiritual world of ideas.

Drawing on Symbolist aesthetics to develop his concept of the icon, Florensky argues that an icon must display a non-naturalistic, "symbolic" style in order for it to represent the spiritual world.[76] "Precisely at the boundary between the two worlds, the soul's spiritual knowledge assumes the shapes of symbolic imagery: and it is these images that make permanent the work of art."[77] According to the symbolic style of icons, figures do not cast shadows as in the real world because "the iconopainter depicts the *being* of a real thing, even the essential *goodness* of the being: a shadow, on the other hand, is not being but the absence of being."[78] Iconic faces are disclosed by otherworldly light, not by a single light source as in the real world and "never by chiaroscuro."[79] In his short essay "On Realism," Florensky asserts that "naturalistic" art can only depict the visible, material world and not the higher spiritual realm of ideas, and is therefore fundamentally deceptive: "the illusion that comes closest to reality is in essence the furthest removed from it."[80] Florensky views naturalism as a Western intrusion that "invaded" and is a "disease" in icons.[81] Linear perspective, which Florensky identifies with humanism, the Italian Renaissance, and the Reformation, exemplifies the deception of naturalism. Florensky instead posits his controversial theory of "reverse perspective" in icons as an expressive, symbolic alternative to linear perspective.[82] For Florensky, it is Russian icons of the fourteenth, fifteenth, and first part of the sixteenth century that exhibit reverse perspective and the symbolic (i.e., non-naturalistic) style that reveals the spiritual world.[83]

Although Florensky's religious writings were suppressed and Florensky himself was tragically persecuted and executed by the Soviet authorities, many of his ideas were adapted and widely popularized by the iconographer and self-styled art historian and theologian, Leonid Ouspensky (1902–1987).[84] Ouspensky, who emigrated from Russia to Paris after the Russian Civil War of 1918–1922, would become the most influential voice in the Orthodox "rediscovery" of the icon, his popular writings translated into numerous languages and achieving almost canonical status among Orthodox Christian readers that continues to this day, particularly in the West.[85] In his writings about icons, Ouspensky draws on Trubetskoy's Solovyovian eschatology and Florensky's Symbolist interpretation of the icon as a window into the spiritual realm.[86] Ouspensky's writings were also strongly influenced by the so-called Neopatristic synthesis that emerged in Paris in the 1930s.[87] Ouspensky was a friend of the Neopatristic theologian Vladimir Lossky with whom he co-wrote *The Meaning of Icons* in 1951, and Ouspensky's rejection of Western art and his argument for a return to "traditional" iconography and icon theology parallels the Neopatristic call for *ressourcement*, a return to patristic sources.[88] In his introduction to *Theology of the Icon*, for example, Ouspensky claims to present historical Church teaching on icons in response to two essential questions: "What does the Church itself think of the art which it has created? What are its teachings on this subject?"[89]

Unlike Trubetskoy and Florensky, Ouspensky dedicates a significant portion of the first volume of *Theology of the Icon* to the history of Byzantine iconography and icon theory. Discussing canon 82 of the Quinisext Council and the Iconoclast controversy of the eighth and ninth centuries, Ouspensky acknowledges that the Byzantine understanding of the icon is based on Christ's Incarnation.[90] Yet in the second volume of *Theology of the Icon*, Ouspensky argues that from the post-Iconoclast period onward, the development of the icon and its theology shifted away from Christ's Incarnation to focus on the Holy Spirit:[91]

> The entire period of the Ecumenical Councils was essentially christological [. . .] The icon, which during this whole era was incorporated into all of christological theology, witnessed above all to the reality of the Incarnation [. . .] The period that followed, extending from the ninth to approximately the sixteenth century, was pneumatological.[92]

Ouspensky argues that the new phase of "pneumatology," by which he seems mainly to mean hesychasm (again reflecting his affiliation with Neopatristic thinkers like Lossky),[93] resulted in an increasingly "spiritualized" style of iconography.[94] Ouspensky attempts to connect a stylistic "spiritualization" of the figure and a rejection of naturalism with the teachings of St. Symeon the Theologian and St. Gregory Palamas.[95] In Ouspensky's view, hesychasm combined with the "spiritual and cultural life of the Russian people" to produce the high point of Orthodox iconography, which, like Florensky, he identifies with fourteenth- and fifteenth-century Russian iconography, and which he describes primarily in modern, formal terms: "It is precisely at this time that the pictorial language of sacred art attained its highest expression; it is noted for its expressive form, its freedom and spontaneity, its purity of tone, its intense and joyful colors."[96] In "The Meaning and Language of Icons," Ouspensky emphasizes the spiritual quality that resulted from this fusion of hesychasm and Russian culture during this time: "It was [. . .] given to Russia to produce that perfection of the pictorial language of the icon, which revealed with such great force the depth of meaning of the liturgic image, its spirituality."[97]

For Ouspensky, Orthodox icons depict the deified saint, the "transfigured state of man," "his sanctification by uncreated Divine light."[98] This is achieved through a stylization of the body, which signifies the spiritual state of the saint:

> Corresponding with this state of the saint, his whole image in the icon, his face and other details, all lose the sensory aspect of corruptible flesh and become spiritualized [. . .] An excessively thin nose, small mouth and large eyes – all these are a conventional method of transmitting the state of a saint whose senses have been "refined" [. . .] it shows not the earthly countenance of a man as does a portrait, but his glorified eternal face.[99]

Ouspensky emphasizes the difference between the spiritualized body of the saint in the icon with the physical body of the viewer: "The icon transmits not the everyday, banal face of man, but his glorious and eternal face [. . .] his flesh is represented completely differently from ordinary corruptible flesh."[100] Ouspensky's rejection of illusionistic depictions of flesh in icons contrasts sharply with

Photios's description of the mosaic of the Virgin at Hagia Sophia when Photios speaks of "the lips" having "been made flesh by the colors."[101] Ouspensky asserts, "The procedures according to which an icon is composed, both in their totality and in the details, exclude all that is illusory, whether it be the illusion of space, that of the natural light, or that of human flesh."[102] And, again, "The colors of the icon convey the color of the human body, but not the natural flesh tints, which, as we have seen, simply do not correspond to the meaning of the Orthodox icon."[103] For Ouspensky, the transfigured body of the saint is distinct from the body of the viewer in the material world, and the iconographer indicates this by stylizing the saint's features to "spiritualize" the holy body.

Ouspensky also departs from the Byzantine traditions of *acheiropoieta* icons and the images of the Virgin painted by St. Luke in his rejection of naturalistic and historical images.[104]

> If, in representing the human aspect of the incarnate God, the icon portrays only the historical reality, as does, for example, a photograph, this would mean that the Church sees Christ with the eyes of the non-believing crowd which surrounded Him [. . .] In sacred art the naturalistic portrait of a person can only be a historical document: in no way can it reflect the liturgical image, the icon.[105]

This rejection of historical images points to Ouspensky's understanding of holiness not as something manifested in or through the body – as narrative and vita icons seem to suggest by depicting saintly figures performing acts of holiness through their bodies in the material and temporal world – but as an invisible quality that can only be represented through a symbolic abstraction of the figure:

> In real life, if we happen to meet a saint, we do not actually see his holiness . . . Consequently, we cannot represent this holiness, which we do not see [. . .] In the icon, it can only be portrayed with the help of forms, colors, and symbolical lines, by an artistic language established by the Church.[106]

For Ouspensky, holiness is a strictly disembodied quality that can only be evoked through abstraction.[107]

In contrast with the emotional, embodied response of Byzantine viewers to icons, Florensky and Ouspensky both describe the viewer's response to the icon in terms of dispassion and transcendence. Ouspensky argues that icons should not arouse emotions in their viewers.[108]

> The icon never strives to stir the emotions of the faithful. Its task is not to provoke in them one or another natural human emotion, but to guide every emotion as well as the reason and all other faculties of human nature on the way towards transfiguration.[109]

For Ouspensky, the viewer responds to the otherworldly appearance of the transfigured saint in the icon with dispassion in order that he or she may likewise be transfigured. According to Florensky, the icon's symbolic representation of the iconographer's mystical vision should likewise awaken in the viewer a consciousness of the spiritual realm.[110] He writes,

> Icons, too, as St. Dionysus Aeropagite says, are "visible images of mysterious and supernatural visions." An icon is therefore always either more than itself in becoming for us an image of a heavenly vision or less than itself in failing to open our consciousness to the world beyond our senses – then it is merely a board with some paint on it.[111]

In contrast with Byzantine texts, then, twentieth-century icon theology redefined both the iconic body and the viewer's response to the icon in terms of disembodiment and transcendence.

Twentieth-century icon theology, therefore, constitutes a sharp departure from traditional Byzantine icon theory. Further, the parallel between modern theologies of the icon and contemporary theories of modern art is striking. Florensky's Symbolist reading of the icon, for example, was anticipated almost point by point by the French Symbolist poet, art critic, and painter G.-Albert Aurier (1865–1892) in his interpretations of post-Impressionist artists such as Vincent Van Gogh and Paul Gauguin. In his seminal 1891 piece "Symbolism in Painting: Paul Gauguin,"[112] for example, Aurier criticizes what he calls "realistic art," including academic painting such as that of Gustave Boulanger, for merely representing the material world: "The goal of their art was nothing but the direct representation of material forms [. . .] what they have called ideal was never anything but the cunning dressing up of ugly tangible things."[113] As Florensky would later argue in "On Realism," Aurier condemns such realistic or naturalistic art as deceptive.[114]

> In consequence certain appropriate laws will have to rule pictorial imitation. The artist will have, necessarily, the task to avoid carefully this antimony of all art: concrete truth, illusionism, *trompe l'oeil*, in order not to give in any way by his painting that deceitful impression of nature that acts on the onlooker as nature itself."[115]

Finally, much as Florensky and Ouspensky would later argue about icons, Aurier asserts that art should represent the heavenly world of ideas through a non-naturalistic, symbolic style:

> Let us leave them to fool themselves in contemplating the shadows that they take for reality, and let us go back to those men who [. . .] ecstatically contemplate the radiant heavens of Ideas. The normal and final end of painting, as well as of the other arts, can never be the direct representation of objects. Its aim is to express Ideas, by translating them into a special language.[116]

These remarkable parallels between Aurier's Symbolist interpretation of Gauguin and the writings of Florensky and Ouspensky demonstrate that twentieth-century Orthodox icon theology not only echoed modernist aesthetic receptions of Byzantine art like that of Greenberg but also adopted contemporary theories of modern art virtually whole cloth. The surprising implication is that what is today commonly assumed by most Orthodox believers to be the Church's traditional theology of the icon dating back to Byzantine times – exemplified by writers such as Trubetskoy, Florensky, and Ouspensky – is essentially Western European modern art theory developed in response to post-Impressionist artists such as Gauguin.

According to James Trilling, it is the particularly modern, rather than medieval, association of abstraction with spirituality that lies at the heart of these Symbolist readings of both Gauguin and the Orthodox icon. While Byzantine theology and cosmology drew deeply from the Platonic and Neoplatonic traditions, the Byzantines simply did not employ a Neoplatonic reading of the icon's style as Trubetskoy, Florensky, and Ouspensky attempted to do in the twentieth century when they argued that icons depict the spiritual world through a non-naturalistic, symbolic style.[117] The figures of Christ and the saints appeared and were described as lifelike, and were not seen or described in terms of an artistic style capable of depicting spiritual realities by means of abstraction. Commenting on Photios's description of the mosaic of the Virgin in Hagia Sophia, Trilling states: "Style as we understand it – something with its own distinctive content, which need not be directly related to the subject of the image – does not exist for Photios."[118] Robert Grigg likewise observes,

> Nowhere in the corpus of Byzantine testimony concerning images do we find evidence that the Byzantines believed that it was necessary to reject "realism" or "naturalism" in order to express the transcendental truths of Christianity. Had this belief existed, one might have expected it to surface during the Iconoclastic Controversy, when questions related to the nature and admissibility of religious images were widely addressed.[119]

The reading of style that equates abstraction with spirituality and stands at the heart of the modern Orthodox understanding of icons is not ancient or medieval, but uniquely modern, and according to Trilling, it was popularized by modern art historians such as Wilhelm Worringer in his hugely influential *Abstraktion und Einfühlung* ("Abstraction and Empathy"), published in 1908, which almost certainly would have been familiar to modern Orthodox writers like Florensky.[120]

So while revivalist iconographers in the twentieth century began creating icons that *looked* increasingly Byzantine, the icon theology popularized by writers such as Trubetskoy, Florensky, and Ouspensky, which claimed to represent traditional Church teaching on icons, in fact marked a sharp departure from historical Byzantine icon theology. Among the first Orthodox writers to interpret the icon through the lens of modernist aesthetics, Trubetskoy described the figures in icons as ascetical and otherworldly, and attempted to link them to Solovyov's vision of all-unity. Florensky adopted Symbolist aesthetics to interpret the icon as a window in the heavenly realm originating in the visionary experience of the iconographer rather than Christ's Incarnation. It is noteworthy that Georges Florovsky, the founder of the Neopatristic movement and one of the most prominent

Orthodox theologians of the twentieth century, criticized Florensky's magnum opus, *The Pillar and Ground of the Truth,* for neglecting Christ's Incarnation in favor of an emphasis on the Holy Spirit: "In a strange way [Florensky] somehow passes over the Incarnation, and from the chapters about the Trinity he immediately moves to teachings about the Comforting Spirit [. . .] The Lord has actually left the world."[121] But it was Ouspensky's widely influential writings about icons that combined Florensky's Symbolism with Neopatristic *ressourcement* and neo-Palamism[122] to produce what has proven to be a well-worn formula of the stylized figure – e.g., enlarged eyes, an elongated nose, small mouth, etc. – as a depiction of the spiritual body in the heavenly realm, defined in opposition to the physical body in the material world. Where the Byzantines viewed Christ's Incarnation as the basis for and central theme of the icon, modern Orthodox icon theology became, in essence, *anti*-incarnational. While Byzantine narrative and vita icons depicting biblical narratives and the lives of the saints bear witness to the embodied God's activity in history and in the material world, Ouspensky's telling statement that "in real life, if we happen to meet a saint, we do not actually see his holiness,"[123] denotes a much different view of God's activity that is primarily ahistorical and invisible. In this modern vision, holiness is not manifested *in* the body, but in spite of it. And the traditional Christian view of the human person as an integrated physical and spiritual being, created as good by the God who himself became embodied, is called into question. While the human body as the outward manifestation of the human person has endured as the central theme in icons from Byzantium to the modern day, the modern Orthodox theology of the icon has redefined both the iconic body and the role of the viewer as fundamentally disembodied.

Notes

1 Jean-Claude Larchet observes that in the Genesis account, God creates the human person by first fashioning man's body, a body that by itself is already recognizable as a human being, even before he breathes life into that body to make it a living being: Larchet (2017), pp. 13–14. Although most Church Fathers identify the image of God with the human soul or mind, some associate the divine image with the human body – e.g., Irenaeus of Lyons in *On the Apostolic Preaching* 11; see also Bouteneff (2008), pp. 82–3; Behr (2013), p. 122; Larchet (2017), pp. 21–2. Whether they describe the human person according to a bipartite division of body and soul or according to a tripartite division of body, soul, and spirit, patristic texts consistently view the human person as a unified composite whole – e.g., see Steenberg (2009), pp. 17, 38–54, 64–8, 142, 167–74; Behr (2013), p. 158; Larchet (2017), pp. 16–21.
2 Ware (1967).
3 Genesis 3.
4 1 Corinthians 6:20; see also Ware (1997); Behr (2006), pp. 141–71.
5 For an in-depth study of the saints' bodies in Byzantine portrait and narrative icons, see Maguire (1996). On the depiction of angelic bodies in Byzantine iconography, see Peers (2001).
6 The intricate desert landscape in the fifteenth-century icon of the Dormition of Saint Ephrem the Syrian at the Byzantine and Christian Museum in Athens (BXM 01545) is primarily an armature for the many activities of the various monks who inhabit the

outdoor space. Later images of *loca sancta*, such as the eighteenth-century icon painted by Iacovos Moskos depicting Mount Sinai with scenes of monastic life, located at the Monastery of Saint Catherine in Sinai, offer a possible exception to this rule, although even this icon is inhabited by saints and monks; see Nelson and Collins (eds.) (2006), cat. no. 43.

7 Such relics included both the actual bodily remains of saints as well as "contact relics," which were not bodily remains themselves but materials considered holy because of their direct contact with holy bodies – e.g., the wood of the cross, saints' clothing or other possessions, or even soil from holy places associated with saints' lives or important events from salvation history. See Barber (2002), pp. 13–24.

8 Barber cites pilgrim objects that combined relics and iconography – e.g., the painted reliquary box at the Vatican with scenes from the life of Christ that contains relics from the Holy Land from ca. 600, a lead-tin ampulla from ca. 600 with an image of the Two Marys at Christ's Tomb that contained holy oil that came into contact with the true cross at Museo Sacro in Monza, Italy, and a pilgrim token from ca. 600 depicting Saint Symeon Stylites the Younger and fashioned from the clay around Symeon's column, today at the Royal Ontario Museum in Toronto: Barber (2002), pp. 16, 20, 22–3.

9 Talbot (2002), pp. 155–6.

10 Kartsonis (1998), pp. 60–7.

11 John of Damascus, Treatise I, 33 in Louth (trans.) (2003), p. 41. For an artistic depiction of this miracle, see the well-known tenth-century icon at the Holy Monastery of St. Catherine in Sinai depicting the Presentation of the Mandylion to King Abgar.

12 Grigg (1987), p. 7. Even to the present day, it is a common practice among pilgrims at saints' shrines to place a small icon of the saint directly on the saint's relics for a moment or two. This can regularly be observed, for example, at the shrine of St. Demetrios in the Church of Hagios Demetrios in Thessaloniki.

13 John of Damascus, Treatise I, 4, Louth (trans.) (2003), p. 22.

14 Grigg (1987), p. 4; Barber (2002), pp. 70–2.

15 Nikephoros, *Antirrheticus* 1.28 (PG 100:277A); Barber (2002), pp. 110–11.

16 Barber (2002), p. 121.

17 Barber (2002), pp. 118–20.

18 Barber (2002), p. 120.

19 Kazhdan and Maguire (1991), p. 6.

20 E.g., Theodorus Lector, *History of the Church* I, 1, as excerpted by Nicephorus Calistus Xanthopoulos (PG 86:165A), trans. in Mango (1972), p. 40; see also Belting (1994), pp. 49, 57–9; Maguire (1996), p. 8. For artistic depictions of such legends, see the miniature showing an artist in Persian garb painting the Virgin and Child in the eleventh-century homilies of Gregory of Nazianzus, Jerusalem, Greek Patriarchal Library, MS Taphou, 14, fol. 107v; see also a miniature depicting St. Luke painting the Virgin and Child in the thirteenth-century Lectionary, Sinai, cod. graecus 233, fol. 87v.

21 Belting (1994), p. 4, see also 53; Maguire (1996), p. 8.

22 Maguire (1996), p. 8.

23 Gilbert Dagron calls this the "hagiographical *topos* of recognition" in Dagron (1991), pp. 30–1.

24 Kazhdan and Maguire (1991), p. 4.

25 Kazhdan and Maguire (1991), p. 5.

26 Kazhdan and Maguire (1991), pp. 5–6.

27 Key texts from the lengthy bibliography of scholarship that has grappled with this challenging question include the following: Mango (1963), p. 65; Beckwith (1970), p. 345; Maguire (1974); Cormack (1977), p. 157; Walter (1984), pp. 266–67; Grigg (1987), pp. 3–9; James and Webb (1991); Kazhdan and Maguire (1991), pp. 1–22; Maguire (1995); Trilling (1995), pp. 57–62; Maguire (1996), pp. 5–47; Nelson (2000).

28 Stallman (1986), I, 442; see also Maguire (1996), pp. 5–6; Efthymiadis (ed.) (2011), p. 251.

29 Within the burgeoning body of scholarship on this topic, see, e.g., Maguire (1981), pp. 22–52; James and Webb, (1991), pp. 1–17; Webb (1991), pp. 59–74; Webb (2009), pp. 81–4.
30 See also recent discussions of the eleventh-century writings of Michael Psellos – e.g., Belting (1994), pp. 261–96; Cormack (2003); Barber (2006); Barber (2007), pp. 61–98; Pentcheva (2010), pp. 191–98; Peers (2012).
31 Photios the Great, Homily XVII.2 in Mango (trans.) (1958), p. 290; see also Mango (trans.) (1972), p. 187. Note a differing translation in James and Webb (1991), p. 13. For the Greek, see Laourdas (ed.) (1959), p. 167.
32 Leo VI, Sermon 34, in Mango (trans.) (1972), p. 205.
33 Downey (1957), pp. 869–70; see also Nelson (2000), pp. 156–61. Although the Church of the Holy Apostles no longer survives, the thirteenth-century Deësis mosaic in Hagia Sophia in Istanbul depicts the figures in the mosaic as if they were illuminated by the actual window in the south wall of the church beside the mosaic, giving the impression that the holy figures occupy the same physical space as the viewer.
34 James (2011), p. 5.
35 Asterius of Amaseia, *Description of a painting of the martyrdom of St. Euphemia* 4, as quoted in Mango (trans.) (1972), p. 39; see also Brubaker (1989), p. 24.
36 Trans. Ihor Ševčenko (unpublished), as quoted in Brubaker (1989), p. 19.
37 Although as James and Webb note, a *topos* should not be taken as a meaningless cliché: James and Webb (1991), p. 3.
38 Grigg (1987), p. 3.
39 Brubaker (1989), p. 25.
40 James and Webb (1991), pp. 9–10.
41 The terminology of the "discovery" or "rediscovery" of the icon is hardly neutral and often reflects an attempt to discredit the icons of the seventeenth and eighteenth centuries by implying that authentic iconography had been forgotten during this period. For more on these terms, see Musin (2005), pp. 7, 18; Jefferson J. A. Gatrall's "Introduction" to Gatrall and Greenfield (eds.) (2010), pp. 4–15.
42 Kotkavaara (1999), pp. 14–17, 124–55; Boeck (2010), pp. 39–41; Billington (1966), pp. 346–58.
43 Gatrall and Greenfield (eds.) (2010), p. 3.
44 Glade (2010); Kotkavaara (1999), pp. 160–70.
45 Nelson (2005), pp. 255–6; Nelson (2015), pp. 15–36; Gatrall and Greenfield (eds.) (2010), pp. 4–7.
46 Greenberg (1961), pp. 167–9.
47 Nelson (2015), pp. 15–36.
48 E.g., Oliver Leaman says of Florensky's writings on the icon, "One would have imagined that Florensky would have interpreted art from a religious perspective, and so argued that icons and church buildings have to be linked closely with their ultimate religious meaning. But he does not argue in this way; on the contrary, he applies a thoroughgoing aestheticism to the analysis of even religious objects, and one cannot tell that the author of these pieces is an Orthodox priest": Leaman (2003), p. 142.
49 Kotkavaara (1999), pp. 2, 38, 247; Musin (2005), pp. 5, 18.
50 Florovsky (1987), p. 276; Coates (2010), pp. 179–80; Nichols (2011), p. 91; Gavrilyuk (2013), p. 17.
51 Trubetskoy (1973); Gavrilyuk (2013), pp. 48–54, 94–5; Musin (2005), p. 10.
52 Trubetskoy (1973); see also Kotkavaara (1999), p. 179; Musin (2005), pp. 9–10.
53 Trubetskoy (1973), p. 16; see also Musin (2005), p. 10.
54 Trubetskoy (1973), p. 21.
55 Trubetskoy (1973), p. 21.
56 Trubetskoy (1973), p. 25.
57 Trubetskoy (1973), p. 21.
58 Trubetskoy (1973), p. 21.

59 In contrast, Florensky's writings focus on the individual panel icon, "released from the strictures of external dependence upon the accidents of architecture." Florensky (1996) [prepared in 1922], p. 133.
60 Florensky (1996), p. 16.
61 Florensky (1996), p. 25.
62 Florensky (1996), p. 22.
63 Florensky (1996), p. 31.
64 Florensky (1996), p. 31.
65 Yet Trubetskoy's essays do not emphasize the dichotomies of abstraction and naturalism or spirit and flesh to the extent that Florensky and Ouspensky would. Nor did Trubetskoy define Orthodox icons in negative terms in contrast with western sacred art of the Italian Renaissance or Reformation as Florensky and Ouspensky did. It is noteworthy that Trubetskoy likens medieval Russian church architecture to the Gothic architecture and the Russian icon to the art of Fra Angelico and Albrecht Dürer. Trubetskoy (1973), pp. 67–8.
66 For a recent biography, see Pyman (2010).
67 Antonova (2010b), pp. 74–5; Antonova (2010a), p. 18; Misler (ed.) (2002), pp. 22–3; Nicoletta Misler, "Pavel Florensky as Art Historian," in Misler (ed.) (2002), pp. pp. 30–1
68 Rosenthal (1994), p. 135; Rosenthal (2002), pp. 64–7, 166–8; Misler (ed.) (2002), pp. 19–21, 31; Pyman (2010), pp. 34–40.
69 Clemena Antonova has also recently argued that Florensky's definition of the "symbol," is taken from German Romanticism: Antonova (2008); see also Antonova (2010b), p. 75.
70 "The point of departure for Florensky's thinking shows what a Platonist and essentialist he was. The basic truth for Florensky is the existence of two worlds, a visible one and an invisible one. The first chapter, or 'letter,' of *The Pillar and Ground* is called 'Two Worlds,' and Florensky's long essay on icons, 'Iconostasis,' begins with reflections on the division of the world into visible and invisible": Cassedy (1990), p. 115; see also Antonova (2010a), p. 17.
71 Florensky (1996), pp. 33–58; see also Misler (ed.) (2002), p. 85. Misler and Antonova have connected Florensky's theory of dreams with Freud's *The Interpretation of Dreams* (1900): Misler (1996), p. 125; Antonova (2010a), p. 18; But dreams were also a preoccupation of the Symbolist movement as well, see Facos (2009), p. 16.
72 Florensky (1996), p. 44; see also Stern-Gillet (2002), p. 43; Antonova (2010b), p. 75; Misler (ed.) (2002), p. 35.
73 Florensky (1996), p. 75.
74 Florensky (1996), p. 82; see also Pavel Florensky, "On Realism" (1923), in Misler (ed.) (2002), pp. 181–82. Ouspensky echoes Florensky on this point in Ouspensky (1992), p. 170.
75 Florensky (1996), p. 76.
76 Florensky (1996), pp. 44–5; see also Musin (2005), p. 11.
77 Florensky (1996), p. 44.
78 Florensky (1996), p. 144.
79 Pavel Florensky, "Reverse Perspective" (1920), in Misler (ed.) (2002), p. 206; Florensky (1996), p. 162.
80 Florensky, "On Realism," in Misler (ed.) (2002), p. 181.
81 Florensky (1996), p. 87, 122.
82 Florensky, "On Realism," in Misler (ed.) (2002), pp. 209–10; see also Florensky (1996), p. 67. Antonova rightly notes, "While reacting against Renaissance premises of art, much of the early twentieth-century theory of Eastern Orthodox art uses without modification concepts and categories deriving from Renaissance theory and practice. Thus, it fundamentally remains within the realm it purports to attack. The very notion of 'reverse perspective' – as inverting the laws of linear perspective – is a telling example in that respect." Antonova (2010a), p. 61.

83 Florensky, "Reverse Perspective," in Misler (ed.) (2002), p. 201; Florensky (1996), p. 86.
84 For a concise biography of Leonid Ouspensky, see Ouspensky (2008), pp. 11–14; see also Musin (2005), p. 11.
85 Shevzov (2010), p. 50.
86 Ouspensky (1992), pp. 285, 489, 493, 508, 512.
87 Ouspensky (2008), p. 12; Kotkavaara (1999), p. 307.
88 E.g., "From the point of view of the Church there was indeed nothing to 'discover': icons have remained in the churches (generally repainted, though some were not), and people prayed before them. It is therefore more correct to speak of a 'return' to the icon." Ouspensky (1992), p. 470; "The renaissance of the icon is a vital necessity for our time . . . As in theology, such a renaissance is contingent upon a return to the tradition of the Fathers," Ouspensky (1992), pp. 512–13. See also Kotkavaara (1999), pp. 31–6, 41; Gavrilyuk (2013), pp. 241–42; Husso (2015), pp. 297–302; Takala-Roszczenko (2015), pp. 303–4.
89 Ouspensky (1992), p. 7.
90 Ouspensky (1992), pp. 95, 127, 129, 138, 146–9, 153, 161.
91 Boris Bobrinskoy has observed that an emphasis on the Holy Spirit was a strong current that ran through many works of Russian theology in the twentieth century. See Bobrinskoy (2000), p. 333.
92 Ouspensky (1992), p. 207; see also p. 217.
93 E.g., Ouspensky (1992), pp. 227–9. As Paul Ladouceur notes, the reappropriation of Palamas was one of the hallmarks of Russian religious philosophers such as Florensky and Sergei Bulgakov, as well as theologians associated with the Neopatristic movement like Georges Florovsky, Dumitru Staniloae, Lossky, and others. Ladouceur (2012), pp. 198–203.
94 Ouspensky (1992), pp. 210, 217, 219, 229, 250.
95 Ouspensky (1992), pp. 229, 235, 237, 249–50; although Ouspensky admits that "neither the Hesychasts nor their opponents have left any writings specifically devoted to art": Ouspensky (1992), p. 243.
96 Ouspensky (1992), p. 257. The nationalistic undertones of Florensky's and Oupsensky's claims regarding the superiority of Russian icons parallel those of contemporary Greek writers such as Photios Kontoglou and his student, Constantine Cavarnos. Cavarnos reviewed Ouspensky's and Lossky's *The Meaning of Icons* favorably but disputed the superiority of Russian icons: "Certain things call for criticism. One of these is the insistence, both by the editor and by the authors, that Russian iconography represents the peak of the whole art . . . Those who have a broad acquaintance with Byzantine as well as with Russian iconography will find such assertions unacceptable. Fotis Kontoglous [sic.], the leading contemporary Greek iconographer, regards Russian iconography as being often 'a light parody of Byzantine.' Byzantine art is masculine and solemn, whereas there is a tendency in Russian iconography to be effeminate and sentimental." Cavarnos (1957), p. 599.
97 Ouspensky and Lossky (1982), p. 45.
98 Ouspensky and Lossky (1982), p. 38.
99 Ouspensky and Lossky (1982), p. 39.
100 Ouspensky (1992), p. 166.
101 See note 31.
102 Ouspensky (1992), p. 498.
103 Ouspensky (1992), p. 184.
104 Ouspensky (1992), p. 170.
105 Ouspensky (1992), p. 171. Oddly, Ouspensky seems to depart here from his earlier interpretation of the *acheiropoieta* icons in vol. 1 of *Theology of the Icon*: "Christianity is not concerned with a 'universal Christ,' a personification of the internal spiritual life, nor with an abstract Christ, a symbol of some grand idea. It is essentially concerned with a historical person who lived in a definite place, at a precise time": Ouspensky (1992), p. 55.

106 Ouspensky (1992), p. 173. The notion that church tradition or canon law has established a particular iconographic style is implied throughout Ouspensky's writings and exemplified by the term "iconographic canon," which Ouspensky deploys repeatedly but rarely defines explicitly. At one point in *Theology of the Icon*, Ouspensky seems to equate his notion of "iconographic canon" with a particular style or artistic language: "The historical course of this artistic language is epitomized by periods of greater precision and purity or, by contrast, of decay and deviation. Indeed, this 'style' and its purity depend on Orthodoxy, on an assimilation of revelation that is more or less complete. This language is thus necessarily subject to change, and what we see along the two millennia of its history are changes within this iconic 'style,' or, more precisely, within the iconographic canon": Ouspensky (1992), p. 470.
107 On the embodied aspect of holiness in Christian theology, see Ware (1992); Behr (2006), pp. 141–71; Larchet (2017), pp. 27–31.
108 Here too Ouspensky echoes modern art historical scholarship rather than traditional Orthodox texts. In his watershed *Byzantine Mosaic Decoration*, Otto Demus claimed, "The individual pictures do not aim at evoking the emotions of pity, fear or hope; any such appeal would have been felt as all too human, too theatrical, and out of tune with the tenor of religious assurance which pervades the ensembles and leaves no room for spiritual and moral problems": Demus (1948), pp. 4–5; see also Mathews' critique in Matthews (1988), p. 12.
109 Ouspensky and Lossky (1982), p. 39; see also Ouspensky (1992), p. 181.
110 Florensky (1996), p. 66.
111 Florensky (1996), p. 65.
112 First published as "Le Symbolisme en peinture; Paul Gauguin": Aurier (1891).
113 Aurier, "Symbolism in Painting: Paul Gauguin" in Chipp (1968), pp. 89–93, here at p. 90.
114 Chipp (1968), p. 91.
115 Chipp (1968), p. 91.
116 Chipp (1968), p. 90.
117 Chipp (1968), p. 58.
118 Chipp (1968), p. 60.
119 Grigg (1987), p. 4.
120 Grigg (1987), pp. 59–61; Misler (ed.) (2002), p. 31.
121 Florovsky (1989), p. 124. "The Weariness of the Spirit" originally appeared in Russian in *Put'* 20 (February 1930) and was later published in English in *Philosophy: Philosophical Problems and Movements*; the first edition of *Puti russkogo bogosloviia* appeared in 1937 and was later published in English in *Ways of Russian Theology* in 1987.
122 Kotkavaara (1999), p. 31.
123 See note 106.

Select bibliography

Antonova, C. (2008), "'The world will be saved by beauty': The Revival of Romantic Theories of the Symbol in Pavel Florenskii's Works," *Slavonica* 14.1, pp. 44–56.

Antonova, C. (2010a), "Changing Perceptions of Pavel Florensky in Russian and Soviet Scholarship," in C. Bradatan and S. A. Oushakine (eds.), *In Marx's Shadow: Knowledge, Power, and Intellectuals in Eastern Europe and Russia*, Lanham MD, pp. 73–93.

Antonova, C. (2010b), *Space, Time and Presence in the Icon: Seeing the World With the Eyes of God*, Farnham, Surrey.

Aurier, G.-A. (1891), "Le Symbolisme en peinture; Paul Gauguin," *Mercure de France* 2, pp. 159–64.

Barber, C. (2002), *Figure and Likeness: On the Limits of Representation in Byzantine Iconoclasm*, Princeton NJ.
Barber, C. (2006), "Living Painting, or the Limits of Painting? Glancing at Icons With Michael Psellos," in C. Barber and D. Jenkins (eds.), *Reading Michael Psellos*, Leiden, pp. 117–30.
Barber, C. (2007), *Contesting the Logic of Painting: Art and Understanding in Eleventh-Century Byzantium*, Leiden, pp. 61–98.
Beckwith, J. (1970), *Early Christian and Byzantine Art*, Harmondsworth.
Behr, J. (2006), *The Mystery of Christ: Life in Death*, Crestwood NY.
Behr, J. (2013), *Irenaeus of Lyons: Identifying Christianity*, Oxford.
Belting, H. (1994), *Likeness and Presence*, trans. Edmund Jephcott, Chicago.
Billington, J. H. (1966), *The Icon and the Axe: An Interpretive History of Russian Culture*, New York.
Bobrinskoy, B. (2000), "The Church and the Holy Spirit in 20th Century Russia," *The Ecumenical Review* 52.3, pp. 326–42.
Boeck, E. (2010), "Strength in Numbers or Unity in Diversity? Compilations of Miracle-Working Virgin Icons," in J. J. A. Gatrall and G. Greenfield (eds.), *Alter Icons: The Russian Icon and Modernity*, University Park PA, pp. 27–49.
Bouteneff, P. C. (2008), *Beginnings: Ancient Christian Readings of the Biblical Creation Narratives*, Grand Rapids MI.
Brubaker, L. (1989), "Perception and Conception: Art, Theory and Culture in Ninth-Century Byzantium," *Word and Image* 5.1, pp. 19–32.
Cassedy, S. (1990), *Flight From Eden: The Origins of Modern Literary Criticism and Theory*, Berkeley CA.
Cavarnos, C. (1957), "Review of *The Meaning of Icons* by Leonid Ouspensky and Vladimir Lossky," *Speculum* 32.3, pp. 597–99.
Chipp, H. B. (1968), *Theories of Modern Art: A Source Book by Artists and Critics*, Berkeley CA.
Coates, R. (2010), "Religious renaissance in the Silver Age," in W. Leatherbarrow and D. Offord (eds.), *A History of Russian Thought*, Cambridge.
Cormack, R. (1977), "Painting After Iconoclasm," in A. Bryer and J. Herrin (eds.), *Iconoclasm: Papers Given at the Ninth Spring Symposium of Byzantine Studies, University of Birmingham, March 1975*, Birmingham, pp. 145–63.
Cormack, R. (2003), "Living Painting," in E. Jeffreys (ed.), *Rhetoric in Byzantium: Papers from the Thirty-Fifth Spring Symposium of Byzantine Studies, Exeter College, University of Oxford, March 2001*, Aldershot, pp. 235–53.
Dagron, G. (1991), "Holy Images and Likeness," *Dumbarton Oaks Papers* 45, pp. 23–33.
Demus, O. (1948), *Byzantine Mosaic Decoration: Aspects of Monumental Art in Byzantium*, London.
Downey, G. (1957), "Nikolaos Mesarites: Description of the Church of the Holy Apostles at Constantinople" XIV.1–2, *Transactions of the American Philosophical Society* 47.6, pp. 855–924.
Efthymiadis, S. (ed.) (2011), *The Ashgate Research Companion to Byzantine Hagiography, Volume 1: Periods and Places*, Farnham, Surrey.
Facos, M. (2009), *Symbolist Art in Context*, Berkeley CA.
Florensky, P. (1996), *Iconostasis*, trans. Donald Sheehan and Olga Andrejev, Crestwood NY.
Florovsky, G. (1987), *Ways of Russian Theology: Part Two*, ed. Richard S. Haugh, trans. Robert L. Nichols, Belmont MA.

Florovsky, G. (1989), "The Weariness of the Spirit: On Fr. Paul Florensky's The Pillar and Confirmation of Truth" in G. Florovsky (ed.), *Philosophy: Philosophical Problems and Movements*, vol. 12 of the Collected Works, Belmont MA, pp. 124–27.

Gatrall, J. J. A. and Greenfield, D. (eds.) (2010), *Alter Icons: The Russian Icon and Modernity*, University Park PA.

Gavrilyuk, P. L. (2013), *Georges Florovsky and the Russian Religious Renaissance*, Oxford.

Glade, S. A. (2010), "Anisimov and the Rediscovery of Old Russian Icons," in Gatrall and Greenfield (eds.) (2010), pp. 89–111.

Greenberg, C. (1961), *Art and Culture: Critical Essays*, Boston.

Grigg, R. (1987), "Byzantine Credulity as an Impediment to Antiquarianism," *Gesta* 26.1, pp. 3–9.

Husso, K. (2015), "Tradition Re-Evaluated: The Discourse on Orthodox Icons in Finland," in Moody and Takala-Roszczenko (eds.) (2015), pp. 297–302.

James, L. (2011), "'Seeing's believing, but feeling's the truth': Touch and the Meaning of Byzantine Art," in A. Lymberopoulou (ed.), *Images of the Byzantine World: Visions, Messages and Meanings: Studies Presented to Leslie Brubaker*, Farnham, Surrey, pp. 1–14.

James, L. and Webb, R. (1991), "'To Understand the Ultimate Things and Enter Secret Places': Ekphrasis and Art in Byzantium," *Art History* 14.1, pp. 1–17.

Kartsonis, A. (1998), "The Responding Icon," in Linda Safran (ed.), *Heaven on Earth: Art and the Church in Byzantium*, University Park PA, pp. 58–80.

Kazhdan, A. and Maguire, H. (1991), "Byzantine Hagiographical Texts as Sources on Art," *Dumbarton Oaks Papers* 45, pp. 1–22.

Kotkavaara, K. (1999), *Progeny of the Icon: Émigré Russian Revivalism and the Vicissitudes of the Eastern Orthodox Sacred Image*, Åbo, Finland.

Ladouceur, P. (2012), "Treasures New and Old: Landmarks of Orthodox Neopatristic Theology," *St Vladimir's Theological Quarterly* 56.2, pp. 191–227.

Laourdas, V. (ed.) (1959), *Phōtiou homiliai: Ekdosis keimenou, eisagōgē kai scholia*, Thessaloniki.

Larchet, J.-C. (2017), *Theology of the Body*, trans. Michael Donley, Crestwood NY.

Leaman, O. (2003), "Review of *Beyond Vision: Essays on the Perception of Art*, by Pavel Florensky, ed. Nicoletta Misler, trans. Wendy Salmond," *The Slavic and East European Journal* 47.1, p. 142.

Louth, A. (trans.) (2003), *John of Damascus. Three Treatises on the Divine Images*, Crestwood NY.

Maguire, H. (1974), "Truth and Convention in Byzantine Descriptions of Works of Art," *Dumbarton Oaks Papers* 28, pp. 111–40.

Maguire, H. (1981), *Art and Eloquence in Byzantium*, Princeton NJ.

Maguire, H. (1995), "Originality in Byzantine Art Criticism," in A. R. Littlewood (ed.), *Originality in Byzantine Literature, Art and Music*, Oxford, pp. 101–14.

Maguire, H. (1996), *The Icons of Their Bodies: Saints and Their Images in Byzantium*, Princeton NJ.

Mango, C. (trans.) (1958), *The Homilies of Photius Patriarch of Constantinople*, Cambridge MA.

Mango, C. (1963), "Antique Statuary and the Byzantine Beholder," *Dumbarton Oaks Papers* 17, pp. 53, 55–75.

Mango, C. (trans.) (1972), *The Art of the Byzantine Empire 312–1453*, Englewood Cliffs NJ.

Mathews, T. F. (1988), "The Sequel to Nicaea II in Byzantine Church Decoration," *Perkins Journal of Theology* 43.3, pp. 11–23.

Misler, N. (1996), "Toward an Exact Aesthetics: P. Florensky and the Russian Academy of Artistic Sciences," in J. Bowlt and O. Matich (eds.), *Laboratory of Dreams: The Russian Avant-Garde and Cultural Experiment*, Stanford CA, pp. 118–32.

Misler, N. (ed.) (2002), *Pavel Florensky. Beyond Vision: Essays on the Perception of Art*, trans. Wendy R. Salmond, London.

Moody, I. and Takala-Roszczenko, M. (eds.) (2015), *Church Music and Icons: Windows to Heaven: Proceedings of the Fifth International Conference on Orthodox Church Music, University of Eastern Finland, Joensuu, Finland, 3–9 June 2013*, Joensuu, Finland.

Musin, A. (2005), "Theology of the Image and the Evolution of Style: the Dogmatic and Canonical Evaluation of Russian Ecclesiastical Art of the Synodal Period," *Iconofile* 7, pp. 5–25.

Nelson, R. S. (2000), "To Say and to See: Ekphrasis and Vision in Byzantium," in R. S. Nelson (ed.), *Visuality Before and Beyond the Renaissance: Seeing as Others Saw*, Cambridge, pp. 143–68.

Nelson, R. S. (2005), "Byzantine Art *vs* Western Medieval Art," in P. Pagès et al. (eds.), *Byzance et le monde extérieur: contacts, relations, échanges : actes de trois séances du XXe Congrès international des études byzantines, Paris, 19–25 août 2001*, Paris, pp. 255–70.

Nelson, R. S. (2015), "Modernism's Byzantium Byzantium's Modernism," in R. Betancourt and M. Taroutina (eds.), *Byzantium/Modernism*, Leiden and Boston, pp. 15–36.

Nelson, R. S. and Collins, K. M. (eds.) (2006), *Holy Image, Hallowed Ground: Icons From Sinai*, Los Angeles CA.

Nichols, A. (2011), *Lost in Wonder: Essays on Liturgy and the Arts*, Farnham, Surrey.

Ouspensky, L. (1992), *Theology of the Icon*, trans. Anthony Gythiel and Elizabeth Meyendorff, Crestwood NY.

Ouspensky, L(ydia). (2008), "A Short Biography: Leonid Alexandrovich Ouspensky," in P. Doolan, *Recovering the Icon: The Life and Work of Leonid Ouspensky*, Crestwood NY, pp. 11–14.

Ouspensky, L. and Lossky, V. (1982), *The Meaning of Icons*, trans. G. E. H. Palmer and E. Kadloubovsky, Crestwood NY.

Peers, G. (2001), *Subtle Bodies: Representing Angels in Byzantium*, Berkeley CA.

Peers, G. (2012), "Real Living Painting: Quasi-Objects and Dividuation in the Byzantine World," *Religion and the Arts* 16, pp. 433–60.

Pentcheva, B. (2010), *The Sensual Icon: Space, Ritual and the Senses in Byzantium*, University Park PA.

Pyman, A. (2010), *Pavel Florensky: A Quiet Genius. The Tragic and Extraordinary Life of Russia's Unknown da Vinci*, New York.

Rosenthal, B. G. (1994), "The New Religious Consciousness: Pavel Florensky's Path to a Revitalized Orthodoxy" in R. P. Hughes and I. Paperno (eds.), *Christianity and the Eastern Slavs, II: Russian Culture in Modern Times*, Berkeley and Los Angeles CA, pp. 134–57.

Rosenthal, B. G. (2002), *New Myth, New World: From Nietzsche to Stalinism*, University Park PA.

Shevzov, V. (2010), "Between Purity and Pluralism: Icon and Anathema in Modern Russia, 1860–1917," in Gatrall and Greenfield (eds.) (2010), pp. 50–73.

Stallman, C. J. (1986), "The *Life* of St Pancratius of Taormina," D.Phil. thesis, University of Oxford.

Steenberg, M. C. (2009), *Of God and Man: Theology as Anthropology From Irenaeus to Athanasius*, London.

Stern-Gillet, S. (2002), "Neoplatonist Aesthetics," in Paul Smith and Carolyn Wilde, eds., *A Companion to Art Theory*, Oxford, pp. 40–8.

Takala-Roszczenko, M. (2015), "'Imported on a Jet-Plane': The Byzantine 'Revival' in Finnish Orthodox Church Music in the 1950s–60s," in Moody and Takala-Roszczenko (eds.) (2015), pp. 303–11.

Talbot, A.-M. (2002), "Pilgrimage to Healing Shrines: The Evidence of Miracle Accounts," *Dumbarton Oaks Papers* 56, 153–73.

Trilling, J. (1995), "Medieval Art Without Style? Plato's Loophole and a Modern Detour," *Gesta* 34.1, pp. 57–62.

Trubetskoy, E. (1973), *Icons: Theology in Color*, Crestwood NY.

Walter, C. (1984), "Expression and Hellenism: A Note on Stylistic Tendencies in Byzantine Figurative Art From *Spätantike* to the Macedonian 'Renaissance,'" *Revue des Études Byzantines*, 42, pp. 265–87.

Ware, K. T. (1967), "The Transfiguration of the Body," in A. M. Allchin (ed.), *Sacrament and Image: Essays in the Christian Understanding of Man*, London, pp. 17–32.

Ware, K. T. (1997), "'My helper and my enemy': The Body in Greek Christianity," in Sarah Coakley (ed.), *Religion and the Body*, Cambridge, pp. 90–110.

Ware, K. T. (1992), "Praying With the Body: The Hesychast Method and Non-Christian Parallels," *Sobornost* 14.2 (1992), pp. 6–35.

Webb, R. (1991), "The Aesthetics of Sacred Space: Narrative, Metaphor, and Motion in 'Ekphraseis' of Church Buildings," *Dumbarton Oaks Papers* 53, pp. 59–74.

Webb, R. (2009), *Ekphrasis, Imagination and Persuasion in Ancient Rhetorical Theory and Practice*, Farnham, Surrey.

11 Nikos Nissiotis, the "theology of the '60s," and personhood

Continuity or discontinuity?

Nikolaos Asproulis

Introduction

Dealing with the multifaceted thought of the late eminent Greek Orthodox theologian and philosopher Nikos Nissiotis (1925–1986) is no easy task. On the one hand, his work extends to thousands of pages in various, mainly foreign language, journals that are not always easy to identify or accessible.[1] On the other, his rich theological and philosophical heritage seems to have fallen immediately after his death, quickly to oblivion. As a result, a comprehensive and synthetic study of his thought in general, and his understanding of personhood in particular, is still missing today.

In this short study, I will first attempt to search for some *methodological* aspects of the anthropological vision of the Greek intellectual, then investigate the way in which Nissiotis understands the meaning of personhood, and conclude with a brief introductory and rather critical assessment and interactive meeting with two of the leading representatives of the so-called theological generation of the '60s in Greece,[2] the eminent philosopher Christos Yannaras (1935–) and the well-known theologian metropolitan John (Zizioulas) of Pergamon (1931–). As it is undeniable that Nissiotis himself belongs to this generation – even if he began his career a little earlier with the defense of his doctoral thesis in 1956 at the University of Athens – I will try to explore to what extent continuity or discontinuity is observed in the personalistic vision of the three eminent theologians.

Some methodological parameters

If one considers that Nissiotis is in a deep and constant dialogue with all the different European pioneering movements and intellectual currents in the postwar era – especially dialectical theology (K. Barth, E. Brunner), neo-thomism, psychoanalysis (C. Jung), existentialism (K. Jaspers),[3] all movements that contributed in one way or another to the "modern turn to subjectivism" ("from the objective world and abstract concepts into the subjective world of human experiences")[4] – one will acquire a satisfactorily complete picture for both his starting point of reflection, and for his long commitment to anthropological issues. At the same time, however, theology and philosophy do not seem to be the only or exclusive interlocutor for Nissiotis. The key dialogical context within which he develops his own anthropological proposal can be found in the "Copernican shift" taking place from the early twentieth century in the fields of natural sciences, psychology, philosophy, and political theory – namely, the theories of A. Einstein, N. Bohr, W. Heisenberg, the depth psychology of S. Freud, the analytic psychology of C. Jung, the individual psychology of A. Adler, the dominant role of existentialism with its pioneering interpretation of the subject,[5] the spread "of totalitarian ideologies and the sovereignty of the massive forms of life,"[6] but also in the progressive emergence and consolidation in the second half of the same century of Western liberal democracy as the most appropriate form for the organization of social life – in short, the achievements of modernity (or post/late modernity), along with the respected variety of anthropological proposals that it brings.[7]

The imperative to investigate the identity and value of the human being over time was the central issue of human reflection, moving from unrestrained *Idealism* and transcendentalism to the newest trend of understanding the human being in the perspective and the spirit of a utilitarian social activism, or as an undervalued number of a neoliberal economy (especially in our time).[8] By taking into consideration the surrounding atmosphere, Nissiotis attempts to reflect on the "mystery" of the human being, away from any ideological bias or preconceptions and one-sidedness, as far as it is possible in any sort of hermeneutical enterprise.

Anthropology then became thereafter for Nissiotis the contact point between his philosophical-theological reflection and secular thought. Nissiotis is not interested in developing a theological anthropology "disconnected" from the existential reflection on life, focused solely on a scholastic, confessional, and abstract interpretation of the Christian faith and church tradition. Instead, he seeks to meet the "challenges" posed by the modern world in order to "form a more authentic Christian anthropology that takes into account the signs of our times."[9] It seems that Nissiotis makes use here, albeit unconsciously, of the "correlation method" of the important contemporary theologian Paul Tillich[10] in order to bring the gospel into a soteriological dialogue with the existential needs of the modern world.

As is well known, the core of Nissiotis's education lies more or less in the field of philosophy, or even in existentialism. However, philosophy does not constitute the sole source of inspiration in forming his anthropological thinking. The Bible and especially *Genesis* and Pauline theology are inviolable parameters that contribute to the consistent building of his complete Christian anthropological view in the context of contemporary debates. Moreover, the language, the means through which his anthropological proposal is presented, is none other than "existential ontology" – a language that adapts ontology to being itself in the perspective of the incarnation of the Word in history.

The philosophical understanding of human being. The concept of personhood

Nissiotis, as has been already noted, does not theologize *in absentia* with regard to the philosophical atmosphere of his time, which he had also studied in all its variety and currents, but always in a critical dialogue with it. In this perspective, and without making, in my view, any philosophical understanding of personhood central or a summary of his whole theological anthropological thinking, Nissiotis does create, in the context of his existential reflection, a very balanced personalistic version, resulting from a critical reading of existential philosophical thought, mainly filtered through the perspective of the Russian philosopher N. Berdyaev as a hermeneutical tool first of the actual human condition and then of theological epistemology.[11]

By understanding the human being as an identity that "begins with a self-affirmation and is fulfilled in relation to others and the ego-world," Nissiotis marks the importance of *self-awareness* and *self-knowledge* for the identity of the subject, as a result of *intra-subjectivity*. The latter is possible only in the perspective of meeting, *coexistence*, communion with other people, the world, and finally the "Other," God. He insists that the subject in his attempt toward self-understanding has to accept its reliance on the necessary *trans-subjectivity*, to the extent that the way toward identity cannot but always go through the Other – the different.[12]

Therefore, he seems to recognize that in order for the subject to be understood as a person, two fundamental dimensions are required: *relationship* and *difference*.

> The relationship with the other is the necessary starting point of existence itself in search of self-affirmation and complementarity. The difference [. . .] is the challenge to being to understand itself more deeply and realize it as a particular subject and this particular I [. . .] that is always in via.[13]

Although not explicitly stated, the human being, for Nissiotis, is, or rather *becomes*, a person to the extent that one opens one's self insofar as the *catholic* is constituted as *coexistence* in communion, freedom, and dialogue with each (O)ther in the now (νυν) of history, in the perspective of a dialogical reciprocity with one's neighbor, the world, and the God. According to Nissiotis, personhood is understood as a *dynamic* reality,[14] an *active* way of being that leaves no room to flourish any passive attitude or rather of any vanishing trends from the exciting adventure of interpersonal relations. In this way, he also keeps the necessary distance from certain one-sided perspectives and the failures of existentialistic philosophy, which tends to adopt unhistorical or individualistic tendencies in dealing with the human existence by trapping it in a sterile immanent *self*-referentiality and a mere subjectivism. At the same time, it is worth noting that Nissiotis, with his personalistic approach, by attempting to overcome extreme idealistic tendencies that seek to cut off the human being from its inner world, thus breaking the psycho-physical totality ("man as a whole"),[15] takes seriously into consideration the inner world of man by studying the unconscious and psychological experiences that contribute to or hinder the formation of the personal identity of man.[16]

At the same time, in the context of (theological) *epistemology*, Nissiotis chooses, not accidentally, the concept of knowledge "as a communion of persons" (c.f. "the epistemological principle of mutually inter-embracing between subjects, considered as persons")[17] and not the competitive relationship between subject and object inherited from the Enlightenment, as a basic condition for the development and fulfillment of authentic spiritual existence. This *personalistic* and *relational* aspect in the field of *epistemology* seems to be the *point* of contact between the philosophical thought of his time and the theological epistemology, which knows God as "personal," by virtue of the revelation of the Triune God and the incarnation of the Word *par excellence* in history. As he briefly states,

> Person indicates not an individual [. . .] but its movement towards also another person. No one exists as a hypostasis if he/she does not pass through the experience of another person. Personality is interwoven with the existence of the other.

Therefore, in the perspective of Christian theology, knowledge of God is understood and realized, particularly in an *ecclesiological* context, primarily as follows: "But now that you know God – or I should say, now that God knows you [. . .] (Gal. 4:9)."[18] This personalistic epistemological approach, which becomes in Christ a historic fact, is able to contribute to the fulfillment of the quests of philosophical reflection about the authenticity of the human being. Nissiotis, however, in the context of his religious-philosophical thinking, does not seem to drift in the hetero-identification of the theological understanding of man by projecting on the Christian understanding and description of man various philosophical readings of the mystery of the human existence. In my view, Nissiotis is not making the concept of the person a summary of his overall theological anthropology but a convenient means or instrument, from the standpoint of philosophy, for a hermeneutical meeting and dialogue with the secular intelligentsia, focusing particularly on epistemology. Therefore, "Orthodox theological epistemology is in a position to develop this theme in every direction and to find in the prolegomena of any separate science an actual contact point."[19]

Nissiotis and the '60s': continuity or discontinuity? A critical reflection

In assessing the contribution of N. Nissiotis to the contemporary Greek theological anthropological reflection, one should avoid hasty, or possibly misplaced, understandings. Nissiotis might fairly be described as the "father" of the so-called theological generation of the '60s in Greece[20] because of the direction he gave, not only in theological reflection by his pioneering critical import and reading of existentialism in the context of the modern Greek intelligentsia but also the agenda he rendered inevitable, which this generation also followed. In this light, I will explore the possible implicit or explicit relationship between Nissiotis and two of the most important representatives of this generation, namely Christos Yannaras and John D. Zizioulas, especially with regards to anthropology.

To summarize briefly how Yannaras and Zizioulas perceive the concept of personhood,[21] one could say that Zizioulas, on the one hand, seems to move between the two main pillars that constitute personhood – namely, communion – relationship and otherness, and while he attempts to balance them harmoniously, he eventually follows indirectly or directly either the first dimension (in his early work, until 1985) or the second (in his later work, culminating in the first chapter of *Communion & Otherness*, 2006, entitled "On Being Other"). Yannaras, on the other hand, seems to insist firmly on an almost exclusive equation of personhood with relation, which brings him closer to various existential philosophies. It seems that he limits the existential event in the tropical (tropos) aspect of relation so that the integrity and wholeness of existence is put into question. By widely approaching the work of these thinkers, one could argue that Yannaras follows Nissiotis, attempting a *philosophical* justification of personhood in the field of theology (by using the queries and the tools offered by the philosophy of M. Heidegger), without, however, taking seriously into account, as a *methodological* starting point, the incarnation of the Word and without being particularly interested in a historical, cosmological or even eschatological approach to the human being. At this point, Nissiotis will warn, "The faithful transposition of Heidegger's lessons in Christian theology, which is based on an historical event and the infinite value of this as a focus around which the whole history revolves [. . .] may have disastrous results."[22]

On the other hand, Zizioulas, by attempting a *theological* foundation in the patristic theology of the personalistic inheritance of personhood, although he reveals with particular emphasis the *cosmological* dimension in the understanding of human being as a *priest of creation*,[23] seems not to take seriously into account Nissiotis's attempted critical correction of existentialism, pointing once, perhaps unconsciously, to an *ahistorical* and *abstract* view of the human being, denouncing more or less the *natural* foundation of personal existence. In this perspective, John Zizioulas will adopt, despite his recent corrective efforts,[24] a rather problematic dialectical relation of *necessity* (nature) and *freedom* (personhood),[25] as a hermeneutical key to his personalistic vision, both in the created and the uncreated realms – a perspective that is not evident, in my view, in Nissiotis's work.[26]

Both the theological thinkers of the '60s seem to adopt a more or less exclusively *ontological* approach to personhood, which limits in both of them, each to a different extent and in different ways, the *ontological* question about the existential event, on the *tropos* ($\pi\tilde{\omega}\varsigma\ \dot{\varepsilon}\sigma\tau\iota\nu$, how) and less on the logos ($\tau\acute{\iota}\ \dot{\varepsilon}\sigma\tau\iota\nu$, what) of being.[27] The fundamental priority of existence against essence, evident in existentialism,[28] finds here a proper fertilization field, although it seems not to be justified in various aspects of patristic thought, presupposed in such a reading. In any case, while Nissiotis seems to refer primarily to the concrete historical human person and surely not to a theoretical or abstract contemplation about the *meaning* of personhood (in other words his perspective focuses on the salvific events and not only or primarily on the divine names),[29] the representatives of the generation of the '60s, despite their sometimes surprising reflections within the overall theological renaissance of their time in Greece, do not always avoid the risk of limiting the debate to a purely theoretical level, without the necessary link with the *ethical* (or in other words "political"), inter alia, effects of their theological or philosophical understanding of personhood. Therefore, the whole issue of the way

Zizioulas and Yannaras understand ontology, primarily the relationship of ontology with history, or even in the Christian understanding of the latter, as a "history of salvation" becomes an extremely urgent methodological question with regard to the very Christian character of Orthodox theology.[30]

At the same time, while Nissiotis does not seem to understand the relationship between *God* and *the human being* through the prism of a vertical and direct reduction, *remoto Christo*, this is not the case with Yannaras especially and less so in Zizioulas. It appears that, through a careful study of their work, their understanding of the human being as personhood images directly, without a solid or always clear Christological mediation, the archetypal mode of existence of the Trinitarian persons, manifested most directly and immediately in the Eucharist event. In this perspective, this last condition (the most widely sacramental and especially Eucharistic – i.e., the experience and emergence of the personal existential mode), although implied, is not sufficiently developed in the context of the anthropological work of Nissiotis, leaving thus outstanding the question about the specific place (the Body of Jesus Christ or the general history of the world) where the transformation of the human being is occurring henceforth. Moreover, it could be argued that this sacramental failure leaves pending the appropriate foundation of the importance of *repentance*, which is pre-conditioned in any synergetic transformation of human existence. It is in this respect where, in my view, the most serious problem in Nissiotis's theological anthropology comes to the fore – namely, the risk of understanding the path of human being toward *theosis*, or deification as an *a priori* prescribed evolution, which constitutes a natural condition, inherent in human existence, which moves ultimately deterministically by virtue of a protological creative energy of God, toward the emergence of its truth. In this case, moreover, one might ask, what is the role played in their entirety of the concrete salvific events of the "mystery of Christ" (Incarnation, Passion, Resurrection, Ascension), to the extent that on the one hand the Incarnation appears isolated from the whole paschal mystery, while on the other, the Resurrection does not entail any ontological "deterioration" in the human being, which moves towards "likeness"?

Despite the pending questions, however, it is obvious that Nissiotis's *anthropological – cosmological* perspective, although initially oriented to ontology, is not solely grounded in the latter so that the rupture between ontology and ethics or ontology and history is finally avoided. An allergy to *ethics* observed in eminent thinkers of the theological generation of the '60s (more in Yannaras,[31] less in Zizioulas)[32] does not find sufficient proportion in Nissiotis's work, who since his early career does not forget to bind his anthropological perspective to history and the particular human being who acts within the respective historical context. This should also not be considered irrelevant to his dynamic understanding of personhood in contrast to its passive foundation in the perspective of Yannaras and Zizioulas, where man becomes personhood by simply participating in the very Trinitarian life at the Eucharistic community, more or less regardless of the overall network of natural and historical relations, which threaten, rather than constitute, its personal identity.

In this perspective, by virtue of the study of Nissiotis's anthropological thought, the once common, with the necessary adjustments, orientation of his personalism toward its encounter with the broader (cf. "secular"), anthropological reflection emerges – a fact that is particularly relevant in the work of John Zizioulas. It is clear that both intellectuals attempt to address, albeit in different ways, the anthropological questions posed by modern existential philosophy, and more widely, by science and culture (Darwinism, sociological and psychoanalytic science, sports, etc.). It is obvious that both Nissiotis and Zizioulas wish to "correlate" the evangelical message by means of a particular understanding of personhood to the urgent existential needs and quests of (post) modern human beings by attempting thus a "translation" of the gospel. Although, however, there seems to be a common perspective in this context, the conditions and the starting point of the relevant reflection differentiate significantly, as we have seen in the two thinkers. At the same time, Yannaras, for his part, does not seem to follow this line, being unable to overcome a culturalistic orientation in doing theology (cf. the East-West bipolarization,[33] the claim for the continuity of Greek culture from antiquity, through the ecclesiastical tradition, until today), insisting, finally, on demonstrating the importance of the ecclesial-cultural experience as the ultimate criterion of his view on personhood.[34]

One of the areas where there appears to be a link between Nissiotis and the representatives of the theology of the '60s, especially Zizioulas, is theological epistemology. It is well known that Zizioulas highlights the importance of knowledge "in person" in the context of theological epistemology in that, as a result of the intra-Trinitarian relationships involved in the Eucharistic community (he will refer to an "epistemological revolution"), "personal knowledge exists only on the horizon of relations" and is not dependent on physical presence, while "it is always free" from any precondition.[35] Yannaras, on the other hand, by adopting the famous fourteenth-century Palamite divine essence-energies distinction[36] as his basic epistemological method of accessing the apophatic mystery of God, speaks of a "participation" in the divine energies and knowledge of the personal mode of existence, which is also presumed empirically by the personal human existence.[37] It is obvious that the "in person" knowledge, when understood as knowledge resulting from the "communion of persons," is a common, despite the differences, epistemological dimension in all the thinkers under discussion. In this case, Zizioulas (less than Yannaras) ascribes a sacramental character to this type of knowledge to the extent that the Eucharist constitutes the *locus* of the coexistence of the persons, an underdeveloped dimension in Nissiotis's work. It is worth noting at this point that Yannaras describes Nissiotis's book entitled *Prolegomena to the Theological Epistemology* as a "landmark of the theological change in Greece," which offers "criteria of theological orthodoxy."[38] In his brief, however, and rather laudatory reference to Nikos Nissiotis, it is not possible to locate an unconditional adoption by the latter of an absolute understanding of the essence-energies distinction as the only legitimate approach to God. Obviously, something that goes rather unnoticed, although observed by Yannaras himself, is that the focus in Nissiotis's theological epistemology is primarily located in the incarnation of the Word in history and certainly not as it is stated as a brief commentary in the "participation of the human being in repentance in the Energy of the divine Essence."[39]

Finally, another point that seems to present certain continuity between Nissiotis's understanding of personhood and theologians of the generation of the '60s is the common attempt, in all three, of overcoming the individualism or collectivism as various deductions of the personal mode of existence of human being. Insofar as Zizioulas will emphasize the importance of communion and Yannaras will identify the person with the relation, the emergence of trans-subjectivity in Nissiotis's perspective cannot but be a key point of the relative perspective in the context of the Greek theological and philosophical thought.

By way of conclusion

Nissiotis's rich theological and philosophical heritage, especially in the anthropological field, still remains largely understudied. His initially biblical, Christocentric, and philosophically personalistic perspective and contribution to the theological and philosophical discussion about human identity invites and challenges us today in a century where anthropology is at the heart of theological and philosophical thought.[40] Contemporary Orthodox theology should reflect carefully on the truth and intentionality of the human phenomenon by staying close to the challenges and needs of postmodern man and the world. Undoubtedly, the theological generation of the '60s is rooted in Nissiotis, who by his pioneering work largely determined the relevant agenda. At the same time, however, theologians and intellectuals of the same generation followed their own path – a development that highlighted the similarities (continuity) but also the differences (discontinuity) between Nissiotis and his companions.

Notes

1 For a comprehensive presentation of his personality, see, for instance, Stransky et al. (1996); Begzos (2015a). For his publications, see Begzos (1994), pp. 17–31 and more recently Begzos (2015b).
2 For a first general evaluation of this pioneer generation of theologians, intellectuals, and spiritual thinkers who mainly under the influence of Russian émigré thought sought the renewal of Greek Orthodox theology on the basis of the patristic tradition, see Kalaitzidis et al. (eds.) (2009).
3 Begzos (2004); Begzos (1991). Cf. Also the collective volume Begzos (1994).
4 Nissiotis (1956), pp. 5–6.
5 Begzos (1991).
6 Nissiotis (1956), p. 5.
7 Cf. Taylor (1992).
8 In this perspective, see Asproulis (2016).
9 Nissiotis (1982), p, 947.
10 Gibellini (2002), pp. 103–29. Cf. Kelsey (2005); Loomer (1956).
11 Begzos (1991).
12 Nissiotis (1996), p. 19.
13 Nissiotis (1996), p. 23.

14 This *dynamic* understanding of personhood can be compared to his "dynamic" ecclesiology in the sense that the (Orthodox) Church cannot be understood as a self-referent and closed reality but as an open one to a lasting relationship with other Christian Churches and traditions and culture in general. In my view, this particular personalistic vision seems to be the presupposition of the related ecclesiological perspective developed within the context of the rich experience of Nissiotis in the Ecumenical Movement. For this understanding of his ecclesiology, cf. Tsombanidis (2013).
15 Nissiotis (2006), pp. 252–58 (in Greek).
16 Toward the recognition of the importance of the psychological world of man seems to be moving inter alia, the work entitled *Psychology of Religion*, posthumously published, and includes his lectures on the topic: Nissiotis (2006).
17 Nissiotis (1965a), p. 44, where he draws on Polanyi (1958).
18 Nissiotis (1965a), p. 45.
19 Nissiotis (1965a), p. 46.
20 See n. 2 and also Kalaitzidis (2014).
21 For J. D. Zizioulas, See Zizioulas (1985), Zizioulas (2006), Zizioulas (2010), and Zizioulas (2013a). For Christos Yannaras, See Yannaras (2008), Yannaras (1984), Yannaras (2011).
22 Nissiotis (1956), p. 182.
23 Zizioulas (2011).
24 Cf. Zizioulas (2013a).
25 Cf. Zizioulas (2013a). For a critical evaluation of the use of this dialectic in Zizioulas work, see Farrow (2007), pp. 109–23.
26 It is noteworthy, however, that Zizioulas in his early work (in his dissertation of 1965) draws from Nissiotis in order to explain the way that he understands personhood in relation to individual. See Zizioulas (2001), p. 32 (n.31). Cf. also Zizioulas (1988).
27 Cf. Loudovikos (2013) and Pinakoulas (2013).
28 N. Nissiotis (1956), p. 156.
29 Agoras (2009).
30 See my book review: Asproulis (2015).
31 Zoumboulakis (2009).
32 Cf. Zizioulas (2013b), as well as his eco-theological studies. See note 23.
33 It is noteworthy to mention here Nissiotis's critical response to Yannaras's argument presented in the *Greek Orthodox Theological Review* on "Orthodoxy and the West": Nissiotis (1972). Nissiotis strongly criticizes Yannaras for various generalizations, radical dichotomies, and one-sideness in his understanding of the Western theological and philosophical tradition, counter-arguing thus for the need of a constant and deep dialogue between East and West.
34 Cf. for instance Kalaitzidis (2013); Petra (2013).
35 Zizioulas (2008), pp. 24–8.
36 The divine essence (God's *ousia*) – divine energies (activities) distinction is a central principle of Eastern Orthodoxy. A doctrine that, although already found in the Cappadocians, has been chiefly popularized by St. Gregory Palamas. By this real and not merely conceptual distinction, the Orthodox maintain that while God's essence (God's very life *ad intra*) as uncreated is inaccessible and incomprehensible *in toto* by the creatures, this is not the case with energies (God's activities *ad extra*), which as uncreated belong to the divine being, but they are radiated to the Creation, being experienced and participated by human beings. For an overall historic and systematic discussion of this distinction, see Lossky (1997); Yannaras (1991), pp. 26–31, 42–5; Ware (1975); Contos (1967), pp. 283–94; Torrance (2009). See also the still classic work on Palamas' thought, Meyendorff (1959) and Yannaras (1975), pp. 232–45.
37 Cf. for instance, Yannaras (2007), pp. 83ff.
38 Yannaras (1999), p. 451.

39 Compare Yannaras (1999), p. 453, to Nissiotis (1965b), p. 76.
40 Ware (2012), pp. 25ff.

Select bibliography

Agoras, K. (2009), "Nature and Personhood, History and Eschata in John Zizioulas and Christos Yannaras: Eucharistic Hermeneutics and Cultural Hermeneutics in theology" in Kalaitzidis et al. (eds.) (2009), pp. 165–234 (in Greek).

Asproulis, N. (2015), "Review of: J. Zizioulas *Communion & Otherness*, T&T Clark, Edinburg 2006," *Orthodoxes Forum* 29.2, pp. 213–16.

Asproulis, N. (2016), "Creation, History and the Church. Towards an Orthodox Eco-Theology and Social Ethics," in D. Werner and E. Geglitza (eds.), *Ecotheology, Climate Justice and Food Security*, Geneva, pp. 187–208.

Begzos, M. (1991), *The Word as Dialogue. A Nikos Nissiotis Portrait*, Thessaloniki (in Greek).

Begzos, M. (1994), *Nikos A. Nissiotis. Religion, Philosophy and Sport in Dialogue*, Athens.

Begzos, M. (2004), "Nikos Nissiotis' portrait (1924–1986)," in N. Nissiotis (ed.), *From Existence to Co-Existence. Society, Technology, Religion*, Athens, pp. 243–9 (in Greek).

Begzos, M. (2015a), "Nikos Nissiotis," *Religion Past and Present*, Brill Online, http://referenceworks.brillonline.com/entries/religion-past-and-present/nissiotis-nikos-SIM_124120.

Begzos, M. (2015b), "Bibliography," in K. Vamvakas (ed.), *Nikos Nissiotis, The Theologian of Dialogue*, Athens, pp. 113–34 (in Greek).

Contos, L. C. (1967), "The Essence-Energies Structure of Saint Gregory Palamas With a Brief Examination of Its Patristic Foundation," *The Greek Orthodox Theological Review* 12.3, pp. 283–94.

Demacopoulos, G. and Papanikolaou, A. (eds.) (2013), *Orthodox Constructions of the West*, New York.

Farrow, D. (2007), "Person and Nature: The Necessity-Freedom Dialectic in John Zizioulas," in D. Knight (ed.), *The Theology of John Zizioulas: Personhood and the Church*, Farnham, pp. 109–23.

Gibellini, R. (2002), *20th Century Theology*, trans. P. Ifantis, Athens (in Greek).

Kalaitzidis, P. (2013), "The Image of the West in Contemporary Greek Theology," in Demacopoulos and Papanikolaou (eds.) (2013), pp. 142–60.

Kalaitzidis, P. (2014), "New Trends in Greek Orthodox Theology: Challenges in the Movement Towards a Genuine Renewal and Christian Unity," *Scottish Journal of Theology* 67.2, pp. 127–64.

Kalaitzidis, P. et al. (eds.) (2009), *Turmoil in Post War theology. 'The Theology of the '60s'*, Athens.

Kelsey, D. (2005), "Paul Tillich," in D. Ford (ed.), *The Modern Theologians: An Introduction to Christian Theology in the Twentieth Century*, Oxford, pp. 62–75.

Loomer, B. (1956), "Tillich's Theology of Correlation," *Journal of Religion* 36.3, pp. 150–56.

Lossky, V. (1997), *The Mystical Theology of the Eastern Church*, Crestwood NY.

Loudovikos, N. (2013), "Possession or Wholeness? St. Maximus the Confessor and John Zizioulas on Person, Nature and Will," *Participatio* 4, pp. 258–86.

Meyendorff, J. (1959), *Introduction à l'étude de Grégoire Palamas*, Paris.

Nissiotis, N. (1956), *Existentialism and Christian Faith According to Soren Kierkegaard and the Modern Existential Philosophers Karl Jaspers, Martin Heidegger και Jean-Paul Sartre*, Athens.

Nissiotis, N. (1965a), *Philosophy of Religion and Philosophical Theology. Reflections on the Position of Philosophy Within Systematic Theology*, Athens.
Nissiotis, N. (1965b), *Prolegomena to Theological Epistemology*, Athens.
Nissiotis, N. (1972), "Orthodox and the West: A Response," *Greek Orthodox Theological Review* 17 (1972), pp. 132–42.
Nissiotis, N. (1982), "Secular and Christian Images of the Human Person," *Theologia* 53, pp. 947–89.
Nissiotis, N. (1996), "From the Consciousness – Through Conscious Alienation – to Identity," *Synaxis* 59, pp. 19–33 (in Greek).
Nissiotis, N. (2006), *Psychology of Religion*, Athens (in Greek).
Petra, B. (2013), "Christos Yannaras and the Idea of 'Dysis,'" in Demacopoulos and Papanikolaou (eds.) (2013), pp. 161–80.
Pinakoulas, A. (2013), "Eucharist and Ethics," in S. Zoumboulakis (ed.), *The Return of Ethics. Old and New Questions* Athens, pp. 180–205 (in Greek).
Polanyi, M. (1958), *Personal Knowledge: Towards a Post-Critical Philosophy*, Chicago IL.
Stransky, T. et al. (1996), "Three Sketches," *The Ecumenical Review* 48.4, pp. 466–75.
Taylor, C. (1992), *Sources of the Self. The Making of Modern Identity*, Cambridge MA.
Torrance, A. (2009), "Precendents for Palamas's Essence-Energy theology in the Cappadocian Fathers," *Vigiliae Christianae* 63, pp. 47–70.
Tsombanidis, S. (2013), "The dynamic ecclesiology of Nikos Nissiotis," forthcoming in the Proceedings "Theological Portraits II: Nikos Nissiotis, The ecumenical theologian of Orthodoxy," organized by the Volos Academy for Theological Studies in Volos, Greece, April 2013 (courtesy of the author, in Greek).
Vasiljević, M. (ed.) (2013), *Knowing the Purpose of Everything through the Resurrection: Proceedings of the Symposium on St Maximus the Confessor, Belgrade, October, 18–21, 2012*, Alhambra and Belgrade.
Ware, K. (1975), "God Hidden and Revealed: The Apophatic Way and the Essence-Energies Distinction," *Eastern Churches Review* 7, pp. 125–36.
Ware, K. (2012), *Orthodox Theology in the 21st Century*, Geneva.
Yannaras, C. (1975), "The Distinction Between Essence and Energies and Its Importance for Theology," *St. Vladimir's Theological Quarterly* 19, pp. 232–45.
Yannaras, C. (1984), *The Freedom of Morality*, Crestwood NY.
Yannaras, C. (1991), *Elements of Faith*, Edinburgh.
Yannaras, C. (1999), *Orthodoxy and the West*, Athens (in Greek).
Yannaras, C. (2007), *On the Absence and Unknowability of God: Heidegger and the Areopagite*, London.
Yannaras, C. (2008), *Person and Eros*, Brookline MA.
Yannaras, C. (2011), *Relational Ontology*, Brookline MA.
Zizioulas, J. D. (1985), *Being as Communion: Studies in Personhood and the Church*, Crestwood NY.
Zizioulas, J. D. (1988), "Nikos Nissiotis' Contribution to Contemporary Theological Thought," *Anisixies* 35, pp. 12–15 (in Greek).
Zizioulas, J. D. (2001), *Eucharist, Bishop, Church. The Unity of the Church in the Divine Eucharist and the Bishop During the First Three Centuries*, Brookline MA.
Zizioulas, J. D. (2006), *Communion & Otherness*, ed. Paul McPartlan, London.
Zizioulas, J. D. (2008), *Lectures in Christian Dogmatics*, ed. D. Knight, London.
Zizioulas, J. D. (2010), *The One and the Many. Studies on God, Man, the Church, and the World Today*, ed. Gregory Edwards, Alhambra CA.
Zizioulas, J. D. (2011), *The Eucharistic Communion and the World*, ed. Luke Ben Tallon, London.

Zizioulas, J. D. (2013a), "Person and Nature in the Theology of St. Maximus the Confessor," in Vasiljević (ed.) (2013), pp. 85–113.
Zizioulas, J. D. (2013b), "Ontology and Ethics," *Frear* 3, pp. 275–86 (in Greek).
Zoumboulakis, S. (2009), "The Journal *Sinoro* and Christos Yannaras: The Theological Proposal of the De-Ethicalization of Christianity," in Kalaitzidis et al. (eds.) (2009), pp. 315–26 (in Greek).

12 Eastern Christian conceptions of personhood and their political significance

Nicolas Prevelakis

To the extent that Eastern Christianity had dealt with personhood before modernity, it had seldom connected this discussion with political questions. This seems to be true throughout the history of Eastern Christian thought, even if, as we shall see, there have been notable exceptions – that is, cases where authors attempted to draw explicit connections between the ways in which they understood personhood and the kind of political arrangements that they thought were consistent with it. The kind of implications that will be discussed in this chapter have to do with the ways in which contemporary Orthodox theology has dealt with modern political ideas in a way that derives from, and attempts to do justice to, its understanding of personhood.

Generally speaking, most modern questions and concepts of political theory were developed first in Western Europe and later introduced in the Orthodox world. This is particularly true of ideas such as the nation-state, liberal democracy, citizenship, pluralism, the idea of a secular space for politics, pluralism, or human rights. All these notions, but most importantly the legal-institutional arrangements that reflect them, were introduced in the Eastern Christian world after the Enlightenment and in large part through the formation of modern nation-states.

There are many narratives about the origins of modernity in the historical and social-scientific literature. One of them is the view that various developments in the West (the Enlightenment, industrialization, modern capitalism) challenged the all-encompassing religious structure of society, which Peter Berger referred to as a "Sacred Canopy,"[1] signaled the appearance of a secular sphere and led to the emergence of the individual as the source of political authority. Some of these narratives see the origins of these developments (secularization, modern capitalism) in the religious history of the West. I am referring, in particular, to the work of Max Weber, in the "Protestant Ethic and the Spirit of Capitalism"[2] or in his "Religious Rejections of the World and their Consequences."[3] To be fair, Max Weber never made a unilinear causal claim, and perhaps no causal claim, at all. His main argument was that there has been, historically, an elective affinity between specific branches of Protestantism and a certain kind of rationalism, which came to prevail in the West.

As pointed out by Vasilios Makrides, within this framework, Orthodox Christianity has often been understood as having had little affinity with modern rationalism.[4] Some scholars have even seen this lack of affinity as an explanation for an alleged reluctance of "Orthodox" countries to modernize. For instance, Samuel Huntington, in his famous *The Clash of Civilizations*, sees the Orthodox world as relatively distinct from the West and its central values.[5]

But while Huntington did not really engage with theology, much less with personhood, other authors have attempted to do so. One such example is that of the well-known psychoanalyst and literary critic Julia Kristeva.

In the midst of the Yugoslav war, when the Western world was trying to understand the mechanisms that brought about the massacres of Sarajevo and Srebrenica, the French newspaper *Le Monde* published an article by Julia Kristeva entitled "The Mysterious Weight of Orthodoxy."[6] Kristeva's argument was that one of the keys to understanding Serbian violence was Serbia's Orthodox legacy. Kristeva's point is that Orthodox theology, more specifically the Orthodox understanding of the Holy Trinity, reflects an understanding of human psychology that bears the seeds of permissiveness and violence on the one hand and of totalitarianism on the other. For that reason, according to the author, the Orthodox churches have been widely instrumentalized by political forces, by the Byzantine Empire in the past, and by nationalism in the present. Kristeva opposes this theological tradition to Western theology, allegedly more prone to the promotion of individualistic societies.

Kristeva suggested that Europe was "facing a difference of cultures, if not an abyss between them, that our hasty universalism would have preferred to ignore." According to her analysis, this difference expresses a "lack of understanding between two confluents of European civilization." The war of Kosovo, therefore, "shows a division of Europe which goes back to the Great Schism of 1054 between Byzantium and Rome, between orthodoxy and Catholicism." The mention of Orthodoxy and Catholicism is very significant. According to Kristeva, under "a secularity on the surface," "the war between Serbs and Kosovars is clandestinely religious," and therefore needs a "religious anthropology" in order to be properly understood. More specifically, what religious differences express is, for Kristeva, different "states of mind." These states of mind are, in turn, differences in peoples' fundamental psychology, which acquire political significance when

> the peoples who wish to integrate tomorrow in an enlarged Europe throw to each other their specific and latent conception of the individual, in the form of conflicts which present themselves (at worse) as religious wars or (at best!) as gravities, incompatibilities which cannot be overcome.

What are these different "conceptions of the individual" that separate the post-Byzantine from the post-Roman world? For Kristeva, the first difference is that, contrary to the West, in which ecclesiastical and political powers were apparently separated, "Orthodoxy" had a "tendency" toward "political instrumentalization, which begins much before the Great Schism of 1054." Kristeva defines "political instrumentalization" as "the ecclesiastical dependency vis-à-vis political power, which has often degenerated into effacement, if not into pure submission." This Orthodox "tendency," according to Kristeva, is what accounts for the contemporary "osmosis between faith and nationalism" inside the "different national Churches – Russian, Greek, Bulgarian, Serbian, Romanian, etc."

Kristeva derives the alleged Orthodox tendency toward "political instrumentalization" from the way the Holy Trinity is understood in Orthodox theology and which, apparently, can best be understood by an "an analytical approach," which could grasp "the psychic dynamics of the subject which is constituted in the Orthodox Trinity, as well as its consequences for the objects of desire and of thought." According to Kristeva,

> The Holy Spirit proceeds from the Father via the Son for the Orthodox ("Per Filium"); the Holy Spirit proceeds from the Father and the Son for the Catholics ("Filioque"). While the Catholic "and" puts Father and Son in equality, and pre-figures the autonomy of the person (that of the Son, as well as that of the faithful) and opens the way to western individualism and personalism, the orthodox "via" suggests a delicious but pernicious annihilation of the Son and the faithful.

Using psychoanalytical terms, Kristeva can therefore write that the psychological effect of Orthodoxy is to stop the process of "individuation" and thus render possible "the expression of more ancient psychic stromata, those of masochism and pre-oedipal depression."

Kristeva's argument is open to many criticisms. First, it is not clear how it avoid the traps of essentialism and anachronism, since they rely on theological debates of fourth-century Byzantium in order to understand political behaviors in late twentieth-century Yugoslavia, as if there was, across these very different situations, a common essence of Orthodoxy that could account for them. Second, even though it is true that religion was instrumentalized during the Yugoslav conflict, this is arguably because religious affiliation has been used as national demarcation – and not because the Serbian authorities had any real interest for, much less engagement with, Orthodox dogma. Third, while it is true that there had been, in Byzantium, a tradition of what some historians have called "caesaropapism," the historical record is arguably more complicated than the way in which Kristeva portrays it and points at numerous cases of tension that appeared early on in Byzantine history, from Athanasius to John Chrysostom.[7]

Pointing out the difficulties of these analyses is, however, not enough. While generalizing arguments of this sort are to be examined with caution, the issue of the kind of elective affinity that may or may not exist between the ways in which Eastern Christianity has understood human personhood and various ethical and political notions of today is important and, to a certain extent, inescapable.

In fact, the question of personhood in Eastern Christianity, its relationship to that of the "West" and its ethical and political implications, have become some of the major topics of Eastern Christian thought since the second decade of the twentieth century. These questions have their roots in the writings of French theologian Theodore de Régnon who, in his *Etudes the théologie positive sur la sainte Trinité*,[8] posited a difference in the ways in which Greek and Latin Church Fathers have approached the relationship between divine essence and divine personhood. According to de Régnon, while the Latin Fathers started from the divine essence and deduced the three Persons, which they saw as internal relations of that essence, the Greeks started from the persons and saw in the divine essence the common nature of these persons. Vladimir Lossky, a Russian theologian who had immigrated to Paris, in his *Essai sur la théologie mystique de l'Eglise d'Orient*, used this analysis to argue that, while the Latin Fathers gave emphasis to the divine *essence*, the Greek Fathers gave emphasis to the *persons* and that their theology was therefore, in a sense, closer to the modern understanding of personhood, understood in terms of freedom and uniqueness, than the Latin one.[9] The idea of an absolute monarchy of the Father, which Kristeva interprets as stopping the process of individuation, is interpreted by Lossky as the very affirmation of the uniqueness of the person and its irreducibility to a divine "essence." According to Lossky, it is therefore the Western conception of the Trinity that emphasizes the divine essence at the expense of personhood, and it is the East, with its emphasis on the monarchy of the Father, that is personalistic. Influenced by Lossky, as well as by such currents as French personalism and existentialism, Greek Orthodox theologian and philosopher Christos Yannaras will later develop the idea that the Greek approach to the Trinity has affinities with modern existentialism, since it sees the person as irreducible to an essence, and thus as being radically free.[10] In the same line of thought, Greek Orthodox theologian John Zizioulas even argued that the Father is the cause of God's existence, that His existence is an act of free choice.[11]

Because of their emphasis on the notion of personhood, the current of thought developed by Lossky, Zizioulas, and Yannaras has often been referred to as Orthodox "personalism." While far from being universally accepted by Orthodox thinkers,[12] it has been extremely influential throughout the twentieth century and has, to a large extent, shaped the way in which Eastern Christianity has come to understand itself.

The theological positions of these authors have led them to different anthropological and political conclusions. For instance, while Lossky has been quite reluctant in drawing parallels between divine and human personhood,[13] Yannaras has often used insights from the "existentialism" of Orthodox Trinitarian thought to draw conclusions about human affairs. Yannaras has seen, for instance, the relations between divine Persons as a model of human relations, and has used the idea of the Trinity, in which persons only exist in relations, to criticize modern individualism, which he sees as one of the most negative features of modern society.

This sort of personalism has also been associated with different philosophical, historical, and political positions. In Greece, Yannaras engaged in a dialogue between Orthodoxy and Marxism; his thought was compared to "liberation theology,"[14] but Orthodox personalism also led to a sort of communitarianism in which many have seen a form of Greek nationalism. Orthodox personalism has taken the form of an engagement with modern Western philosophical movements, such as Marxism, personalism, and existentialism, and in that sense has helped modern Orthodoxy open itself to the modern world; at the same time, critics have pointed out that it has also led to the idea of a sharp dichotomy between Orthodox Christianity and the West, a rejection of the West, and thus an Orthodox isolationism.

The moral and political implications of Eastern Christian personalism are far from being self-evident. In the rest of this chapter, I will focus on one particular issue: that of human rights. There are three reasons for this. The first is that this is a relatively circumscribed, and therefore manageable, question. The second is that there have been at least two important books in the last decade specifically dealing with the connection between modern human rights and Eastern Christian understanding of personhood. I am referring to Christos Yannaras's *The Inhumanity of Rights (Η απανθρωπία του δικαιώματος)*[15] and to Aristotle Pananikolaou's *The Mystical as Political. Democracy and Non-Radical Orthodoxy.*[16] The third is that the two aforementioned authors, while sharing similar theological and anthropological views, differ in their overall analysis. Yannaras sees human rights as fundamentally incompatible with Eastern Christian notions of personhood, whereas Pananikolaou, while raising some reservations, thinks that they are.

The issue of human rights is extremely important in today's world. The language of human rights is dominant in modern international politics and, to a large extent, frames the way in which we understand ourselves in the world. They are an important aspect of what Durkheim called the modern "cult of the individual."[17] Marx criticized the French declaration of the Rights of Man and of the Citizen for being egoistic, and for serving the interests of a specific class.[18] Other authors have questioned whether human rights are truly universal and objective, or whether they express the subjectivity and values of a specific culture.

While it is obviously impossible to summarize the works of Yannaras and Papanikolaou in such a small space, I will attempt to point out what I think are the central elements of their argumentations for our discussion.

Yannaras makes the following claims:

> First, Eastern Christian understanding of personhood is based on the idea of relation and that this understanding is at odds with the individualism of human rights. At the level of society, Yannaras argues, Eastern Christianity focuses on the idea of communion, while the philosophy of human rights sees society as a sum of self-enclosed, and only superficially related, individuals.
>
> Second, according to Yannaras, the roots of this individualism are to be found in the Middle Ages, when religious institutions provided an authoritative institutional and ideological framework for human coexistence. The way religious institutions did this, according to Yannaras, was by appealing to metaphysical dogmas as the foundation for morality. For Yannaras, the notion of natural rights, which later led to human rights, emerged mainly as a reaction to this framework. It replaced religious authority with the authority of the rational individual and considered that this would be sufficient to provide moral foundations for society. Human rights are thus inherently individualistic.

Yannaras's critique cannot be separated from his broader philosophical project, which is to make the category of relation central not only in human personhood but also in theology (through his analysis of divine personhood), metaphysics (through his idea of an ontology of relation), and epistemology (by insisting that truth is not to be understood as "adequatio intellectus rei" but as inherently linked to inter-subjectivity). His critique of human rights is thus part of a broader critique of modernity and its tendency to separate (individuals from each other, humanity from transcendence, and reason from communion).

Papanikolaou, on the other hand, has a very different evaluation of human rights. He sees them as fundamentally compatible with an Eastern Christian conception of personhood, stressing, for instance, the notion of human dignity, a central element in both Christian conceptions of personhood (and directly linked to the idea of man as "imago Dei") and in most current understandings of human rights.

As said before, it is interesting that Papanikolaou bases his anthropology on very similar premises to those of Yannaras. For Papanikolaou, an Orthodox understanding of personhood shares the following presuppositions: a) the possibility of human-divine communion (theosis), an important characteristic of Eastern Christian thought, which arguably found its clearest expression in the essence-energies distinction of Gregory Palamas; b) an emphasis on the uniqueness and the freedom of the human person; and c) an understanding of human personhood as fundamentally relational – i.e., defined by, and existing in, its relations (with others as well as with God).

Drawing explicitly on the work of Christos Yannaras, as well as John Zizioulas Papanikolaou writes,

> Although there has been much debate over the patristic pedigree of this theological notion of person, a convincing argument has yet to be put forth that would refute the understanding of divine-human communion as a relational event of love of God and love of neighbor in which a human being – and through the human, all of creation – is personalized, that is, constituted as irreducibly unique and ecstatic.[19]

Like Yannaras, Papanikolaou explains that these principles would be incompatible with the idea of human rights if human rights were to be understood as a) secular/atheistic and b) individualistic – that is, applying to man defined as an individual whose private sphere has to be systematically protected from the others. With this in mind, Papanikolaou's argument consists in challenging these claims.

Regarding the first one – that is, the alleged atheism of human rights, Papanikolaou makes a historical and a philosophical argument. Historically, he shows that, contrary to what is commonly believed, human rights were not initially conceived of as secular, but where formulated from within an explicitly religious perspective. Philosophically, he argues that human rights cannot be founded on reason alone and thus presuppose some transcendent foundation if they are to make sense at all.

Regarding the second point – i.e., the alleged individualism of human rights – Papanikolaou's thought is more complex. He acknowledges that human rights define a framework within which humans appear as separated entities who relate to each other legally and that this is very different from the Eastern Christian emphasis on communion. However, he sees this as a broader characteristic of human politics, which, given the imperfection of human nature, require arrangements that are very different from the kind of communal life the Church represents. He thus sees human rights as a "minimalist morality," rendered necessary by the fact that it is impossible to "sacramentalize in fullness the political."[20] And while agreeing that human rights do not reflect the full potential of Christian communion, he argues that, when implemented, they do shape a community in which Christian "ascetical struggle to love" is facilitated.[21]

Despite the strong disagreement on the surface, there are, I think, significant agreements between the two authors. First, while showing the compatibility between human rights discourse and Eastern Christian anthropology, Papanikolaou is very careful to show the limitations of this discourse. Toward the end of the chapter on human rights, he writes,

> The above endorsement of human rights seems half-hearted, but it must be conceded that the Orthodox resistance to human rights language contains a kernel of truth: there needs to be a greater recognition that human rights language cannot be so easily spliced onto Christian understandings of God and the human person, especially if the Christian God is one of incarnation and communion.[22]

While Papanikolaou's endorsement may seem, in his own words, "half-hearted," the same could be said about Yannaras's rejection of human rights. While raising significant concerns, Yannaras explicitly acknowledges that human rights are an important achievement – even while calling that achievement "pre-political." And while Yannaras's conception of the "political" (that is, of a political community defined by relations of communion) may seem utopian, his criticism of human rights is very different from radical contestations that may stem from moral relativism, or from a general defense of the collectivity against the individual.

It is important to point out that, to a certain extent, human rights discourse has tried to move away from the kind of individualism that its critiques have traditionally accused it of. For instance, the mention of "brotherhood" in the very first article of the United Nations Declaration of Human Rights, as well as the recent focus on cultural and collective rights, as well as the environment, may be seen as pointing in this direction. And in terms of philosophical foundations, the United Nations Declaration of Human Rights does not claim any other source except, perhaps, the "endowment of human beings with reason and conscience." The source of this endowment is not discussed, thus leaving room for both a secular and a religious interpretation.

What conclusions can one draw from this study? The first is that the notion of personhood still dominates most engagements of Eastern Christianity with modern political questions. The second is that there is significant divergence of opinions regarding the specific assessments so that one should be very careful not to see the social and political thought of Orthodox Christianity in monolithic terms. The third is that the Eastern Christian notion of personhood is often linked to a) a critique of individualism, b) the idea of a *personal* relation between God and the world, and c) the idea of a distinctive nature of Eastern Christianity vis-à-vis the West. To a certain extent, this conceptual framework informs the ways in which twentieth and twenty-first-century Eastern Orthodoxy has engaged not only with human rights but also with modernity more broadly.

Notes

1 Berger (1990).
2 Weber (2001).
3 Weber (1958).
4 Makrides (2005).
5 Huntington (2011).
6 Kristeva (1999); translation mine.
7 See Dagron (2007).
8 Régnon (1892, 1898).
9 See Lossky (1957), p. 57.
10 Yannaras (2008).
11 Zizioulas (1985), pp. 40–1.
12 See Halleux (1975); Larchet (2011); Torrance (2011).
13 So Lossky (1974), pp. 109–21.
14 Clément (1985).
15 Yannaras (2006).
16 Papanikolaou (2012).
17 Durkheim (1964), p. 407.
18 Marx (1843).
19 Papanikolaou (2012), pp. 113–14.
20 Papanikolaou (2012), p. 40.
21 Papanikolaou (2012), p. 130.
22 Papanikolaou (2012), p. 130.

Select bibliography

Berger, Peter (1990), *The Sacred Canopy. Elements of a Sociological Theory of Religion*, Anchor.
Clément, Olivier (1985), "Orthodox Reflections on 'Liberation Theology'," *St Vladimir's Theological Quarterly* 29.1, pp. 63–72.
Dagron, Gilbert (2007), *Emperor and Priest. The Imperial Office in Byzantium*, Cambridge.
Durkheim, Emile (1964), *The Division of Labor in Society*, New York.
Halleux, André de (1975), "Orthodoxie et Catholicisme : du personnalisme en pneumatologie," *Nouvelle Revue Théologique de Louvain* 1, pp. 3–30.
Huntington, Samuel (2011), *The Clash of Civilizations and the Remaking of World Order*, Simon & Shuster.
Kristeva, Julia (1999), "Le Poids mystérieux de l'Orthodoxie," *Le Monde*, 17 April 1999 (in French).
Larchet, Jean-Claude (2011), *Personne et nature. La Trinité–Le Christ-L'homme*, Paris.

Lossky, Vladimir (1957), *The Mystical Theology of the Eastern Church*, Cambridge and London.
Lossky, Vladimir (1974), *In the Image and Likeness of God*, New York.
Makrides, Vasilios (2005), "Orthodox Christianity, Rationalization, Modernization: A Reasssessment," in Victor Roudometov et al. (eds.), *Eastern Orthodoxy in a Global Age. Tradition Faces the Twenty-First Century*, Walnut Creek CA, pp. 179–209.
Marx, Karl. (1843), "On the Jewish Question," in R. Tucker (ed.), *The Marx-Engels Reader*, New York, pp. 26–46.
Papanikolaou, Aristotle (2012), *The Mystical as Political. Democracy and Non-Radical Orthodoxy*. Notre Dame IN.
Régnon, Théodore de (1892, 1898), *Etudes de théologie positive sur la Sainte Trinité*. Paris.
Torrance, Alexis (2011), "Personhood and Patristics in Orthodox Theology: Reassessing the Debate," *The Heythrop Journal* 52:4, pp. 700–7.
Weber, Max (1958), "Religious Rejections of the World and Their Directions," in *From Max Weber*, Oxford, pp. 323–59.
Weber, Max (2001), *The Protestant Ethic and the Spirit of Capitalism*, Routledge.
Yannaras, Chrestos (2006), *The Inhumanity of Rights*, Athens (in Greek).
Yannaras, Chrestos (2007), *Orthodoxy and the West*, Brookline MA.
Yannaras, Chrestos (2008), *Person and Eros*, Brookline MA.
Zizioulas, John (1985), *Being as Communion*, New York.

13 Consubstantial selves

A discussion between Orthodox personalism, existential psychology, Heinz Kohut, and Jean-Luc Marion

Nicholas Loudovikos

After the almost total fragmentation of human subjectivity, either *from above*, according to Jean-Michel Besnier's expression, through social sciences, or *from below* through psychology and neurobiology, foretold by Heidegger, and, in another way, also by Foucault, the question of the possibility for an ontology of subjectivity is almost explicitly raised again. The West desperately needs a new anthropology and contemporary philosophical and psychological quest have been trying over the last decades to advance beyond what Charles Taylor called *a detached self* – i.e., the transcendental subject of Western metaphysics.

I prefer to call this transcendental subject *the self-referring subject*. Born within Christian theology, when the gospel met Plotinian introversion in Augustine's thought, this self-referring subject described human essence as a willing thought, the image of a strongly introvert God, who unites Himself in the strong external acts of His will. This willing thought dominates what is not *spiritual* – i.e., human and worldly nature along with state and history – as I strove to show elsewhere.[1] Moreover, the self-referring subject did not initially lack divine participation, but when it was secularized step by step, through Descartes, Leibniz, and German Idealism, it became the modern "we-less I," according to Norbert Elias's fine expression,[2] and even a "worldless I," according to Fergus Kerr's expression.[3] This kind of subject creates only indirect relationships with beings outside itself, in the sense that the act of relating does not enter the very definition of selfhood, but follows as a possible choice, something that is made more decisively evident in Thomas Aquinas's thought. In order to understand this, we need to compare Maximus the Confessor's understanding of God's relation with creation with that of Aquinas. I mean the *immediacy of relation* between God and the world, or, better, the *immediate facing* of the world by God in Maximus. As I have claimed elsewhere,[4] this is a highly delicate point of the patristic doctrine of creation, related to the way the Areopagite has been understood in different theologico-philosophical traditions. There somehow exist, as I believe, two different ways of understanding the Dionysian metaphysics of creation in the fifth chapter of his *On the Divine Names*, where we read that

> the principles of things participate in being, and they first do so and then they exist as principles. And if you like, the principle of the living things as such is

self-life, and of similar things self-similarity, and of united things self-unity, and of ordered things, self-order.[5]

For a certain Western and more or less Thomist understanding of this passage, common in medieval as well as some modern theologians, these primary divine attributes marked by the initial prefix *self-* belong to the essence of God, if they are seen ontologically, but they also form *common natures* of sorts, which are participated in by the individual creatures in order for them to exist as such. This interpretation is not, of course, Platonic, although it seems perhaps at first sight to come very close to Platonism; what is meant here is not that those *common natures* are in a way separate beings such as *self-life, self-wisdom, self-goodness* etc., but that they are communions, participations, advances, preexisting in God as separate forms and ideas, according to which, in a second step, things are created through participation. However, Maximus seems to claim something even more profound when he writes, interpreting the Areopagite, "Since He is intellect, then indeed He thinks of entities inasmuch as He Is. *And if He thinks of entities in the process of thinking of Himself, then He is those entities.*" In consequence, "he thinks of entities inasmuch as He thinks of Himself, and is connected to what is innate to Him; for this intellection of His is the genesis of things that exist."[6] Beyond any objective and necessary existence of *logoi*, reminiscent of the Platonic ideas, Maximus accepts the term "ideas" for the *logoi*, interpreting them as "everlasting intellections" of the personal Word[7] – i.e., his "good wills" and his "divine purpose" for each separate created thing – into which He pours his "innate wisdom" and "innate life" through his *logoi*, thus demonstrating His good "preeternal intention."[8]

The difference between the two approaches seems worth noting, not because the first is wrong, as both traditions insist that God is participated in, but because the Maximian view seems to me closer to the deeper intentions of Areopagitic thought, since it reveals an impressive turn concerning *the immediacy of God's facing of creation*. Maximus seems to simply think that God does not need to think of whiteness, or goodness, or wisdom as sorts of common ideas of being when he wants to create white and good and wise creatures. Rather, as we saw earlier, his intellections are *immediately* existent things. The consequences of this position are enormously important. The divine *logoi* are much more immediate than any preexisting *common ideas*, precisely because they portray an incredibly spontaneous act of creation *in favor of creation*, an immediate explosion of love *giving selfhood(s) to nothingness*, without this sort of well-structured pre-thinking, a good preliminary study or premeditation of all possible inadequacies of his new enterprise. The world has been created, in a way, first and foremost, for its own sake: God here creates a primordial dialogical relationship with creation, through an *ecstasis* out and not of His essence, but of the exclusivity of His love for Himself. Furthermore, this is precisely the consequence of the rejection, made by the Bible, of any understanding of creation as *emanation* from the One, as this happens in Neoplatonism. Divine emanation means precisely lack of any possibility for real otherness/selfhood for the creature, while creation through the divine *logoi*/wills means creating an *antithesis* of the divine *thesis* – i.e., someone who can agree but also totally disagree with his Creator, to wit, an independent intention/selfhood.

Thomas concurs with the Greek Fathers in that creation means creating an otherness/selfhood outside God, but here this otherness/selfhood is not so clearly stressed as it is in Maximus[9] and Palamas,[10] and since God is the supreme being and the supreme good, it is impossible for Him to find something higher than Himself to love, and thus God's love is His self-love. Thus, according to Thomist thought, even our love for God is a limited participation in his infinite love for Himself. But thus a serious antinomy seems to exist between our natural love for ourselves and our love for God. Gilson, who notes the problem, gives also the Thomist answer to it: "Loving yourself means to love something analogous to God, and that means that finally you love God."[11] This sort of *erotic solipsism* (to love the other through loving yourself), common for both man and God, represents the peak of what I have called *the self-referring subject* earlier, although this will become manifest only after the modern secular revolution of "purely self-sufficient humanism," in Charles Taylor's words.[12]

***

This self-referring subject needed Marx to remind him of his forgotten roots in community, Darwin to remind him of his inextricable bonds with the natural world, and Freud to show him the limits of his conscious spirit, deeply undermined and determined by his unconscious substratum. What this sort of subject first and foremost lacks is *the other*, whether divine, human, or worldly: possessive, dominating, transcendental, and detached selfhood is formed through its will to power, without or before his relationship with the world. The end of this metaphysics of transcendental subjectivism comes nowadays with the end of the reign of the disembodied mind, as this end is described by modern neuropsychology and cognitive science, but also by the most significant part of modern depth psychology, along with phenomenology, which still prevails in contemporary philosophy, since both of them seek, successfully or not, to overcome this metaphysics of detached selfhood. It is perhaps the most important task of Orthodox theology today to decisively help toward this direction. To help, in other words, to construct a *nonmetaphysical* ontology of *selfhood*, since any *transcendental* metaphysics of personhood, either divine or human, seems totally absent from the Greek patristic theological horizon.

Speaking of modern Orthodox personalism, I have many times in the past stressed its positive aspects, some of which are the connection of personalism with Christology and Trinitarian theology, its connection with eschatology, ecclesiology, and theology of sacraments. But the crucial problem arises precisely here: do we understand the patristic concept of person as it really exists in patristic thought? There are two ways, as I think, to understand personhood, concerning Trinitarian theology, in the context of modern Orthodox theology. The first is exemplified by the foremost of its exponents as follows:

> Trinitarian freedom is, negatively speaking, freedom from the given and, positively, the capacity to be other while existing in relationship and in unity

of nature. In as much, therefore, as unity of nature provides sameness and wholeness, Trinitarian freedom, as the capacity to be other, can be spoken of as freedom from sameness. And in as much as otherness provides particularity, Trinitarian freedom can be spoken of as freedom from selfhood and individuality.[13]

Here nature (even divine nature) is a passive given of necessary sameness, which cannot *actively* be included in hypostatic otherness and which has to be escaped from through the "personal" capacity to be other. This ontological scheme seems Levinasian, not patristic: freedom from sameness/totality and then freedom from selfhood for the sake of the infinity/other. If we apply Ricoeur's criticism in relation to this scheme, we shall be forced to admit that this entails an even more decisive subjectivism, as it shows an initial will of self-enclosure and separation from the other (the "moment" of ecstasis from sameness) in order for the other to be understood as radical exteriority (the "moment" of "freedom from selfhood and individuality").[14] It is precisely this danger of an ecstatic and separated subjectivism that the patristic notion of the Trinitarian homoousion saves us from, as this subjectivism shows a subject who never really meets the other, as he, first, avoids the others' existence (ecstasis above sameness), and then he avoids his own existence (denial of selfhood) – in both cases, either the other is absent or the self is missing. On the other hand, not only Levinas, along with the Orthodox personalists noted earlier, but also even perhaps Ricoeur, cannot avoid self-enclosure, since they, and most of all the Orthodox personalists, embrace the other in the very moment they (and in order for them to) move toward the freedom from sameness. Thus, in that case, on the one hand, our understanding of person needs to detach it from the natural *atomon*, and, on the other hand, the other's otherness becomes a *dictated otherness*, as I have called it elsewhere.[15]

The other possible way of understanding personhood-in-communion, in the context of Orthodox theology, considers nature as actively included in Trinitarian personal communion. Thus, concerning divine essence, the Confessor avers, "Though it stays in immovable rest, the divine essence seems to move, moving toward each other" (*ἐν τῇ ἀλλήλοις χωρήσει*, where χωρώ is a verb meaning both *move* and *contain*).[16] This "movement" is called "convergence (*σύννευσις*) to the one, of those who originate from him," by Gregory Nazianzen.[17] So this is what homoousion is: a timeless intra-Trinitarian movement, as the affirmation, by the Son, of His nature as the Father's nature; an affirmation, by the Spirit, of His nature as the Father's nature; and a reciprocal affirmation by the Son and the Spirit of their essence as that of the Father, following timelessly the *causal* affirmation, made by the Father of his nature as the Son's and the Spirit's nature through *generation* and *ἐκπόρευσις* (procession). This reciprocal affirmation of nature as immovable movement – i.e., as *χώρησις* (movement toward and mutual containment) and *σύννευσις*/convergence between the three – is initiated by the Father: this is the principle of the Monarchy of the Father, on which we all agree; i.e., the Father's absolute *monocausality*, which, at the same "moment," timelessly, actively and not passively, is reciprocally affirmed by the two Others. This affirmation represents the intra-Trinitarian love – i.e., the *free natural dialogical reciprocity* between the three Persons, which can be also perhaps called *reciprocal intergivenness* – in the sense that it is a timeless reciprocal essential dialogue on the ontological level, constituting God's very mode of being. In this sense, it is absolutely wrong to interpret the homoousion as any sort of Hegelian *kenosis*, since it represents precisely the opposite, a timeless πλήρωσις (fullness) – i.e., the mutual dialogical affirmation/fulfillment of otherness on the level of nature, without which any "personal" otherness is a transcendental σχέσις (relation), or, better, a narcissistic, imaginary inclusion of the other in the agent's subjectivity. Thus the divine homoousion does not mean sameness, but a pre-eternally achieved and timeless reciprocal, interpersonal, essential χώρησις/movement, containing σύννευσις/convergence, or dialogical reciprocity, or, simply, inter-giveness. And it is of course senseless to think that the homoousion/consubstantiality, understood as it was understood earlier, occurs "before" the communion of the persons, thus forming a sort of "cause" of their communion: it is precisely this personal communion that occurs as consubstantiality.

***

But how is this ontology of persons in communion, based on consubstantiality, to be applied to creation? At this point, we need to explore the Areopagitic ecclesial ontology of charisms in order to show how we can articulate a full theory of consubstantial communion, where both selfhood and otherness coexist, mutually verifying the true being of a person, who is thus formed as, simultaneously, *participation and distribution.*[18] Thus, whereas in Proclus the sanctifying power of the orders depends in a pagan and naturalistic way on the ontological level that they occupy, in Dionysius, the purifying and illuminating activity of these orders depends absolutely on their participation in God, or rather it is God himself (in Christ) who brings about purification, illumination and perfection in the faithful through the agency of the hierarchic orders. This mode of operation of the superior orders "teaches [. . .] them to perform all the hierarchic functions *as if acting under God*, having him as their guide in all things as they accomplish their own functions."[19]

Each rank through God and in God is thus, for example, valid as a reference to the whole – each rank subsists and operates *with God* – that is to say, as a unified manifestation of the divine energy universalizing particular charisms. Each priestly rank thus presents, in each of its forms, the whole of God's universalizing act/energy: the hierarch presents the whole of the divine energy as perfecting; the priest, the whole of the divine energy as guiding by light/illuminating; and the deacon, the whole of the divine energy as purifying. Thus the whole of God is apparent by grace in each of the particular grades of each order, universalizing it, that is to say, making it in turn inclusive of the whole of ecclesial being in a specific manifestation, or rather, charism. Each charism, then, is an aspect of the whole of ecclesial being, in communion with the others, since it implies a deep communion of all of them in each one.

This means that the participatory aspect of selfhood, as a charism-bearer member of Christ's body, brings about the *distributive* aspect of this ecclesial constitution of selfhood. In other words, this constitution of the charisms of each order through participation is strengthened by the existential interior structure of the orders as reciprocally *gift-giving*. Each gift of grace that is received by each division of these orders is not received unless it can be presented anew to the other divisions. By each gift of grace, each rational division receives the same kenotic love of God, the whole of God as gift, which is preserved only under the condition that it will be handed on again and indeed as a catholic self-offering of each division to the other divisions and orders. This gift-receiving reciprocity ends up again eucharistically in its original gift-giver, who is God, creating, we can perhaps say, the fundamental pattern of an "Eucharistic ontology" of hierarchies and orders. Because each gift-receiving division receives the fullness of God's love eucharistically, it is this same fullness of divine love that it hands on itself in its turn, making a gift simultaneously of its own self to the other divisions. What we thus have is an ontological understanding of selfhood not as a transcendental imaginary schesis/inclusion of the other in my ecstatic "person," which is, as we are to see next, forever narcissistic, but as a participation-in-distribution, in the sense of *so much distribution, so much participation*.

It is precisely this Eucharistic ontology of selfhood, based on *participation-in-distribution*, where we have *so much distribution, so much participation*, that lies, as I think, behind Maximus the Confessor's "eucharistic ontology of dialogical reciprocity," as I have termed it elsewhere.[20] This participation-in-distribution manifests, in Maximus's thought, the possibility of conveying the Trinitarian homoousion to creation, as *inter-giveness* through Christ. Since human nature is in fragmentation after the Fall – following the gnomic/personal fragmentation of humanity, as the Confessor claims[21] – in order for this anthropological homoousion to be achieved, we need to practice our ascetical *distribution of/as gifts* (and that means that the whole selfhood becomes a gift) to others, instead of ecstatically *relating* with them, following Christ who gathered the broken parts of humanity through his Cross. Consequently, homoousion is now *to be achieved*, since after the Fall the primordial unity of created nature was broken, and hypostatic/natural otherness cannot safeguard the unification of the broken parts of creation without the ascetical struggle for selfless love, which is precisely the way for participation to become distribution, thus in turn increasing participation. So homoousion is an absolutely dynamic existential concept for Maximus, giving us the essential base for this ontology of selfhood as participation-in-distribution; the oneness of humanity is not just given as essential sameness, but remains to be achieved as *so much distribution, so much participation* in Christ, in the Spirit, in the Church.

But what is the shape this ontology of selfhood-in-communion takes in St. Gregory Palamas? Gregory precludes any possibility of a merely intellectual ascent to God, since this is, for him, only imaginary. Any real ascent to God has to happen by the grace/energy of the Holy Spirit, in Christ, and that means that man has to bring with him "every kind of creature."[22] In this remarkable passage, horizontal distribution – since to *bring* the other *with you* simply means to *offer yourself/to distribute your charisms* to the other – becomes an absolute prerequisite for vertical participation, and indeed, we see again applied the axiom *so much distribution, so much participation*, in both ecclesiological and ascetical terms, simultaneously, since, in this way, the Church becomes the very inner spiritual structure of man, as I have claimed elsewhere.[23] The difference between this understanding of personal communion and that of the Orthodox personalists earlier is enormous: while, according to the latter, the other is met in my moving toward a (more or less crypto-individualistic) freedom from essence/sameness, and he supports it, according to the former, it is precisely my "distribution" to the other that offers me not simply a detached otherness but a deeper unification of nature, in my way toward a deeper participation in God.

***

After the remarks made earlier, it goes without saying that the strength of the patristic position concerning personhood lies precisely in its remarkable understanding of consubstantiality as the model of not only the divine, but also human *koinonia*. This goes in parallel with its equally remarkable *nonmetaphysical holism* concerning its understanding of the human person, against the latter's philosophical fragmentation, made by the (always) transcendental philosophical metaphysics, a (Platonizing) fragmentation into parts ontologically superior or inferior, where the false question of domination, or possession (who dominates or possesses whom), subsequently rises. Some theological exponents of such a transcendental metaphysics seem to claim that there exist two possible approaches to a theological ontology of personhood based on a supposedly patristic and, especially, Cappadocian and Maximian juxtaposition between individual or atomon and person. According to the first, which is for them right, we must depart from person as it is understood in Trinitarian theology and Christology – i.e., as supposedly possessing and dominating nature; according to the second, which seems to them to be wrong, we depart from atomon, which the Fathers connect, as they claim, only with nature, forming just a part of it and totally subjugated to it. As I claimed elsewhere, it has been impossible for me to find in the Cappadocians or even more in Maximus, who explicitly identifies atomon and person in his Christology, even *one* text proving any differentiation between person, atomon, and hypostasis.[24] However, the real problem with this approach is that we thus lose the reality of *natural otherness*, which forms the very ontological content of personal otherness, thus indissolubly connecting personal fulfillment with the consubstantial healing of nature's fragmentations. For Maximus, hypostatic particularity is then bound with *natural particularity*, and it is inconceivable without it. Finally, human being in communion with other human beings "saves the natural otherness of the difference of his personal parts unconfused."[25]

As we are all formed in the tradition of Western transcendental subjectivism, it is difficult for us not to connect personal freedom with a sort of ecstasis – an outlet from something that seems to be necessarily somehow *given to us*. However, it is nature personally conceived that is freedom; nature, in its theological sense, means, *ex definitio*, gift, love, call, promise – i.e., *all the names personal freedom can acquire*. Maximus proposes to our philosophically corrupted minds to *listen* to nature, to *follow* nature, to restore our will's personal choice *according to nature*,[26] which reveals God to us, precisely because nature is not anymore a metaphysical τόδε τι, but a personal manifestation. Thus a person who chooses in freedom does this *according to nature, and listening to it, and not against it, or above it, or without it, or, even, for it.*

This is why the patristic insights concerning selfhood as distribution-in- participation, where we have *as much participation, as much distribution*, are so valuable. Any transcendental construal of personhood fails precisely to see that it is finally nature that is fulfilled and divinely realized, that personal communion means consubstantiality, that otherness is not simply "personal" but also natural, and it is precisely because of this that it can become a gift to the other, thus healing our fallen natural fragmentation. Any transcendental construal of person finally loses the other, for reasons that depth psychology will explain to us presently. We shall also see that psychology or modern philosophy deeply need theology in order to really achieve what they struggle for.

***

The reason for the great success of psychoanalysis and depth psychology in the West lies perhaps, as I have claimed in one of my books in the past,[27] in its biblical presuppositions. It is precisely because of these presuppositions that all of us (believers or nonbelievers) are ready to believe, for example, that our nature can be finally (or, if you like, eschatologically) fulfilled through our conscious work on it. It is also because of these presuppositions that all of us are ready to be convinced that there exists an *inherent wisdom* in our nature, as if it is an image of a supreme divine being, and so we must listen to it before we change it.

The question of personhood has been the central issue raised by modern existential psychology in all its forms and schools of thought. The whole discussion seems to include the search for the possible relationships between person and communion, or between the self and its fundamental relation to others. What is crucially important for Orthodox theology is that somehow the main trends of clinical research and theory seem here to result in a dilemmatic bifurcation of questions: do we need either transcending person toward relationship/communion in order to find the ultimate meaning that constitutes personhood, or, on the contrary, do we need first to search for a genuine personal selfhood in order then to authentically search for communion/relationship?

These two main theoretical tendencies are represented, respectively, by, I would say, Irvin Yalom and Carl Rogers. Irvin Yalom in his *Religion and Psychiatry*[28] criticizes the vanity of the young technology tycoon's aspiration toward self-fulfillment without an acquaintance with the deep meaning of life that only self-transcendence can provide. In this article, Yalom asserts that the "encounter between I and Thou," either in group psychotherapy or in a certain community, forms a basic characteristic that psychotherapy shares with religion. This existential connection brings about the hidden meaning of existence that cannot be found otherwise. Drawing on Winnicott, Mitchell, William James, and Harry Stack Sullivan, group therapy aims at correcting interpersonal distortions, as an existential broadening of the self in order to really relate to others, though maintaining its own integrity. This full self-expression is the main criterion of the truth of this interpersonal relatedness, while even the cure of the mental disease is a consequence this time of the invention of a series of new existential goals of interpersonal character.[29] This invention must also rely upon a *corrective emotional experience*, since intellectual cognition alone cannot correct the traumatic effect of previous interpersonal failures. Thus the psychotherapeutic group becomes a kind of social microcosm where therapy is experienced as an interpersonal, both intellectual and emotional, corrective experience. The mechanism of interpersonal learning as a therapeutic factor is as follows: we have realized that the mental disorder stems from distorted interpersonal relationships; the goal of psychotherapy is to help the patient learn how to acquire satisfying interpersonal relationships without distortions. The members of the social microcosm of the psychotherapeutic group, through reciprocal interaction as well as self-reflection, realize these distortions, and through intellectual and emotional corrections, change toward a more authentic reconstruction of relationality. As the interpersonal distortions decrease, the need for self-concealment decreases too, while self-respect and the ability of social adaptation through *empathy* increase.

The earlier positions highlight the discovery of intersubjectivity in American psychology of the self. What is of crucial importance for us here is that the ground of personal realization is relatedness: all the, first, existential and, second, psychological disorders are ultimately disorders of relatedness. It is only after the cure of this distorted ability of relationship (a cure that itself takes place in a context of relations) that the person can return to creativity, self-fulfillment, etc. It is obvious that here we have the awareness of a fundamental disease lying behind the idealized American *detached self*, which self is of course in absolute continuity with the European detached self of modern continental philosophy. It is precisely this self, in its basically *imaginary constitution*, which collapses in its narcissistic self-enclosure. Thus a fundamental question is raised: is this a possible healing of relatedness that precedes the constitution of the self, or the opposite? In other words, can we say that a possibly healthy and full relatedness forms the very core of personal self-awareness? Is the meaning of selfhood fulfilled in relatedness?

If Yalom's reply to this question tends, at least at first sight, to be affirmative, then Carl Rogers's reply does not seem similar.[30] In Rogers's psychology, it is precisely this restoration of the detached self that seems to be the primary goal of psychotherapy. The healed person finds the center of self-evaluation inside him, without asking the others for his decisions and choices. What we thus have has been rightly called "client-centered therapy," in the sense that it wants to assist the emergence of the client's "true self" beyond the masks it wore and the disguises he needed to take in his alienated everyday existence. Rogers has a disarming optimistic belief in the autonomous and self-existing wisdom of human nature. He believes that human nature is absolutely reliable when it is left free to express itself, and he is hostile to anyone who claims that man is basically irrational. The only possible answer that can be traced in Rogers's writings is that this distortion has been caused through communion with others, which "objectifies" the human self. As a healing, Rogers proposes a type of, as I call it, *mythical individualization*, in the sense of an out-of-the-world self-discovery, through the mythical out-of-the-world encounter with a therapist who plays here the role of a midwife, who assists in the birth of this mythical self. It is noticeable that the function of the other here is characteristically *nonreal*; he is not the real everyday other, but a paid psychotherapist who pretends to function as a primordial womb for the rebirth of the absolutely alienated client within the mythical wisdom of his lost self – the other here only forms a sort of stage for my self-fulfillment.

Can we say that we thus have two opposite approaches to the question of the relationship between person and relatedness? I am not quite sure that we have an absolute opposition here. I am not quite sure, in other words, that Yalom's intersubjectivity really opposes Rogers's self-directive self-fulfillment, although it is clear that in Yalom's thought relatedness is much more stressed than in Rogers's psychology. If Yalom's patient needs his therapeutic community, the Rogerian client needs his midwife therapist – in both cases, the other is desperately needed. In theological terms, we could say that consubstantiality, or the other as a gift, is desperately needed in order for the subject to be affirmed – and this is perhaps the most astonishing discovery of modern psychology. Surely, in Yalom's thought, the *distributive* element, in our theological terminology, is clearly prevailing, while in Roger's system, the *participatory* element is stressed, in the sense of an individual, "vertical" participation in a personal myth or meaning; thus, we never have a personality as *distribution-in-participation*, and, moreover, the other is always needed in a *narcissistic* way. Narcissism, or self-love, seems to prevail in both sorts of relating earlier, since in both we simply *need* the other for us, and since narcissism does not mean lack of intersubjectivity, but, on the contrary, it is the usual type of intersubjectivity. Thus we tend *to use the other*, either as a source of information and help for our narcissistic *social* balance (i.e., for a *pseudo-distribution*), or as a means for our self-fulfillment (i.e., for a *pseudo-participation*). Even if we completely ascribe an existential or ontological priority to the other by almost effacing the self, as some of the most advanced contemporary existential thinkers did, we still use him in order for us to acquire this sort of catholicity that the narcissistic self needs in order to feel more "intersubjectively" balanced. But is then the other real?

In an effort to answer this question, we must now switch to perhaps the most advanced modern analysis of narcissism, that of Heinz Kohut. I have chosen Kohut precisely because his work represents, as I think, the most dramatic clinical description of the desperate need of narcissism for moving toward an always fuller realization of a sort of consubstantiality, as we shall see, where both selfhood and otherness can really not only be maintained but also existentially interwoven. Defining narcissism as the libidinal investment of the self,[31] Kohut differs from Freud in that he does not reject so-called *secondary* narcissism, but considers it to be a necessary part of selfhood throughout human life. Man tries to restore his *primary narcissistic bliss* as an infant, disrupted unavoidably because of a caretaker's failed ministrations, through two unconscious *configurations* (a term meaning a cluster of needs, wishes, feelings, fantasies, and memories within the unconscious). These are the *grandiose self* and the idealized *parental imago*, both forming what Kohut called *the bipolar self*. The grandiose self arises from the fantasy of a perfect and omnipotent self, an *expansive self*, seemingly possessing something like the exaggerated superqualities and superpowers of comic strip superheroes who can accomplish anything. This exhibitionistic form of narcissism is finally modified and integrated into the personality as self-esteem and ambitions. The idealized parental imago contains the fantasy of a perfect other with whom union is sought, as a wish to merge with the perfect other who possesses wisdom, kindness, vast knowledge, unlimited strength and a capacity to sooth, settle, and help maintain emotional balance. This idealizing form of narcissism is finally internalized creating ideals. Kohut refers to the grandiose self and the idealized parental imago as the "archaic narcissistic configurations," arising from the early unconscious attempt to preserve the original blissful perfection. Their core may be phrased as "I am perfect" = grandiose self; "you are perfect, but I am part of you" = idealized parental imago.

Kohut emphasizes that the key to understand the narcissistic disorders inheres in the idea that the objects that perform psychological functions for the child are experienced in terms of the functions they perform and not in terms of their particular personal qualities. They are experienced by the child as parts of the self. When they fulfill their functions, they are taken for granted, as is a limb or any other body part. Only when an object fails in its functions does it draw notice. Kohut names the objects experienced as part of the self, "selfobjects": the expression was originally hyphenated, but finally, Kohut decided, in 1977, to remove the hyphen, since he wanted to convey the sense that the object is not experienced as being separate from the self in terms of the psychological function it provides. Man's need for selfobjects is, according to Kohut, lifelong. In his own words,

> Throughout his life a person will experience himself as a harmonious firm unit in time and space, connected with his past and pointing meaningfully into a creative-productive future, [but] only as long as at each stage in his life, he experiences certain representatives of his human surroundings as joyfully responding to him, as available to him as sources of idealized strength and calmness, as being silently present but in essence like him, and, at any rate, able to grasp his inner life more or less accurately so that their responses are attuned to his needs and allow him to grasp their inner life when he is in need of such sustenance.[32]

In theological terms, this sort of communion in and through selfobjects can perhaps be termed *an imperfect consubstantiality*, which is imperfect precisely since, though the presence of the other is proved to be absolutely necessary for selfhood to exist psychologically, this other is not real in terms of his particular personal qualities. Thus in our terminology here, we have individual *participation* in a "meaningful creative-productive future" through a *pseudo-distribution* of feelings and understanding to the (nonreal) others. But after the psychological restoration of a certain personal integrity, a new element is inserted in personality: the establishment of "empathic" communication between the self and its selfobjects on mature adult levels instead of the level of repressed or split-off, unmodified needs. *Empathy* is now the psychological acknowledge of the existence of the other – a means of knowing about his humanness and his particularity; for Kohut, one can say that the more empathy, the more psychological maturity. Empathy thus forms the psychological edition of *accomplished consubstantiality*, or, better, the accomplished *need* for consubstantiality, since it is still far from our theological concept of subjectivity as distribution-in-participation. It still seems difficult, in other words, to fathom the function of selfhood and otherness as a unique event of actively receiving and sharing each other as gift on the level of our fragmented nature, as an act of participation in a common (divine) meaning, or, to put in patristic terms, *as an essential act of unification of the very nature of beings that inserts the other's natural otherness in my very hypostatic natural identity through a dialogical syn-energy without spoiling his or my own natural and hypostatic integrity, in a way toward divine participation.*

This dialogical syn-energy keeps communion undivided and unconfused, with both of its parts active – both I and Thou are real, mutually receiving each other through their personal natural energies. The problem is that while psychology can perhaps point in this direction, only theology can provide us with the tools for such a dialogical *inter-meaningfulness*, as I have termed it elsewhere – i.e., a real intersubjectivity – not for the sake of my narcissistic balance, where even *empathy* is unconsciously used in order to keep the other in my service, through fulfilling his psychological "needs," but as a raising of another previously unknown common meaning for all of us. What we have in psychology instead is an acknowledgment of the other's otherness, which we need for our narcissistic balance – though this acknowledgment can be taken, as I think, in the form of *empathy*, as a first step in the right direction. The underlying problem is always that psychoanalysis, along with self-psychology and existential psychology, is likewise close to the original sin of Western thought, which is the underlying superexaltation of detached selfhood, within or outside the frame of metaphysical transcendental subjectivism – though they condemn it. Modern Orthodox personalism, on the other hand, through its *ecstatic* understanding of person as freedom from (or dominion over) the necessity represented by the common human nature, has not yet crossed the borders of the aforementioned transcendental subjectivism. In addition, it also seems to ignore even the earlier psychoanalytic realism, which attributes all the difficulty of having a real other and a real selfhood together to its right cause, which is the difficulty of having a spiritually *mature narcissism*, as it were – something that the ascetical tradition knows very well.

My reference to Jean-Luc Marion will be brief, but necessary.[33] Marion is perhaps the only Western thinker, as I believe, who deeply realized the loss of the real other in Western thought and tries to create a new horizon, through phenomenology, in order to save otherness in deed. Marion aspires to go beyond Husserl who avers, "We never directly experience the other as another ego. Instead we have a direct intentional experience of the other as another body, and only an appresentation, or indirect assimilation, of the other as another ego like me."[34] That is, what I have from the other is my own constitutional experience of him. Marion, instead, tries to give the other a meaning precisely as other.[35] He does this by following and correcting Levinas, who asserts that the ego is *called* by the other, along with Ricoeur for whom the self is not self-identical, but becomes itself through the other.[36] Marion replaces the term "subject" with the term *gifted*, in French, *l'adonné*, constituted as such by a *given*. Thus for Marion,

> In effect *l'adonné* does not see himself before receiving the impact of the given. Relieved of his royal transcendental status, it no longer precedes the phenomenon, or even accompanies it any more as a thought already in place. Since he is received from what he receives, he does not precede it and especially not by a visibility prior to the unseen of the given.[37]

But for Marion, this sort of constitution of the gifted by the given is utterly *passive* and the only "active capacity" Marion allows is "just in order to make sure that this (passive reception) happens."[38] Thus through this new axiom "I am loved, therefore I am," which has recently also been utterly transferred to Orthodox personalism by some of its foremost exponents, *we finally sacrifice full selfhood in order to save the other*. In our terminology, we have *distribution-in-passive-participation*. However, while for Maximus there is an absolute *koinonetic* dimension in his concept of gnomic will, this *koinonia* needs two *active* dialogical poles in order for it to function properly, as I have claimed elsewhere.[39] This quasi-Thomistic passivity of the self also proves, I am afraid, that, in psychoanalytic terms, communion, again, is not fully real – the selfobject has now become a superego, swallowing up the poor ego.

Conclusion

The modern psychological and philosophical quest has at least proved that the human person remains a mystery. In the context of contemporary thought it seems impossible to maintain the dialectic between I and Thou balanced and real, and through self psychology, we know precisely why this happens. It is only a careful study of the theological notions of natural otherness, natural and gnomic will, homoousion and dialogical syn-energy that can, in my view, help theology claim something that is truly different from what Western thought has already said. The almost total impasse of transcendental subjectivism, and the failure of phenomenology to correct it convincingly, force us to take seriously, beyond any conception of ecstatic personal *schesis*, the patristic suggestion of *subjectivity as distribution-in-participation*, where we have *so much distribution, so much participation*, fully saving the reality of both selfhood and otherness in a manner more successful than perhaps any other attempt in the history of modern thought.

Notes

1 See my work Loudovikos (1999), ch. I,1,5.
2 See Elias (1991), pp. 198–201.

3 See Kerr (1986), pp. 7–23.
4 See my work Loudovikos (2015a), pp. 213–32.
5 Dionysius the Areopogaite, *Divine Names* 5 (PG 3:820B).
6 Maximus, *Scholia on the Divine Names* 5.7–8 (PG 4:324A, 325AB).
7 Maximus, *Ad Thalassium* 13 (PG 90:296AB).
8 See Maximus, *Scholia on the Divine Names* 7.3 (PG 4:352B).
9 See my article Loudovikos (2016).
10 See my book chapter Loudovikos (2015b).
11 Gilson (1989), p. 280.
12 See Taylor (2007), pp. 18–21.
13 Zizioulas (2012), p. 206.
14 See Ricoeur (1990), p. 387.
15 See my article Loudovikos (2011).
16 Maximus, *Scholia on the Divine Names* (PG 4:425A).
17 Gregory Nazianzen, *Oration* 29.2 (PG 36:76).
18 For this topic in more detail, see my work Loudovikos (2015a), pp. 34–42.
19 Dionysius, *Ecclesiastical Hierarchy* 5.3.3 (PG 4:512A).
20 In my work on eucharistic ontology: Loudovikos (2010), ch. 5.3.
21 See, for example, Maximus, *Ad Thalassium* 40 (PG 90:397BCD, 401CD).
22 Gregory Palamas, *Against Acindynus,* 7, 11, 36.
23 See my work on this in Loudovikos (2015a), pp. 21–33.
24 See my article on this issue: Loudovikos (2013), pp. 271ff.
25 Maximus, *Ep.* 15 (PG 91:553BC).
26 See Loudovikos (2013), pp. 280ff.
27 See Loudovikos (2002), ch. 3.
28 Yalom (2002).
29 See Yalom (2005).
30 I am referring to Rogers's masterpiece, *On Becoming a Person*: Rogers (1995).
31 See Siegel (1996), p. 59.
32 Kohut (1984), p. 52.
33 See Marion (2002).
34 Marion (2002), p. 33.
35 Marion (2002), p. 46.
36 See Marion (2002), pp. 40, 115.
37 Marion (2002), p. 116.
38 See Marion (2002), p. 118.
39 In Loudovikos (2010), ch. 6, 3–4.

Select bibliography

Elias, N. (1991), *The Society of Individuals*, London.
Gilson, E. (1989), *L'Esprit de la Philosophie Médiévale*, Paris.
Kerr, F. (1986), *Theology After Wittgenstein*, Oxford.
Kohut, H. (1984), *How Does Analysis Cure?* Chicago and London.
Loudovikos, N. (1999), *Closed Spirituality and the Meaning of the Self*, Athens (in Greek).
Loudovikos, N. (2002), *Psychoanalysis and Orthodox Theology: On Desire, Catholicity and Eschatology*, Athens (in Greek).
Loudovikos, N. (2010), *Eucharistic Ontology; Maximus the Confessor's Eschatological Ontology of Being as Dialogical Reciprocity*, Brookline MA.
Loudovikos, N. (2011), "Person Instead of Grace and Dictated Otherness: John Zizioulas's Final Theological Position," *Heythrop Journal* 52.4, pp. 684–99.

Loudovikos, N. (2013), "Possession or Wholeness? St Maximus the Confessor and John Zizioulas on Person, nature and Will", *Participatio* 4, pp. 258–86.
Loudovikos, N. (2015a), *Church in the Making: An Apophatic Ecclesiology of Consubstantiality*, Crestwood NY.
Loudovikos, N. (2015b), "Inter-Meaningfulness: Re-Reading Wittgenstein Through Gregory Palamas's and Thomas Aquinas Readings of Aristotle," in S. Mitralexis (ed.), *On Wittgenstein*, Cambridge, pp. 151–66.
Loudovikos, N. (2016), "Being and Essence Revisited: Reciprocal Logoi and Energies in Maximus the Confessor and Thomas Aquinas, and the Genesis of the Self-Referring Subject," *Revista Portuguesa de la Filosofia* 72.1, pp. 117–46.
Marion, J.-L. (2002), *Being Given. Toward a Phenomenology of Givenness*, trans. J. Kosky, Stanford CA.
Ricoeur, P. (1990), *Soi-même comme un Autre*, Paris.
Rogers, C. (1995), *On Becoming a Person*, 2nd ed., Boston and New York.
Siegel, A. (1996), *Heinz Kohut and the Psychology of the Self*, London and New York.
Taylor, C. (2007), *A Secular Age*, Cambridge MA and London.
Yalom, I. (2002), "Religion and Psychiatry," *American Journal of Psychotherapy* 56.3, pp. 301–21.
Yalom, I. (2005), *The Theory and Practice of Group Psychotherapy*, 5th ed., New York.
Zizioulas, J. D. (2012), "Trinitarian Freedom: Is God Free in Trinitatian Life?" in R. J. Wozniak and Giulio Maspero, eds., *Rethinking Trinitarian Theology; Disputed Questions and Contemporary Issues in Trinitarian Theology*, London and New York, pp. 193–207.

Index

accidents 56, 57
acedia 24
adoption by God 20
Akathist 70
Alexander of Aphrodisia 39
analogy 104, 106
Andrew of Crete 70, 73, 86
Andrew Paleologos 119
Andronicus II 119
Andronicus III 116, 119, 121
angels 107–8
Anna Palaiologina 116, 119
Annunciation 72–3
anthropology 162
apocrypha 69, 85, 91
Apollinarius 36, 37
apostle: Paul as 10
Aristotle 24, 33, 38–9, 58, 105, 107, 120, 124, 129
Arius 50
asceticism 108
Athanasius of Alexandria 20, 175
Athanasius of Mt. Athos 140
atomon 58, 63, 188; see also individual; particular
atonement 122; *see also* Passion of Christ
Augustine 24, 25, 29, 182
Aurier, G. Albert 149
autexousia 104–5, 108; *see also* freedom as necessary for virtue
authority 177–8

baptism 13
Barber, Charles 139
Barlaam the Calabrian 109
Barth, Karl 29–30, 161
Basil of Caesarea (the Great) 23, 32, 35, 37, 39, 52–3, 63, 120; *see also* Cappadocians

begotten 47; Belting, Hans 139
Berdyaev, N. 163
Berger, Peter 173
Besnier, Jean-Michel 182
Bessarion 129
body in relation to soul 20–1, 103–5, 107, 109, 137; depicted in icons 137–51; embodying 21, 138–42
body of Christ 13, 20
Boethius 38
Bulgakov, Sergius 90

caesaropapism 175
Calvinism 128
capitalism 173
Cappadocians 24, 29–30, 31–40, 52–3, 121, 188
Caro, Roberto 73
Catholicism 174
causality 129–32, 185
Chalcedon, Council of 30, 31; anti-Chalcedonians 35–6, 38; diffference without division 50; union without confusion 50; *see also* Christology, miaphysite
Charles Taylor 68, 182, 184
Chesnut, Robert 37
Chionios 117
Christology, miaphysite 30; of Cappadocians 30, 31–5; Chalcedonian 30, 35–6, 38; hypostatic union 31; of Maximus 49–51; monophysitism 31; Nestorian 31; person in 54; of Philoponus 38–40; of Severus 31; *see also* hypostatic union
church architecture 143
Church of the Holy Apostles 141
citizenship 173

communion in Paul 11; divine-human 178, 188, 192; in human beings 105, 179, 163, 185–7, 188, 192; in Trinity 52, 184
compassion 24
conscience 23, 25
Constantine Harmenopoulos 120, 121
Constantinople, First Council of 53
consubstantiality 103, 107, 109, 110, 186, 192; *see also* homoousios
coworker (with God) 21, 109, 128, 132; *see also* synergeia
creation 70–1, 74, 81, 83, 91, 106, 107, 122, 129, 131, 137, 182, 187
creativity 107
cross *see* Passion of Christ
Cunningham, Mary B. 86
Cyril Lucaris 128
Cyril of Alexandria 31, 35–6, 37, 58

Darwin 184
death 81, 85, 86–7
debt 121, 122
deification 21, 106, 108–11, 122, 147, 166, 178
Demetrios Kydones 116, 117, 122, 123
Demetrios the Myrrh-Streamer 114, 115, 117–18
Demosthenes 120
de Regnon, Theodore 175–6
Descartes 182
desire 105; *see also* emotions; passions, as part of human nature
determinism 130–2
dialogue 186
Didymus the Blind 22
Dionysius the Areopagite 149, 182, 186
disposition: moral 24, 25
distribution 185–9, 190
divided self 24
divine ideas 24; *see also* logos
divine presence 183
Dodson, Joseph 80–1
Dorotheos Vlatis 116–17, 123
Dositheos 128
dreams 145
dualism of body-soul 104, 137, 187
Durkheim, E. 178

East *vs.* West 29, 176–80
ekphrasis 69, 140–2
emanation 183
emotional scripts 19, 22–4
emotions: as part of human nature 21; in response to icons 148; usefulness of 22–4; *see also* passions, as part of human nature
empathy 189, 192–3
energies 50, 51–2, 57, 60, 107–8, 110, 178, 186; *see also* operations
enhypostatic 56, 62
enkrateia 108
Enlightenment 164, 173
Entrance of the Theotokos 70, 91
envy 23
epistemology 164–8
eros 105
eschatology 20, 103, 108, 143–4
essence 47, 49, 51, 55–6, 60–2, 139, 178, 185; *see also* ousia
ethics 165–6
ethopoiia 69, 71–3, 81, 84
eucharist 166–8, 187; *see also* communion in Paul
eulogy 117–18, 120
Euphemia the Martyr 141
Eutychian 31; *see also* Christology, miaphysite
Evagrius Ponticus 23
exclamatio 69
existentialism 47, 54, 62, 64–5, 105, 161, 165, 176

Fall 104, 108, 137, 187
family 10
fate 129
father: ancient conceptions of 10–11; imitation of 10–11, 14; *see also* spiritual father
Ferrrara-Florence, Council of 115, 129
Florensky, Pavel 137, 143, 144–46, 149–51
Florovsky, George 150–1
foreknowledge (divine) 128, 130–2, 183
Foucault, Michel 182
Frank, Georgia 85
freedom as necessary for virtue 21; determinism 129–32, 165; in nature 38, 188; *vs.* of persons 178, 188–9; Trinitarian 184–5; undermined by vice 23; *see also* autexousia
Freud 184, 190

Gaugin, Paul 142, 149–50
Gemistos Pletho 128
generation 185
Gennadios Scholarios 128–32
genus 47, 55, 56, 58, 60–4; *see also* species
George Amiroutzes 129

George of Nicomedia 68, 73–4
German Idealism 182
Germanos of Constantinople 70, 73
gift 187, 193
Gilson, Etienne 184
gnomē 64; *see also* will
Gnosticism 137
grace 110, 132, 185
Great Schism 174
Greenberg, Clement 142, 149
Gregory Nazianzen (the Theologian) 21, 35, 39, 52–3, 185; *see also* Cappadocians
Gregory of Nyssa 20–1, 23, 32, 35, 38, 39, 53, 55, 63, 120; *see also* Cappadocians
Gregory Palamas 103, 105–11, 116, 123–4, 147, 151, 178, 184, 187
group therapy 189

habit 23, 24, 25
Hades 81, 85, 86–7
Hagia Sophia (church) 140, 148, 150
hagiography 140
Hagios Demetrios (basilica) 114, 117
heart 109
Heidegger, Martin 165, 182
hesychasm 103, 108–11, 114, 117, 147
hierarchy 186–7
Holmsgaard Eriksen, Uffe 85
Holy Spirit 115
homily 71–3
homoousios 32–3, 185, 186–7, 189; *see also* consubstantiality
human rights 173, 177–80
Huntington, Samuel 174
hypostasis 1; and energies 50, 51; and individual 56–64; and *ousia* 29–30, 32–4; and *physis* 31, 32–3, 35–6, 38–40, 104, 185, 192; and *prosopon* 47–56; and will 51, 54; *see also* person; *prosopon*
hypostatic union 31, 38, 49, 51, 58–9, 69, 104; *see also* Christology, miaphysite

iconoclasm 138, 147
icons 137–51; not made by hands 138, 148
idiomata see particular
image, of God 20–1, 107–8, 137, 178; and likeness 20–1, 108
imagination 107
imitation, of Paul 10–15; as a chain 13–15; of Christ 12–15, 105; of saints 14–15
Impressionism 142

Incarnation 70, 73, 165; in defense of icons 137–42; as predetermined 106, 122; *see also* Christology, miaphysite; hypostatic union
individual: Christ as 55, 58–60; Eastern vs. Western view of 174–5; individuation 34; as opposed to universal 30, 32; and person 56–64, 176–8; properties of 47–51, 52, 58; *see also* particular; person
individualism 176–9, 182
individuality 30
Industrialization 173
intellect 104, 107–9; *see also nous;* reason
Irenaeus 20
Isidore Boucheiras 117

James, Liz 141
John VI Catacuzenos 116, 119, 123
John Apokaukos 119
John Cassion 22
John Chrysostom 120, 130, 175
John Geometres 69
John of Damascus 56, 64, 70–1, 129, 138–9
John Paleologos 119
John Philoponus 38–40
John the Baptist (Forerunner) 115
John the Monk 73
Joseph (the Patriarch) 88–90
justice 119–20, 122
Justinian 120

Kannengiesser, Charles 90
Kaster, Robert 22
Kazhdan, Alexander 140
kenosis 74, 187
Kerr, Fergus 182
knowledge: according to the flesh 13; scientific 106; theological 110; *see also* reason
Kobusch, Theo 30
Kohut, Heinz 190–1
Kontoglou, Photios 143
Krausmüller, Dirk 39
Kristeva, Julia 174–6
Krug, Gregory 143

law 119–21
Lazarus 86–7
Lebon, Joseph 31
Leibniz 182
Leo VI the Wise 140
Leontius of Byzantium 55, 104
Leontius of Jerusalem 55, 63

Levinas, Emmanuel 185, 193
liberal democracy 162, 173
liberation theology 176
likeness 139–40; *see also* image, of God
liturgy 68; canons 86–7; emotional involvement in 69, 72–3, 82, 86; *kontakia* 84, 85, 87; timelessness of 69
logismoi 22, 23
logos (or *logoi*) 21, 24, 25, 49, 53, 56, 62, 63, 81; incarnate 104, 105, 183
Lossky, Vladimir 21, 29, 146, 176
Loudovikos, Nicholas 26, 103
love 10, 12, 15, 68, 75, 89, 178, 184–5

MacIntyre, Alisdaire 24
Maguire, Henry 140
Makrides, Vasilios 173
Manuel II Paleologos 123, 128
Manuel Cantacuzenos 119
Marion, Jean-Luc 192–3
Mark Eugenikos (of Ephesus) 130
Marxism 176
Mary 68–75; grief of 68, 73–4; humanity of 73–5; icons of 139, 140–1, 148; as meeting place of divine and human 70–2; Old Testament types of 71–2, 90–1; as purpose of creation 122; as special protector of Constantinople 90
Matthew Vlastaris 120
Maximos of Simonopetra (Nicholas Constas) 74
Maximus the Confessor 21, 23, 25, 47–65, 103–5, 107, 182–4, 187, 193
mediation 103, 107
mercy 24
Meyendorff, John 105
Miaphysitism 30, 35, 38–9; *see also* Christology, miaphysite
microcosm 24, 103–4, 106, 107–8
miracles 138, 140
modern art 142–3
modernity 162
monarchy of the Father 176
monasticism 25
monphysitism 31, 35; *see also* Christology, miaphysite
moral identity 21, 24–5
moral integrity 19, 24
moral psychology 19
Murdoch, Iris 68

narcissism 190–1, 192
nationalism 175
nation-state 173

Nativity of Christ 70, 72
naturalism 142, 143, 146
natural law 104, 109
natural sciences 162, 167
nature, human 20–1, 23; above 110; according to 104, 110; against 105, 106; as gift 26; and *hypostasis* 35–7, 38–40, 47–56, 59–64, 104, 184–5; not eclipsed by grace 110; and person 31–2, 54, 188–9, 192; powers of 23; as synthetic in humans 103–5, 106; two natures of Christ 31, 35; and virtue 25; and will 50, 51, 54, 60; *see also ousia; physis*
Nelson, Robert 143
Nemesius of Emessa 22
Neo-patristic synthesis 146, 151
Neoplatonism 58, 145, 151
Nestorianism 31, 35, 53; *see also* Christology, miaphysite
Nicene 31; *see also* Christology, miaphysite
Nicephorus Gregoras 123
Nicholas Cabasilas 114–27
Nicholas Mesarites 141
Nicholas of Methone 130
Nikephoros I of Constantinople 139
Nikephorus Choumnos 119
Nil Cabasilas 115, 116, 117
Nissiotis, Nikos 161–8
nous 21; *see also* intellect

One, the 128–9, 183
ontology, revolution of 30, 35, 37; of Cappadocians 32–4, 38, 40; and ethics 166; eucharistic 187; existential 162; of persons 182, 184, 186–8; relational 178; of Severus 35–7
operations 50, 51, 57, 60; *see also* energies
Origen 20–2, 32, 38, 62, 103, 104, 110, 130
other, the 68–9, 163, 184–5
otherness 185, 188, 192
ousia 29–30, 32–4; *see also* essence
Ouspensky, Leonid 137, 143, 144, 146–51

paganism 89
Pankratios of Taormina 140
Papanikolaou, Aristotle 177
parousia 13–14
participation 21, 183, 186, 188–9, 190, 192
particular: as opposed to universal 29–30, 32–4, 38, 39–40, 56, 63; *see also* individual; person

passibility *see* passions
Passion of Christ 70, 71, 73, 83, 86, 122, 166, 187
passions: as part of human nature 21, 22, 137; suscepibility to 104; usefulness of 22–4, 104–5, 109; *see also* emotions
Paul 9–18
perfection 20–1
person: as both soul and body 103; as centre of self-consciousness 29; in Christology 30, 49, 51; in context 114; as free 54; and individual 56–64, 176–8, 188; as rational 54; as relational 10, 68; in Severus 37; as translation of *hypostasis* 29, 47–56; transformation of 68; in Trinitarian doctrines 29–30, 47–51; *see also hypostasis*; individual; *prosopon*
personal relationship 10–15, 68, 71, 189; among all humanity 105, 163; with Christ 12–15; and knowledge 163–4; necessary for personhood 163–4, 184–5; in New Testament 9; between parents and children 10–11
personalism 5–6, 47, 54, 62, 64–5, 176–80, 184–6
personality: associated with moral order 38; in Severus 35–7; and the will 39
personhood 29, 68–9, 163–4
personification 80–93
Philokalia 22, 23
Photius the Great 140, 148, 150
physis 31–8
pity 24
Plato 21, 105, 120, 124, 128, 129, 137, 145, 150, 183, 188
Platonic ideas 183; *see also* logos
Plotinus 110, 128, 182
pluralism 173
pneumatology 147
political instrumentalization 174–5
politics 165, 173–80
Porphyry 38, 58, 103
prayer 109
Presentation of the Lord 91
Presocratics 37
priest of creation 165
procession 47, 185
Proclus 128, 129, 186
Proclus of Constantinople 70, 73
prosopography 114, 115
prosopon 1, 9, 47–56
prosopopoeia 80–2, 86
providence 20, 128–32

psychoanalysis 162, 174–5, 188–90, 192

Quinisext Council 147

Rahner, Karl 29–30
rationalism 173
reason: moral 24; as natural 38; as part of the soul 21; *see also* intellect; *logos*
Reformation 145
relics 138
Renaissance 145
repentance 25, 166
responsibility: moral 107
ressourcement 146, 151
resurrection 111, 137, 166
rhetorical devices 69, 80, 82, 140
Ricoeur, Paul 185, 193
Rogers, Carl 189–90
Romanos the Melodist 71–3, 80, 82, 83, 85, 86, 87
Russian Religious Renaissance 144

Sabellius 50, 53
Satan 85
Scholasticism 128
secularization 173–4, 182
self-determination *see autexousia*; freedom as necessary for virtue
self-identity 19
self-knowledge 22, 23, 163
Ševčenko, I. 121
Severian of Gabala 75
Severus of Antioch 31, 35–7, 38, 50
Skliris, D. 53, 55
slave 10, 12–13
Slavophiles 142
soghyatha 73
solipsism 184
Solovyov, Vladimir 143–4, 146
sophia 81, 89, 90; *see also* wisdom
Sophronios of Jerusalem 73
Soskice, Janet 68
soteriology 122; *see also* atonement
soul: of Christ 58; as divine 129; parts of 21, 24, 104, 108–9; pre-existence of 20–1; in relation to body 20–1, 51, 103–5, 107, 109–111
species 47, 55, 58, 60, 63, 104; *see also* genus
spiritual father: immitation of 10–12; Paul as 10–13
stavrotheotokia 73
Stoics 21–2, 105, 130

subjectivism 184–5, 188, 192
subjectivity 182
suffering 11
symbolism 144
Symbolist art 145, 149
Symeon the New Theologian 74–5, 147
synergeia 21

Tarasios the Martyr 141
teleology 20–1
telos 104, 110; *see also* eschatology ; teleology
Theodore Metochites 130
Theodoret of Cyrrhus 63
Theology of the '60's 164–8
Theophany 83–4
Theotokos *see* Mary
Thessaloniki 114–20
Thomas Aquinas 122, 182–4, 193
Thomas Magistros 120
Thomism 184
Thunberg, Lars 103, 104
Tillich, Paul 162
Timothy 14
toponym 81, 83
Törönen, Melchisedec 54, 104
Torrance, Alexis 25
totalitarianism 174
traditionalism 143
Trilling, Jacob 150
Trinity: danger of tritheism 29, 34, 39; individuality of 30; energies in 51–2; as inspiration for view of person 166–7, 174–6; properties of persons in 47–51, 52, 184–5; social views of 29
tritheism 29, 34, 39

Trubetskoy, Evgeny 137, 143–4, 146, 150–151
typology 69–71, 82, 90–3

uncreated 105, 106, 109, 110, 147; ontological gap with created 129
union with God 22; *see also* deification
universal: as opposed to individual 30, 32; as opposed to particular 29–30, 32–4
univocity of being 129, 131, 183
usury 121
utilitarianism 143

Van Gogh, Vincent 149
virtues 21–2, 24–5
visions 145
Vlatadon Monastery 116, 123
von Balthasar, Hans Urs 103, 105, 106, 109

Warner, Marina 90
Weber, Max 173
will: of Christ 50; gnomic 51; and nature 50, 51, 60
wisdom 81, 89; *see also sophia*
World War I 143
Worringer, Wilhelm 150

Yalom, Irvin 189–90
Yannaras, Christos 47, 68, 161, 164–8, 176

Zealot Crisis 119
Zizioulas, John 1, 29–30, 34, 47, 53–5, 68, 161, 164–8, 176